GOD SPEAKS OF LOVING

HIS CREATION

ANTHONY A EDDY

Copyright and Publishing

© 2020 by BookWhip Publishing.

All rights reserved. No part of this book may be reproduced or transmitted in any form or by any means, electronic or mechanical, including photocopying, recording, or by any information storage and retrieval system without express written permission from the author, except in the case of brief quotations embodied in critical reviews and certain other non-commercial uses permitted by copyright law.

Printed in the United States of America

Soft Cover ISBN: 978-1-950596-17-1
Hard Cover ISBN: 978-1-950596-18-8
Ebook ISBN: 978-1-950596-19-5

8. "GOD Speaks of Loving His Creation"

A Part of 'The End-time Psalms of God' as named by God, *or 'The End-time Homilies of God' as named by man - in being 'Religious discourses which are intended primarily for spiritual education rather than doctrinal instructions'.*

Cover design, Manuscript Content and Layout, Conceptual Related Imagery and titling texts, ©® Copyright May 2014, Jan 2016, Aug 2017, Apr 2018, 2019 by The Advent Charitable Trust, CC45056, Hamilton, New Zealand. All rights reserved worldwide.

www.thewebsiteofthelord.org.nz

Prepared on a 27in iMac™© with the use of Nisus®© Writer Pro. All trademarks™ and intellectual rights remain the property of their respective owners.

Printed in the United States of America.

To order additional copies of this book, contact:
Bookwhip
1-855-339-3589
https://www.bookwhip.com

GOD Speaks of Loving

The Family of The Loved of God have His heart declared
in embracing the Secured with a common destiny
led past the markers on the journey home
where The Inheritance of The Saints
of God receive their honouring
in the reaching of the goal.

His Creation

The supreme reward for Faith is laid out:
the future life of man as he inherits
that which has been stored in
readiness of achievement;
all has been prepared
as set in Eternity.

Anthony A Eddy
(Scribe)

Dedication

*I again have very real cause for gratitude in offering
the preparation of this, His eighth, book also into His care.*

*To our God of love, of justice, of redemption
who is very interested in all we do
and in our achieving our return home.*

For He alone is worthy of the devotion of Man.

"For God so *loved*‡ the world that He gave His only begotten Son, that whoever believes in Him should not perish but have everlasting life.
For God did not send His Son into the world to condemn the world, but that the world through Him might be saved.
He who believes in Him is not condemned; but he who does not believe is condemned already, because he has not believed in the name of the only begotten Son of God."
Jesus, The Christ, The Bible: John 3:16-18 (NKJV)

‡***Scribal Note:*** loved, '*agapao* (ag-ah-*pah*-oh); Strong's #25: Unconditional love, love by choice and by an act of will. The word denotes unconquerable benevolence and undefeatable goodwill. *Agapao* will never seek anything but the highest good for fellow mankind. *Agapao* (the verb) and *agape* (the noun) are the words for God's unconditional love, it does not need a chemistry, an affinity, or a feeling. *Agapao* is a word that exclusively belongs to the Christian community. It is a love virtually unknown to writers outside the New Testament.'

New Spirit Filled Life Bible, (NKJV): Word Wealth 3:16

Acknowledgements

Here, acknowledgment of effort and thankfulness of heart is very much due to everyone who has helped in assisting in the completion of these eight books. I had no idea, when the first one started to come forth, that there were to be eight, let alone nine!

Current positions on personal privacy and its legal protection in many jurisdictions, to both wide and varying degrees, precludes their naming and public thanking. They are certainly deserving of full honouring for their efforts, and I am sure there are records written in the heavens that will, in due course, be declared.

One, however, does stand out above all others and due of very special honour and gratitude from a very thankful heart. Here I am speaking of The Lord Jesus, The Christ, with The Holy Spirit as sent to be with man, and of The Father who sent His Son to Earth.

May the fruit of everyone's work be blessed by The Lord within the lives of those in receipt of this and the other books.

May all be blessed by God as they witness this new beginning with the completing of the coming forth of an extensive and detailed end-time vision dictated in English by The Lord in these— His nine books — the volumes each forming a part of The End-time Psalms of God. These may probably be better known by man in his naming as 'The End-time Homilies of God' - in being 'Religious discourses which are intended primarily for spiritual education rather than doctrinal instruction'.

May God, our loving Father, Jesus Christ, His Son, together with the Holy Spirit as our counsellor—bless and favour His wider family in all they do and bring to pass in the growth and development of His kingdom here in New Zealand and around the world. Marana tha— O Lord, come!

The Banner of The Kingdom was first flown as a flag at
10:30 a.m. on Monday, 1st September 2008
in Hamilton, New Zealand.
The Banner of The Kingdom was first flown as His flag on His Church
in the village of Burripalem near Tenali, Andhra Pradesh, in India
on Sunday, 31st July 2011
in unity with Reaching Forward Ministries
of Tenali, Andhra Pradesh, India.

Contents— Order Received

(2, 3, 4 ...) Denotes following items with a similar or same name as earlier ones

Title 'GOD SPEAKS OF LOVING HIS CREATION'	I
Copyright and Publishing	*II*
GOD Speaks of Loving His Creation	*III*
Dedication	*IV*
Acknowledgements	*V*
Content— Order Received	*VI*
Content— Alphabetical	*VIII*
Content— Category	*X*
Free In Deed	*XII*
Introduction	*XIV*

01. Days of Embit'ment and Accord	1
02. Entry to My Garden	4
03. Sparkle of A Diamond	6
04. Terror of The Seas	9
05. Variations in The Sea Level	12
06. Sequences in My Garden	15
07. Beating of A Drum	18
08. Swan of Regality	21
09. Comfort of The Lord (3)	23
10. Life within My Garden	25
11. Cheerleader of My Garden	28
12. Achieving of My Garden	31
13. Crying of The Whales	33
14. Fields of Wonder	36
15. End-time Psalms of God	39
or End-time Homilies of God	
16. Missing from My Garden	42
17. My Light Within My Garden	44
18. Maestro of The Intellect	46
19. Arrowheads of God	49
20. Wishing of Man	52
21. Whistler in The Wind	55
22. Temperature of The Day	58
23. Withering of The Vine	61
24. Bleating of My Sheep	64
25. Reins of Power	67
26. Beauty of My Garden	70
27. Lining of Peru (Nazca Lines)	73
28. Visiting My Garden (2)	76
29. Vacancies within My Garden	79
30. Snowfields in My Garden	81
31. Food Source of My Garden	84
32. Sourcing of Evil	87
33. Visions for The Future	90
34. Pathway of The Stars of God	93
35. Days of Thunder (2)	95
36. Tin-lizzies of The Skies	98
37. Relat'shps W'in My Garden	101
38. Meeting of The Minds	104
39. Songsters of God	107
40. Rewards of Faith	110
41. Gardens of God (2)	113
42. Movement of The Soul	116
43. Coming of The Tulips	119
44. I, The Lord Jesus (3)	121
45. My Sheep w'n The Saleyards	125
46. Settlers within My Garden	128
47. Apocrypha of Man	131
48. Passing of a Cloud	134
49. Sustaining of a Vision	137
50. Management of God	140
51. Gardening of Man	143
52. Tableting of Man	146
53. Bow of a Ship	149
54. Dressing of My Garden	152
55. Requiem of Man	155
56. Garden of The Cross	158
57. Glory of My Garden	161
58. Sea of Faces	164
59. Scream of Agony	167
60. Example of the Philistines	170
61. Superintendency of God	173
62. Election of a Man	176
63. Secrecy of God	179
64. In The Sights of God	182
65. Figurines of Man	185
66. Hearing of My Call	188
67. In The Service of God	191
68. Ageing of Man	194
69. Window of Opportunity	197
69a. Floodgates of God	197
70. Keepsakes of Life	200
71. I, The Lord Jesus (4)	202

72. New Beginnings	205
73. Greetings From Your King	208
74. Welcome to My Garden	211

My End-time Environment for Man: *215*

Of Temples	216
Of End-time Prophecies	218
Coming Day of The Lord	222
Of End-time Events	225
Cutover of God	229
Dissemination of The Multi'des	232
Wisdom Sought and Found	234
My Heralds with The Parts	237
What are The End-time Psalms of God?	241
Habakkuk 2:1-3	242
Renaming of The Book Series	243
My Nine Volumes' Indexing	244
Cross-Index Content Study Aid	246

Appendix: *247*

Alphabetical Item Titles Listing of The End-time Psalms of God	248
or as The End-time Homilies of God	
9 Books of End-time Psalms of God	261
or as The End-time Homilies of God	
4 End-time Flowers of God	262
Synopses of The Flowers of God	*262*
About the Scribe	*263*
Journaling and Notes (1)	*264*
Journaling and Notes (2)	*265*

Contents— Alphabetical

(2, 3, 4 ...) Denotes following items with a similar or same name as earlier ones

Title 'GOD SPEAKS OF LOVING HIS CREATION'	I
Copyright and Publishing	II
GOD Speaks of Loving His Creation	III
Dedication	IV
Acknowledgements	V
Content— Order Received	VI
Content— Alphabetical	VIII
Content— Category	X
Free In Deed	XII
Introduction	XIV

A
Achieving of My Garden	31
Ageing of Man	194
Apocrypha of Man	131
Arrowheads of God	49

B
Beating of A Drum	18
Beauty of My Garden	70
Bleating of My Sheep	64
Bow of a Ship	149

C
Cheerleader of My Garden	28
Comfort of The Lord (3)	23
ET Coming Day of The Lord	222
Coming of The Tulips	119
ET Cross-Index Study Aid	246
Crying of The Whales	33
ET Cutover of God	229

D
Days of Embitterment and Accord	1
Days of Thunder (2)	95
ET Dissem'on of The Multi'des	232
Dressing of My Garden	152

E
Election of a Man	176
ET End-time Events	225
ET End-time Prophecies	218
End-time Psalms of God or as *End-time Homilies of God*	39
Entry to My Garden	4
Example of the Philistines	170

F
Fields of Wonder	36
Figurines of Man	185
Floodgates of God	197
Food Source of My Garden	84

G
Gardens of God (2)	113
Gardening of Man	143
Garden of The Cross	158
Glory of My Garden	161
Greetings From Your King	208

H
ET Habakkuk 2:1-3	242
Hearing of My Call	188

I
I, The Lord Jesus (3)	121
I, The Lord Jesus (4)	202
In The Service of God	191
In The Sights of God	182

K
Keepsakes of life	200

L
Life within My Garden	25
Lining of Peru (Nazca Lines)	73

M
Maestro of The Intellect	46
Management of God	140
Meeting of The Minds	104
Missing from My Garden	42
Movement of The Soul	116
ET My Heralds with The Parts	237
My Light Within My Garden	44
ET My Nine Volumes' Indexing	244
My Sheep within The Saleyards	125

N
New Beginnings	205

P

Passing of a Cloud	134
Pathway of The Stars of God	93

R

Reins of Power	67
Relationships Within My Garden	101
ET Renaming of Book Series	243
Requiem of Man	155
Rewards of Faith	110

S

Scream of Agony	167
Sea of Faces	164
Secrecy of God	179
Settlers within My Garden	128
Sequences in My Garden	15
Snowfields in My Garden	81
Songsters of God	107
Sourcing of Evil	87
Sparkle of A Diamond	6
Superintendency of God	173
Sustaining of a Vision	137
Swan of Regality	21

T

Tableting of Man	146
Temperature of The Day	58
ET Temples	216
Terror of The Seas	9
Tin-lizzies of The Skies	98

V

Vacancies within My Garden	79
Variations in The Sea Level	12
Visions for The Future	90
Visiting My Garden (2)	76

W

Welcome to My Garden	211
ET What are The End-time Psalms of God?	241
Whistler in The Wind	55
Window of Opportunity	197
ET Wisdom Sought and Found	234
Wishing of Man	52
Withering of The Vine	61

My End-time Environment for Man: *215*

Temples	216
End-time Prophecy	218
Coming Day of The Lord	222
End-time Events	225
Cutover of God	229
Dissemination of The Multi'des	232
Wisdom Sought and Found	234
My Heralds with The Parts	237
What are The End-time Psalms of God?	241
Habakkuk 2:1-3	242
Renaming of The Book Series	243
My Nine Volumes' Indexing	244
Cross-Index Content Study Aid	246

Appendix: *247*

Alphabetical Item Titles Listing of The End-time Psalms of God *or as The End-time Homilies of God*	248
9 Books of End-time Psalms of God *or as The End-time Homilies of God*	261
4 End-time Flowers of God	262
Synopses of The Flowers of God	*262*
About the Scribe	*263*
Journaling and Notes (1)	*264*
Journaling and Notes (2)	*265*

Contents— Category

(2, 3, 4 ...) Denotes following items with a similar or same name as earlier ones

Title 'GOD SPEAKS OF LOVING HIS CREATION'	I
Copyright and Publishing	II
GOD Speaks of Loving His Creation	III
Dedication	IV
Acknowledgements	V
Content— Order Received	VI
Content— Alphabetical	VIII
Content— Category	X
Free In Deed	XII
Introduction	XIV

Edifice of God (1)

38. Meeting of The Minds		104

My Creation (9)

04. Terror of The Seas		9
05. Variations in The Sea Level		12
08. Swan of Regality		21
13. Crying of The Whales		33
22. Temperature of The Day		58
27. Lining of Peru (Nazca Lines)		73
43. Coming of The Tulips		119
47. Apocrypha of Man		131
50. Management of God		140

My Garden (22)

02. Entry to My Garden		4
06. Sequences in My Garden		15
10. Life within My Garden		25
11. Cheerleader of My Garden		28
12. Achieving of My Garden		31
14. Fields of Wonder		36
16. Missing from My Garden		42
17. My Light Within My Garden		44
26. Beauty of My Garden		70
28. Visiting My Garden (2)		76
29. Vacancies within My Garden		79
30. Snowfields in My Garden		81
31. Food Source of My Garden		84
34. Pathway of The Stars of God		93
37. Relat'ships W'in My Garden		101
41. Gardens of God (2)		113
46. Settlers within My Garden		128
54. Dressing of My Garden		152
56. Garden of The Cross		158
57. Glory of My Garden		161
71. I, The Lord Jesus (4)		202
74. Welcome to My Garden		211

My Grace (3)

64. In The Sights of God		182
69. Window of Opportunity		197
69a. Floodgates of God		197

My Love (5)

15. End-time Psalms of God		39
or as *End-time Homilies of God*		
49. Sustaining of a Vision		137
53. Bow of a Ship		149
58. Sea of Faces		164
67. In The Service of God		191

My Return (6)

Free In Deed		XII
01. Days of Embit'ment and Accord		1
07. Beating of A Drum		18
09. Comfort of The Lord (3)		23
61. Superintendency of God		173
73. Greetings from Your King		208

Preparation (21)

03. Sparkle of A Diamond		6
19. Arrowheads of God		49
20. Wishing of Man		52
21. Whistler in The Wind		55
23. Withering of The Vine		61
24. Bleating of My Sheep		64
25. Reins of Power		67
33. Visions for The Future		90
36. Tin-lizzies of The Skies		98
39. Songsters of God		107
40. Rewards of Faith		110
42. Movement of The Soul		116
48. Passing of a Cloud		134
60. Example of the Philistines		170

62. Election of a Man	176
63. Secrecy of God	179
65. Figurines of Man	185
66. Hearing of My Call	188
68. Ageing of Man	194
70. Keepsakes of Life	200
72. New Beginnings	205

The End-time (22)

18. Maestro of The Intellect	46
32. Sourcing of Evil	87
35. Days of Thunder (2)	95
44. I, The Lord Jesus (3)	121
45. My Sheep w'n The Saleyards	125
51. Gardening of Man	143
52. Tableting of Man	146
55. Requiem of Man	155
59. Scream of Agony	167

My End-time Environment for Man: *215*

ET Of Temples	216
ET Of End-time Prophecies	218
ET Coming Day of The Lord	222
ET Of End-time Events	225
ET Cutover of God	229
ET Dissemination of The Multi'des	232
ET Wisdom Sought and Found	234
ET My Heralds with The Parts	237
ET What are The End-time Psalms of God?	241
ET Habakkuk 2:1-3	242
ET Renaming of The Book Series	243
ET My Nine Volumes' Indexing	244
ET Cross-Index Content Study Aid	246

Appendix:	*247*
Alphabetical Item Titles Listing of The End-time Psalms of God	248
or as The End-time Homilies of God	
9 Books of End-time Psalms of God	261
or as The End-time Homilies of God	
4 End-time Flowers of God	262
Synopses of The Flowers of God	*262*
About the Scribe	*263*
Journaling and Notes (1)	*264*
Journaling and Notes (2)	*265*

Free In Deed

"I,
  The Lord Jesus,
    speak to all who hold this the eighth book as dictated to,
                          and recorded by,
                          My servant,
                          Anthony.
        For mighty is his effort in his perseverance and commitment with his one
                                                    finger typing.

I,
  The Lord Jesus,
    cause this,
      My end-time record for man,
        to be brought before him:
        for his perusal in order he may come to an understanding—
      of his prospects for a future life with Me.

I,
  The Lord Jesus,
    recommend man's examination carefully and with attention:
        for all that is declared to man in these eight books—
      emanating from The Throne Room of God.

For these,
  My end-time scrolls,
    impart knowledge of what man should expect prior to My return:
          of how to dwell in Righteousness,
          of the importance of The Truth,
          of the gifts of My Spirit,
          of the prospects for My Bride,
          of the achievement of Eternal Life,
          of how to uplift The Promises of God,
          of how to accept My gift of Grace while it is today.

I,
  The Lord Jesus,
    would not have man in ignorance,
    would not have man in fear,
    would not have man falling for the devil's lies,
              for the devil's temptations,
                  for the devil's capturing of the soul of man.

I,
  The Lord Jesus,

have the angelic hosts of Heaven in their thousands of thousands
on their thousands of thousands:
who are assigned to attend to the welfare of
My people—
upon receipt of a request.

I,
 The Lord Jesus,
  anticipate with great joy the likelihood of meeting My spirit children:
in My garden as accompanied—
each by an embodied soul.

I,
 The Lord Jesus,
  proclaim to those with unbelief,
   to those with non-belief,
    to those who know not Faith developed to the fore:
to search,
to seek,
to knock,
to commit,
to grow,
 to develop to live within
  the field of Faith:
where as neighbours does the field of Righteousness
prevail alongside the field of Truth.

For as Righteousness prevails so Peace becomes secure.
For as Truth prevails so Lies lose control.
For as both dwell at home within My Temple so My Spirit leads and counsels.
For Freedom is welcomed as Captivity departs.
For Grace befriends and cleanses when The Anguish of the heart beseeches.

I,
 The Lord Jesus,
  would welcome all those in captivity,
as the devil supervises evil:
to join the flock of The Good Shepherd—
and so come to participate in the freedom known to God."

My Content Study Aid

_____

_____

Introduction

These Divine texts mostly consist of Truth Statements intermixed with counselling and are presented for serious contemplation as to their ramifications and how we approach them in the conclusions we may draw. For they are filled with great significance for these present times.

I testify here to one and all that these texts are not of my writing nor instigation. These texts do not stand alone but smoothly build on the preceding ones as if designed as an unfolding story with an establishing foundation. On the original individual documents the scribe has begun each Divine call with the words: 'And I hear The Lord Jesus saying,' "...". It does not appear necessary to have this phrase repetitively introducing each call in this book. Please take it, therefore, as a 'given' as to the stated origin both by testimony and by claim.

The style of the book preserves the scribal comments in italics; while double quotation marks " " denote and enclose text of a Divine origin. British spelling is used for reasons of national culture. Layout simplifies ease of reading and personal study. Each call itself may be accurately searched from within His website. A concordance or a thesaurus has not been used at any stage prior to, during, or after the receiving of these texts. A dictionary (Oxford Concise™) has sometimes been used to comprehend fully, the words of the Divine voice used in expressing His intent. Because the texts have been received via dictation spoken by the Divine voice directly into the mind, the punctuation is subject to human interpretation. Occasionally however, when required for clarity or emphasis, the capitalisation of words, together with the paragraphing, have also been indicated by the Divine. Minor spelling 'typos' are scribal and the punctuation, together with the titles, usually are, but not always. Multiple subject matters sometimes occur in a particular call which precludes the call's naming being entirely appropriate with respect to descriptive accuracy. There are nine parts within the series which The Lord has named 'The End-time Psalms of God'. These may probably be better known by man in his naming as 'The End-time Homilies of God' - in being 'Religious discourses which are intended primarily for spiritual education rather than doctrinal instruction'.

Attached to the end of most items is 'My Content Study Aid' inserted at the request of The Lord Jesus to enhance the benefits found in meditating on and understanding the 'Hows' and 'Whys' of the truth statements and His counselling as found herein. If no such Study Aid exists at the end of an item then there are additional Journaling & Notes pages provided in the Appendix. Please remember this is your book to use in the way which best serves your growth within the discipleship of God.

Great care has been taken to ensure scribal accuracy in hearing and transcribing what are now these printed pages of Divinely originated texts. Every word is as received without later omissions, additions, substitutions or edits. May The Holy Spirit so testify as such to every enquiring soul.

The Scribe,
Hamilton, New Zealand

The Days of Embitterment and Accord

"The days of embitterment filled with dissatisfaction—
                are about to come as thunderstorms within the sky,
                are about to overshadow those who will succumb,
                are about to spread discontent leading into violence,
                are about to bear the hidden self into the sunlight—
                              as each is met with a coming dawn,
                are about to bear the pain of suffering into the
                              hearts of innocence,
                are about to bear the jewels of Satan into the
                              refiner's fire.

The days of embitterment rest upon the mountains at home with man,
                rest upon the snow tops to career down the slopes of snow,
                            to career down the ice formations,
                            to career down among the avalanches
                                which sweep all before to darkness.

The days of embitterment are soaked in self-pity,
                are registered with like for like,
                are gathered in The Multitudes who are registered as
                                disaffected souls—
                    which have squashed their spirits—
                    which have squandered their opportunities of success:
                    which have rejected—
                    which did not see—
                    which did not hear:
                    that which has been placed before them at the
                                thresholds of their dwellings.

The days of embitterment broach the boundaries of the fields of Righteousness:
                attempt to conquer and to disperse,
                attempt to fell and to trample,
                attempt to hack and to hew so to cause to fall,
                attempt to search for dissatisfaction,
                        for dismay,
                        for the distraught—
                among the fallen and the suffering:
                    where thanksgiving is not heard,
                    where both praise and worship is strangled in
                                  the throats:
                    of those who should know better.

The days of embitterment will come to an end;
>   are as The Fire feeding on the wood,
>   >   the hay,
>   >   >   the straw:
>   which fail to pass the reason for the mustering,
>   which fail to find a contrite heart,
>   which fail to exhibit either a call for Mercy or for Grace.

The days of embitterment exhaust the fuel of Satan,
>   exhaust the things of Satan,
>   exhaust the academies of Satan held responsible for the
>   >   spreading of the lies.

The days of embitterment peter out,
>   fade away,
>   >   as their will is spent to languish by the roadsides travelled
>   >   >   in despair.

The days of embitterment have their mountains demolished,
>   have their havens melt,
>   as the winter passes into the dawning of a spring;
>   where summer will no longer look down on the tragic plight
>   >   of others,
>   >   no longer to experience the numbers to
>   >   >   enforce an evil will,
>   >   no longer to be forced to open a door so
>   >   >   locked in fear.

The days of embitterment lead into the days of accord:
>   >   where raised voices are no longer heard,
>   >   where raised fists are no longer seen in streets,
>   >   >   in pounding on the doors,
>   >   >   in the grabbing hold of children,
>   >   >   in the flinging out from the havens
>   >   >   >   thought to be secure.

The days of accord are days of reconciliation,
>   of forgiveness,
>   of assimilation,
>   of harmony without the trials,
>   >   without the subjugations,
>   >   without the threats of death,
>   >   without the shows of hatred arising from the
>   >   >   souls of man.

The days of accord see the clearing of the landscapes;
>   the cleansing of the cityscapes;
>   the redressing of the seascapes:

the repairing of the damage so witnessed within the turmoil
of embitterment.

The days of accord speak of changes in reaction,
    of changes in the positioning of threats,
    of changes in the casting of the challenges,
    of changes from the violent modes of behaviour.

The days of accord re-establish Righteousness with Peace;
    re-establish love and care,
    re-establish consideration for the helpless and infirm,
    re-establish the calls of God upon the willing and committed.

The days of accord testify that the worst is over,
    that a reign is near,
    that a kingdom vibrates in readiness for its king,
    that a people of purity await the bridal gathering,
    that Satan's freedom days are numbered,
    that the flowering of The Earth is ready to proceed,
    that Grace still lingers only to recede.

The days of accord render unto Caesar and render unto God,
    acknowledge both within their varied habitations,
    search for both in line with inclinations,
    greet each according to The Fear so held.

The days of accord witness the wonders of recovery,
    the miracles of healing,
    the signposting of the way to an eventual home:
        prepared and waiting—
        for the occupants both eager and expectant.

The days of accord see the closing of the door of preparation,
    the raising of the veil of eternity,
    hear the trumpet blast of angels that reverberates around The Earth.

The days of accord are to welcome the second coming of The Lord on the clouds
of conquest.

The days of accord are a time of the refreshing of The Earth—
    as it is prepared to welcome The Coming King foretold."

My Content Study Aid

_____

_____

Entry to My Garden

"Entry to My garden is at The Will of God.

Entry to My garden is protected from the gate-crashers,
        is protected from those who carry sin,
            is protected from those of whom I do not testify to The Father.

Entry to My garden can be by invitation in mortality which affects the entity of being;
        can be by Martyrdom,
        can be by entry from a grave for the committed and professing.

Entry to My garden should be the goal of man.

Entry to My garden is qualified by the footprint of discernment;
        is qualified by the mark of acceptance for the hallowed and the sacred;
        is qualified as the just reward for all who trod the road of Discipleship
                when Freewill choice was exercised;
        is qualified by Love within The Grace accepted,
            within The Grace attributed,
            within The Grace which settled on a contrite heart.

Entry to My garden has acceptance unlimited by time,
        unlimited by health,
        unlimited by age,
        unlimited by premature presentation where Freewill is
            soundly based for honouring.

Entry to My garden is open to the young and innocent whose spirits still are seeking,
                whose souls are unimpaired by the
                shortened time spent in mortality.

Entry to My garden is closed from a recanted soul within mortality not subjected
                      to intimidation,
        not subjected to pain imposed by satanic forces,
        not subjected to threats of harm to family members.

Entry to My garden is closed to those who procrastinated past the use-by date of Grace,
            past the use-by date of Faith,
            past the use-by date for
                acceptance of The Inheritance
                    of The Cross.

Entry to My garden is closed to those with an appeal for Mercy unsustained by the
                evidence as marshalled from a life.

Entry to My garden is assured for those who use the gift of tongues;
  who seek fluency in the gift of tongues;
  who establish the interpretations of the gift
          of tongues;
  who recognise the languages in their varying
          within the gift of tongues,
  who establish inflexions of expression within
          the gift of tongues,
  who practise repetition,
    pronunciation,
      vowels and consonants within the
          gift of tongues.

Entry to My garden is at The Will of God as I uphold My Word.

Entry to My garden opens vistas to facilities galore;
  opens portals where travellers begin;
  opens scopes of vision and of sound abounding on every hand;
  opens the time spheres of man to be visited at leisure;
  opens the fields of introduction and of recognition where tears and
          hugs mingle for attention;
  opens access to the lands of might and majesty—
    where The Power and Authority of God is evident to all;
  opens examination of the small and beautiful as details are absorbed.

Entry to My garden opens the existence of eternity—
    with all which God has planned—
  for the return of man to be within The Family of God.

Entry to My garden sets the showcase for My stars,
  sets the showcase for the best attributes of man,
  sets the window dressing as it was first set to be—
    now man is again reconciled with the living love of God.

Entry to My garden opens eyes to the polishing of light;
  opens ears to the delights of the choreography of sounds;
  opens hands of friendship and relations;
  opens skilled tongues to express communication levels;
  opens taste buds for the furnishing of sensations;
  opens the sixth sense where thought ensures tongues are to the fore.

Entry to My garden is the introduction to life within the garden categories of God.

Entry to My garden is at The Will of God:
  where Faith with Righteousness and Freewill testimonies open the
          new beginnings—
    as found in the household known of God."

The Sparkle of A Diamond

"The sparkle of a diamond as cut and polished by man is beautiful to behold,
>is beautiful to wear,
>is beautiful to own,
>is beautiful as a repository
>>of wealth,
>is beautiful as the size increases,
>is beautiful as it transfers through
>>the generations.

The sparkle of a diamond as prepared by God is not limited by size,
>is a blaze of light,
>is triumphant in its presence,
>is not contaminated by value,
>is spectacular in appearance,
>is a raiser of appreciation,
>is seen in decoration of My garden.

The sparkle of a diamond reflects the eyes of God,
>reflects The Light of God,
>reflects the purity of God.

The sparkle of a diamond is the standard of eternal life set for existence in My garden.

The sparkle of a diamond neither fades nor wears away within eternity of My garden,
>only is besmeared within mortality:
>>where it is treated as a depository—
>for that which would diminish its sparkle as prescribed
>>by man.

The sparkle of a diamond is not an innate property of a diamond;
>depends upon The Light available for re-direction,
>depends upon the source,
>depends upon intensity,
>depends upon surroundings,
>depends upon the size,
>depends upon the purity,
>depends upon the cut.

The sparkle of a diamond is the end result of skill:
>governed both by knowledge mixed with wisdom—
>to release the sparkle from what lies upon a bench.

The sparkle of a diamond emerges from the rough:
>>under hands of capability both guiding and directing;
>>under hands born both of practise and experience;

> under hands both persevering and completing.

The sparkle of a diamond is substantive in its presence.

The sparkle of a diamond has its parallel in man:
> has its parallel in his birth into mortality;
> has its parallel with his development from the rough;
> has its parallel with care in loving hands;
> has its parallel with the shedding of impurities;
> has its parallel with the ability of his shining;
> has its parallel with the brightness of his light;
> has its parallel with his selection for presence in My garden;
> has its parallel as he dwells within the purity of eternity—
>> so enabling a reflection in the eyes of God.

The sparkle of a diamond should not remain hidden in an unfound stone,
> should not remain lying without an opportunity to change,
> should not forever be remaining as it was—
>> never to attain its full potential so its Glory may shine forth.

The sparkle of a diamond should be the goal of man:
> to be found both ready and waiting and willing to be
>> changed by A Master Craftsman;
> to attain the fullness of the promise as purity is achieved;
> to be selected to dwell forever within My garden—
>> in a place which is prepared.

The sparkle of a diamond sparkles still in the presence of man:
> is no longer overshadowed by man;
> is no longer gathered selfishly by man;
> is no longer placed where the sun can no
>> longer reach—
> where trips outside are mostly in the darkness:
>> when only lit by the lights of man.

The sparkle of a diamond is designed to sparkle all its life,
> is designed to remind man of its being,
>> of the changes wrought,
>> of how it has been changed.

The sparkle of a diamond is subject to how man's possessive strength has overlain
>> its freedom—
> to keep it in the darkness where its sparkle is not seen,
> to hide it in a vault from where it is not easily released,
> to prevent admiring eyes appreciating its history of creation:
>> and the testimony it bears.

The sparkle of a diamond still keeps its affinity with the parallel of man:
> who is also designed to sparkle all his life;
> to remind man of the changes made within a life;
> of how such display in fullness with amazement
> on completion.

The sparkle of a diamond has its parallel in The Freewill of man:
> his coating of the contaminants of life which
> prevent his shining;
> of his imprisonment within the vaults of Satan
> where his Glory is not realised,
> where his testimony is not
> established for qualifying a
> future both in time and space.

The sparkle of a diamond should be sought by man:
> that he too should sparkle as he was born to do;
> that he may participate in The Bride of Christ—
> to be part of The Glory of the sparkling that
> will surround The Bridegroom—
> in The Presence of The Father where the
> testimonies are heard in
> receiving His acceptance."

My Content Study Aid

The Terror of The Seas

"The terror of the seas is present in My gardens of example,
        is present in the seas of man's mortality,
        is present in the fears of man,
        is present when outside the ability to control,
        is present when man resorts to weapons which result in death.

The terror of the seas is mostly one of imagination,
            of the unknown and imperilled,
            of the stupid and at risk.

The terror of the seas is a mixture of both silence born with speed,
            of both size and frenzy,
            of both the horror laid before the eyes in quest of
                  wealth and the images of teeth built to catch the prey.

The terror of the seas has to eat to live,
        has its niche wherein it feeds,
        keeps the shoals clean and tidy where stragglers do not
                              long survive.

The terror of the seas is the survivor from a time of vulnerability
                where smallness was an invitation to a meal,
                where smallness sought protection,
                where smallness needed mothering,
                where smallness beat the odds and grew into
                          a monstrous size.

The terror of the seas is not afraid of that which is encountered,
        will maul and leave in tatters if taste is not to liking,
                if texture as such was previously unencountered,
                if the presence as such arises unexpectedly yet
                        justifies a snap in passing.

The terror of the seas vibrates and skirmishes,
        approaches and retreats,
        passes and returns.

The terror of the seas is thinking of its mouth when on patrol in its domain.
The terror of the seas visits repeatedly where its mouth is filled without much effort.
The terror of the seas does not rest when nourishment is plentiful until appetite is sated.

The terror of the seas is sensitive to blood within its path,
        has the source located accurately,
        notes the issue of an invitation accepted for partaking,
        awaits the joining of the throngs so mayhem may commence.

The terror of the seas circles in assessment,
        awaits an opportunity judged as free from threat,
        plunges to attack,
        seizes what protrudes,
        tries to shear it free,
        lingers for remains.

The terror of the seas is a repository of instinct,
        is a recaller of success and failure,
        evaluates a food source on what has gone before.

The terror of the seas crosses boundaries unaware,
        crosses rivers flowing underneath,
        crosses ribbons of food both plentiful and cheap,
        crosses others with similar motivations,
        crosses to the breeding grounds where warmth bespeaks
                        of shallowness,
          where shallowness bespeaks of safety,
          where safety bespeaks of food chains aplenty
                      among the waving fronds,
          where waving fronds bespeak of masking and
                protection when it is most needed.

The terror of the seas is an apex predator,
        is powerful and able,
        is at home within its environment,
        is in need of food to sustain its body weight and drive,
        is there to curb the deformed,
            the sick,
            the elderly,
            the strays,
            the injured,
            the exposed—
        those who have lost the protection of the masses and were
                      discovered when alone.

The terror of the seas vanquishes and vanishes,
        mauls and mutilates,
        seeks and searches.

The terror of the seas comes and goes upon a quest,
        grows and develops with each day,
        knows immunity from attack because of size.

The terror of the seas is not a plaything in a bath,
        is not a plaything found at sea,
        is not a plaything to be trapped,

is not a plaything where numbers may lead to thoughts of safety,
where each circles with much patience to await
the brash and immature.

The terror of the seas is to be respected for its position,
not to be teased or encouraged by those thought safe within
a boat."

My Content Study Aid

Variations in The Sea Level

"Variations in the sea level should be of concern to man,
        are of concern to God,
        are of concern to all who watch and wait.

Variations in the sea level have gone beyond the control of man,
        are the result of man's pumping of his dirt into the air which he
                must breathe,
        of his contaminating that which should be pure,
        of his dirty washings left to dissipate in the air,
        of the exhausting of his engines,
        of the belching of his smoke stacks,
        of the deforestation
            where there is no replenishment,
            where none do stand as proxy,
            where there is no funding of regeneration
                to keep a silent vigil
                so stability is retained.

Variations in the sea level measure the rubbish thrown away by man on a daily basis:
        with which the cleaning lady can no longer cope:
        as her cloths and dust bins are removed from
            her jurisdiction,
        with cloths too dirty to absorb,
        with lids removed and blown away.

Variations in the sea level sees lands removed of mass which weighs them down,
        sees water encountering recirculation after centuries of rest,
        sees land now under threat of reclamation by the seas,
        sees man to be forced to flee where imprudence placed
                a home—
            where the sea can reach only
                to dismantle.

Variations in the sea level are not a blessing to man,
        are a reaping of his harvest of neglect,
        are a reaping of his carelessness in stewardship,
        are a reaping of not accepting responsibility—
            when the patterning cried out for attention,
        are a reaping of unwillingness to act—
            to set a house in order,
        are a reaping of the blaming of others who also fail to act—
            to condemn another,
        are a reaping of the harvest which is prepared and ready,

                                            which will be painful
                                                                       and prolonged,
                                   which will no longer be delayed.

Variations in the sea level are the responsibility of all those:
        who sought and are instated as leaders of the nations;
        who have accountability for the plundering with the burning,
            the utter lack of care,
            the extinction of the mantle on vast areas of Earth,
            the draining of the lakes and rivers which threaten—
                    both dependent life and related habitations,
                    the destruction of the water resources where
                most is dissipated in the morning mists:
                    which are no longer to be seen by man,
            the mining and emissions from the smokestacks—
                where scrubbers are not installed as polishers of
                              all which seek escape.

Variations in the sea level are composed of snow storms of the past,
        are built upon a rise in temperature where ice cannot survive,
        are calling to the vigilant to prepare for
            the inrush of the waters,
            the invasions becoming common,
            the ineffectiveness of barriers,
            the unwillingness of man to submit to lowering
                    projections for the future—
            prior to the onset of disasters where 'relief'
                can no longer meet demand.

Variations in the sea level will bring forth the arguments of diplomacy:
        of the threats of wars both civil and as clashes across the
                borders installed by man,
        of refugees who are forced to flee yet with no land set aside,
        of the disowned and the despairing who know not what to do:
                with but a billycan for each to bail.

Variations in the sea level is a disaster facing multitudes in the cities of The Earth—
        where the shoreline marks a threat which will not go away.

Variations in the sea level will attack the roads and the engineerings of man—
        the wharves and the jetties,
        the harbours and the bridges,
        the concentrations of man:
            who sought the presence of the sea—
                soon to be no longer seen where advances
                          result in full retreat.

Variations in the sea level call for attention to the details,
> attention to the handling of relocations,
> attention to the preservation of life known to be
>> under threat,
> attention to ensuring the preservation of livelihoods
>> about to change,
>> about to need assistance,
>> about to need the funding necessary to comply:
>>> with safety from invasion;
>>> with removal beyond the threat;
>>> with the answering of the questions—
>>>> 'to where' and 'when' and 'how'.

Variations in the sea level are known by The God of Heaven and The Earth with all
> which is implied:
>> as the changes wrought by man impact on The Earth.

Variations in the sea level are a warning to man:
> to assist all those so afflicted—
> in doing unto others that which they are unable to do
>> for themselves—
> to move into a new beginning necessitated by circumstances
>> not of their own making."

My Content Study Aid

_____
_____
_____
_____
_____
_____
_____
_____
_____
_____
_____
_____
_____

Sequences in My Garden

"Sequences in My garden depend upon location.

Sequences in My garden are sorted by intent,
                are submitted upon acceptance,
                are imposed upon surroundings,
                are withdrawn upon completion of either inspection
                                            or participation.

Sequences in My garden may be either short or long,
                have indefinite extension,
                have rewards for concentration,
                have selections based on The Will of God:
matched to the interest span of the uniqueness of each individual resident within
                                                    My garden.

Sequences in My garden are not constrained by time,
                involve participation in the present—
                          which is different from the experience of time
                                      within mortality,
                are retained within the memories of all who see and hear as
                          they come to understand that in which they dwell.

Sequences in My garden are wonders in progress,
                are signs of marvels readied for assimilation,
                are displays prepared for absorption and interaction.

Sequences in My garden are eternal in their nature,
                are amazing in complexity,
                are thorough in refinement.

Sequences in My garden love to have responses,
                are excited by affirmations,
              are in agreement with exclamations of delight.

Sequences in My garden do not vie with one another,
                do not have hesitations,
                do not have collapses of integrity,
                do not have seesaws with their ups and downs,
                do not have roundabouts which travel round in circles,
                do not have 'Oops!' which indicate mistakes,
                do not have power failures leading to frustrations.

Sequences in My garden sprout from The Will of God within the blessing of
                                                          The Residents.

Sequences in My garden are secure in their destiny,
        have not been patched together,
        have not been assembled with mosaics to the fore,
        have not been trimmed to fit,
        have not been limited by editing,
        have not been excised to fit a file of audio,
        have not been shrunken for a time slot set by
                            external influences,
        have not been modified to link-in with an explanation,
        have not been tied to a particular presentation.

Sequences in My garden are not recursive,
        are not disjointed,
        are not the subjects of complaint.

Sequences in My garden give rise as if to flights of imagination where realities
                            are intermingled,
        where realities are searchable and verifiable,
        where realities are dependent on missions based on Truth,
        where realities are birthed with the fragile and the delicate.

Sequences in My garden bring surprises galore,
        can fill an afternoon with stories as if for three months
                            in mortality,
        can stretch the vistas before the eyes until the eyes are
                            fully open.

Sequences in My garden leave museums in the dark,
        leave zoos not worth a visit on the morrow,
        leave funfairs unattended—
                all alone and so forlorn.

Sequences in My garden have floral arrangements not presently visible on The Earth,
        have decorators trying out their layouts and their plans with
                            much excited talk,
        have the specialists at entertaining who generate
                            mysteries aplenty:
            in defying of the senses as attached to evaluations.

Sequences in My garden are endemic on the entering of Heaven,
        on the exploring of the vastness of arrays,
        on discovering the hidden waiting for a search.

Sequences in My garden are there for the interest and the amusement of The Residents of
                            My garden,
        are there to learn and to mature without the bounds of time
                            knocking on the doors—
            where deadlines are queuing for attention.

Sequences in My garden open portals to a completely different way of life:
one which is the way of God,
where Truth with Righteousness and Mercy continue
there to rule and judge—
in the new environment for My Bride—
there where The Testifiers of The Lord are welcomed,
as they come to dwell within The Family of God."

My Content Study Aid

The Beating of A Drum

"The beating of a drum signifies a march within a street,
                a march into a field of battle,
                a march of death which bears a coffin high,
                a march of movement with stragglers aplenty,
                a march embracing a call to arms,
                a march all out of step with a procession of a wedding,
                a march within The Call of God where the young at
                                  heart do skip and dance.

The beating of a drum denotes the thump of feet,
        denotes the clap of hands,
        denotes the sounds of accompaniment,
        denotes the setting of the drum in measuring the human
                              voice released.

The beating of a drum denotes a warning of assault from a watch tower wide awake.

The beating of a drum warns of an approach while out of sight.

The beating of a drum salutes the objective of the marching,
        salutes the preparation,
        salutes the equipping,
        salutes the uniforms and dress codes,
        salutes the abilities and training.

The beating of a drum passes a message across a distance without undue delay,
            from a locality difficult to assess,
            to the target of the drummer where access
                              is impeded.

The beating of a drum shrinks and expands an audience,
        magnifies the sound of repetition,
        emphasizes what is about to be,
        praises The Works of God,
        is fun to beat and sound.

The beating of a drum sharpens senses,
        arouses curiosity,
        can seek an investigation.

The beating of a drum imparts a threat to silence,
        imparts a threat to peace,
        imparts a threat from a reason still unknown.

The beating of a drum is an intrusion to the soundscape,
        is an intrusion to activities,
           is an intrusion where the source remains a query.

The beating of a drum carries the rhythm of the drummer,
        feeds the sound waves with intent,
        cycles until the circle is complete,
        rouses as the tempo changes,
            as the tempo increases,
                as the tempo reaches a crescendo which climaxes on
                                the ears.

The beating of a drum assails the environment of man,
        speaks of many things,
        suggests many things,
        calls to many for whom it is intended,
        hinders conversations with intensifying loudness,
        is accompanied by relief as it is heard to fade away—
                into distance owning its possession.

The beating of a drum signals and withdraws,
        marshals and attends,
        times both the step and style of pace.

The beating of a drum can have many different sounds,
        many differing temperaments,
        many different sources at home within the family
                of drums.

The beating of a drum takes ownership of the pitch at which it's tuned,
            at the 'voice' constructed for
                its footprint,
            at its placement in a band where
                drumming is extensive.

The beating of a drum can dominate,
        can shrink into a background,
        can re-emerge into the sound sphere when it's input is essential
                and the timing is bespoke.

The beating of a drum can imitate the human voice:
        can serve up the commas and fullstops;
            the drum rolls of announcement as the marks
                of exclamation;
            the drumbeats crowded in where percussion wins the
                solo of the day.

The beating of a drum has time accompanied by intervals,
                intermixed with the velocity of the beat,
                overseen by pauses for an instructed rest.

The beating of a drum has long been an accompaniment of man,
        has long been an instructor of man,
        has long been at the demand of man,
        has long been in the service of man,
        has long been the supporter of the battles,
                the initiator of the fights,
                the signal to withdraw.

The beating of a drum extends the voice of man,
        replaces the voice of man,
        superimposes on the voice of man,
        accompanies the voice of man,
        leads in timing the voice of man,
        shepherds the voice of man.

The beating of a drum by a child can be boring and trying of one's patience,
                is of much interest and achievement to the child,
                is a measure of discovery and with an imprint
                                          on attention.

The beating of a drum comes in many different guises,
        in many different tunings,
        in many different sizes,
        in many different sounds,
        in many different cultures,
        in many different uses of accessories to life.

The beating of a drum once was as a heartbeat on a tree,
        the heartbeat of a life,
        the heartbeat that was stilled,
        the heartbeat that had to rest;
                the heartbeat that started up again,
                the heartbeat that lives for evermore—
                the heartbeat that arose as proxy for all the rest—
                the rest,
                        committed to selection,
                        as those who would have it so."

My Content Study Aid

The Swan of Regality

"The swan of regality sets the stage as her platform of presentation,
                                    of a queenly stance upon the water,
                                    of both preened and aligned
                                                        with care.

The swan of regality watches,
                listens,
                repositions herself with dominance and grace,
                moves in style and splendour worthy of the scene.

The swan of regality is dressed in white,
                knows her cousin garbed in black with a beak still dashed with red.

The swan of regality is ready for inspection,
                is ready for her photograph,
                is ready to highlight life upon a pond.

The swan of regality is used as an example,
                has all her curves in place,
                has nothing out of place to form a basis of distraction.

The swan of regality is equipped for her environment,
                can feed where others cannot,
                can feed in deeper waters where the short necks go elsewhere,
                can feed without a threat from poachers,
                can feed at her leisure with a minimum of fuss,
                can feed where her preference is not grazed by others,
                can feed until her appetite is sated by her fare.

The swan of regality cruises slowly past,
                is not in a hurry to complete her journey,
                has time to consider all which venture in her path,
                will peck to scatter the intruders who come within her zone
                                                   of influence.

The swan of regality is assessed by her appearance and her 'looks',
                is the appropriate colour as favoured by the righteous,
                has a history of being admired by man,
                has a history of being prized upon a lake.

The swan of regality can easily wear a crown,
                is commemorated by man as 'an ugly duckling',
                has a future where it is selectively protected by man.

The swan of regality is visited by children equipped with bags of bread,
        equipped with time and willingness to feed,
        equipped with manifestations of delight as the swan responds.

The swan of regality raises her cygnets with great care,
    raises her cygnets near the water,
    raises her cygnets to pay attention,
        to be wary of the dangers encountered:
            whether in childhood,
        or in the responsibilities of adulthood—
            which maturity imposes.

The swan of regality has feet designed for travelling in the water,
    has wings designed for travelling through the air,
    has a beak designed for shovelling entrapments—
        within the venue where the food is found.

The swan of regality is not known for its chattering,
    is not known for excessive friendliness,
    is not known for seeking the company of man.

The swan of regality has a reserve of fear close to the surface of behaviour,
    has caution as its catchphrase where relationships are sought,
    has monogamy of bonding throughout the times of rearing.

The swan of regality is not antagonistic,
    is not unduly protective of its territory,
    is not prone to attack except when on a nest,
        except when with cygnets trailing
            along behind,
    except when threatened by the predators of
        which they are aware."

My Content Study Aid

The Comfort of The Lord (3)

"The comfort of The Lord rests within My garden,
      rests with fellowship and trust,
      rests with significance and worth.

The comfort of The Lord speaks to My companionship:
   with those I know who committed to the values which I taught,
   with those I know who lived in Faith,
   with those I know who perceived The Truth of The Apostles,
   with those I know who died to self for their beliefs,
   with those I know who persevered until each grave was filled.

The comfort of The Lord speaks with those within whom My Spirit was made welcome,
        within whom The Fire of My Spirit burnt
           brightly without faltering,
        within whom My Call to servanthood was
           obeyed without delay.

The comfort of The Lord speaks with such as these on matters arising for discussion,
       on histories vividly recounted,
       on divine appointments long kept but
          not forgotten,
       on ministries as encountered in
         reality with the assistance
         of My guiding counsel,
       on ministries dependent on My
         answering of prayers.

The comfort of The Lord is at home with My people whom I love,
    with My sheep for whom I died,
    with My Praisers and My Worshippers bringing
       Glory to My Name—
    so I may so bring Glory to The Father.

The comfort of The Lord reaches out to embrace the new arrivals,
    listens attentively to all such would impart,
    encourages them to be at home within the being
        of surroundings—
    yet to transition from the strange to the familiar.

The comfort of The Lord sees The Apostles up and serving,
    sees the angels busy with their ministering,
    sees The Comforters in action,
    sees The Inheritance of My Disciples becoming evident within
       the various fields of jurisdiction,

        sees The Gowns of Life embellished as deserved,
        sees The New Names established as The White Stones are
                                  carried
                                    carefully to and fro,
        sees The Garlands placed with care on The Victors' Heads—
                those who were honoured in the running of their race.

The comfort of The Lord knows The Presence of My Spirit,
        knows The Presence of The Father,
        knows all which comprise The Edifice of Heaven.

The comfort of The Lord soothes and pacifies all I know who were subjected to violence
                                    which terminated in the
                                    immediacy of death,
        all I know who were tortured unto death
                with angels leading them to Heaven,
        all I know who were martyred unto Glory for
                My Name without wilting in their Faith.

The comfort of The Lord welcomes The Presence of The Saved of God:
        welcomes those who qualified during the tribulation;
        welcomes those who called on The Website of The Lord;
        welcomes those who were instated through The Psalms of God;
        welcomes those who accepted Grace with a contrite heart;
        welcomes those who responded to The Call of God within
                                    the fields—
                so visited by God within My servants;
        welcomes those who confessed their love of
                                The Living Loving God.

The comfort of The Lord is neither shallow nor withdrawn,
        is deep and understanding,
        is laced both with Mercy and with Justice,
        is administered between the twins of Righteousness with Truth.

The comfort of The Lord is secure in the destiny of choice,
        honours all who are enabled to enter through the gate,
        honours all who have an entry in The Lamb's Book of Life.

The comfort of The Lord welcomes My returning citizens as adoptees
                into The Family of God,
                into The Kingdom of The King of kings,
                into The Inheritance of The Cross as
                        promised and upheld."

Life Within My Garden

"Life within My garden is not crowded.

Life within My garden has space aplenty for any and all activities,
        has space aplenty for displays of interest,
                of grandeur,
                      of tableaux fit for gardens.

Life within My garden does not create a chorus of cries for help,
        speaks of contentment in surroundings which are neither spared
                for comfort nor of interest,
        speaks of interactions with neighbours of sensitivity who can
                sense and respond accordingly.

Life within My garden is not a static scene,
        can change depending on the viewpoint,
            depending on the settings of the time spheres,
            depending on the shadows lengthening or shortening,
            depending on the travelling where the 'who' or 'what'
                is set as the objective.

Life within My garden surmounts the difficulty of sameness,
        the difficulty of portraying the interest of the day,
        the difficulty of identity where the family members
            have features of great similarity.

Life within My garden is neither bereft of movement nor the sounds of thought.

Life within My garden is the immersion of the senses in the perceiving of surroundings:
        together with the interactions galore which hold
            the eyes in movement and
            the 'uncertain' ones at bay.

Life within My garden has no walls of containment,
        is not a zoo in just another setting,
        is not arranged to satisfy the gapers and the gawkers.

Life within My garden is arranged so all may feel at ease,
        all may be welcome and 'at home',
        all may be comfortable and secure in their being.

Life within My garden is not a place for boasting of past endeavours,
        is not a place where pride describes the exploits,
        where success is the sole reason for emphasis,
        where the power of thought is first to be fully understood,
        where poor thought control can lead to the embarrassment
            of leakage without intent.

Life within My garden converses with understanding of The Tongues of Heaven
        as encountered in mortality:
        as practiced there for fluency;
        as expanded there in expression;
        as tried there in the achieving of interpretation;
        as tested there for articulation of the many
               different tongues:
         with enunciation cleared for use and purpose;
        as sought for both speaking and translating,
          for both translating and speaking—
             as 'both sides of the coin'.

Life within My garden is a possession prized by God,
    is a time of relaxation in both the scheduling of man and the
               scheduling of God,
    is an example of where both God and man can come together—
        in the closeness of a shared experience—
        where man depended on The Son of God,
        where The Son of God depended on The Father:
        where both had to arise from the grave of man—
          in order to fulfil their chosen destinies
            which dwelt within Freewill.

Life within My garden is an exciting place to be,
    is a location which befriends The Stars of God,
      which encapsulates the 'be-all' of existence yet
          negates the 'end-all' of validity,
      which reaches out to where the starbursts cluster
            in assembly,
      which makes practical the visiting where close-up
          views are both interesting
          and appealing:
      where the discoveries associated with the
         touch and feel of visits
         are not easily forgotten.

Life within My garden is far-reaching:
    extending well beyond the stars—
      as an extending sphere whose components were seen
              in mortality;
    extending into galaxies which the telescopes of man had neither
          pierced nor imaged;
    extending well beyond the imagining of man where the infinite
          is difficult to grasp.

Life within My garden is sprinkled with life forms according to The Will of God;
     are scattered out of reach of one another;
     are scattered so they cannot coalesce to form
          a grand alliance—
    which would decry the creation power of God.

Life within My garden is awesome to behold,
    is awesome to dwell therein with trips both far and wide,
    is awesome to study the creativity of The Living Loving God—
      at the centre of His Creation with all which that entails.

Life within My garden has no equal anywhere in existence,
    has nothing in existence where other life forms welcome visitors:
        to share their being in existence,
    has no entities of life occurring without input from
         The Living Loving God.

Life within My garden marks the grand designs of God,
    marks life within its fullness—
      complete and opened out,
      magnified and developed—
      both in intelligence and the freedom of Freewill.

Life within My garden honours both My Spirit and The Father:
     where The Three unite in unity—
     and My people of The Father's flock are held in
        His proxy of adoption."

My Content Study Aid

The Cheerleader of My Garden

"The cheerleader of My garden is My Spirit in His fullness.

The cheerleader of My garden is significant in His abilities,
        knows the placement which obviates a search,
        knows the specifications both for location and the access,
        knows the introductory details for journeying among
                the stars,
        knows the being of a presence in the home base
                which presents.

The cheerleader of My garden is not a sluggard in attention,
        is not the subject of complaints,
        is not the instigator of misdirection.

The cheerleader of My garden answers all the queries with precision and delight,
        rarely has a follow-up requesting further detail,
        never has to update a previous solution.

The cheerleader of My garden is knowledgable and trustworthy,
        will not be misunderstood,
        will not implant an error in directions,
        is well informed on the placements in and of My garden.

The cheerleader of My garden considers all the implications surrounding each request—
    as examples:
        of temperature,
        of lighting,
        of gravity,
        of the source of energy,
        of the means of access and return,
        of the circumstances of the welcome of the visitor,
        of the activation of the senses in tune with the viewing of surroundings
                with all which is encountered.

The cheerleader of My garden knows all there is to know,
        is not stumped for lack of knowledge,
        is not misled through lack of wisdom for discernment.

The cheerleader of My garden knows how to gather retinues,
        how to place them to the best advantage,
        how to secure for a two-way journey all invited
                to attend.

The cheerleader of My garden is still the overseer of construction,
> the enrober of My Creation as progressive
> completion is evidenced to all within My garden.

The cheerleader of My garden knows the choristers available,
> knows the music master's plans,
> knows the festivities to soon be due as the introductions
>> to the ceremonies—
>> the ceremonies of welcome,
>> the ceremonies of rejoicing,
>> the ceremonies of dance,
>> the ceremonies of song,
>> the ceremonies of music,
>> the ceremonies of exaltation,
>> the ceremonies of praise and worship—
>>> which come under the auspices of The Edifice
>>>> of God.

The cheerleader of My garden is My gardener-in-chief,
> is My chief sounding board of intent,
> is My plumb line and My level which holds to the straight
>> and true.

The cheerleader of My garden is honoured for His efforts,
> as measured by results,
> as evidenced by the landscaping,
>> the seascaping,
>> the spacescaping wherein all
>>> are confirmed to dwell.

The cheerleader of My garden checks that all is well within The Heavens and on Earth,
> that all complies with the standards of
>> The Kingdom,
> that all may arise and bless:
> The Holy of Holies which no longer is enclosed;
> The Sanctuary of The Sacred where Glory now reposes;
> The Altar of The Lamb where The Ark of The Covenant now resides.

The cheerleader of My garden is at home within My garden of tranquility wherein is the
> residence of God;
> from where radiates Righteousness with Peace;
> from where radiates well-being with Truth;
> from where radiates the eternity of existence:
> from The Presence of The Loving Living God.

The cheerleader of My garden stands upright and upholds—
> the equilibrium of Creation and of Evolution,
> the equilibrium of Eternity and of Mortality,
> the equilibrium of Heaven and of Hell.

The cheerleader of My garden knows these are some of the equilibriums of God;
> knows these are all of the equilibriums of man."

My Content Study Aid

Achieving of My Garden

"Achieving of My garden can be the fulfilment of a dream.

Achieving of My garden can be the guiding light within a life within mortality,
        can be the motivation which dwells within a heart,
        can be the motivation for a family at large.

Achieving of My garden sees the spirit and the soul,
            united with the body,
            being honoured for the destiny as sought.

Achieving of My garden sees the wonderland as opened for inspection,
            opened with a dwelling place apportioned,
            opened with the fullness of relationships
                      and friendships,
            opened upon promises oft times repeated,
            opened with the gates of Heaven spreadeagled wide
                      and inviting,
            opened at the ending of mortality for all who placed
                their Faith in The Son-rise of The Son.

Achieving of My garden is the destiny of choice within the fields of Discipleship,
        is the destiny within the fellowship of God,
        is the destiny with adoption into The Family of God,
        is the destiny preferred for man to seek within his existence
                      in eternity.

Achieving of My garden should not produce a heartfelt sigh,
        should not produce a sense of relaxation,
        should not produce a sense that Discipleship has ended.

Achieving of My garden opens new beginnings,
        opens different ways of living,
            different ways of addressing the familiar challenges
                      of yesteryear,
            different ways and means to be applied with
                understanding to the ways and means of God.

Achieving of My garden is not a lifestyle in the making,
        is a lifestyle of presentation readied for adoption.

Achieving of My garden is not dependent on a culture being carried forward,
        has the culture already instated so to impact on the entrants to
                      My garden.

Achieving of My garden incurs an orientation to be successfully concluded,
        where failures have already been prevented by exclusion,
        where qualifying failed to gain an escape pass through
              the flames,
        where there could not be surmounted the hurdles born
            of dissatisfaction—
        in the presence of a heart unknown to contrition.

Achieving of My garden reflects the success of Righteousness with Faith,
        of Truth bound up with Love,
        of Sincerity within The Fear of God,
        of Intent surrounded by Commitment in the
            heart where gratitude prevails.

Achieving of My garden is as a lightning bolt to the spirit soul and body
        as they awaken from their sleep,
        as they step up to all which rests in storage,
        as they prepare to receive the fullness of
            their inheritance just waiting
            for the here and now.

Achieving of My garden is not a let-down to expectations,
        is not a frown of disappointment,
        is not a scowl with understanding,
        is not a dismissal without approval.

Achieving of My garden is as the epitome of the offering of God,
        is as the rewarding of the being of a true and faithful servant,
        is as the treasure stored in Heaven awaiting a release."

My Content Study Aid

_____
_____
_____
_____
_____
_____
_____
_____
_____
_____
_____

The Crying of The Whales

"The crying of the whales is not heard proclaiming a loss within My garden.

The crying of the whales is heard within the seas of mortality,
    is heard within the oceans of The Earth,
    is heard within the submarines which burrow through the
              whales' domain.

The crying of the whales is heard within the reach of dolphins,
    within the reach of identity commensurate
         with understanding,
    within the reach of all who can identify a distress call
         when heard impinging on the ear.

The crying of the whales is heard within the ranges of the ships of death:
      striking death to the mature,
      striking death to the young at tail still drinking milk,
      striking death to the largest selected both for size
            and bulk.

The crying of the whales speaks of the cries of loss,
    of the cries for babies still remembered as they were,
      as the cries for family members
        no longer in relationship,
      as the cries for the elderly stolen
        from their time of
         grandparents to the pod.

The crying of the whales arises from activities of the pirates of the seas:
        those who hunt and kill to sell munching on the
          parents of the seas,
        those who hunt within the bounds of deceit,
        those who satisfy The Multitudes as the liars of
          their nations,
        those who would hide under the research of
          the scientists—
        who do not examine with integrity the
         necessity of the killing
         sprees of the ships of death.

The crying of the whales is the signature of the witnessing of death,
                                 of the witnessing of the pain and suffering,
                                 of the smell of blood upon each breath
                                                     intermingled with the taste
                                                     of blood within the water,
                                 of the distress calls for help and assistance
                                          beyond the capabilities of the mothers:
                                                           who circle in despair.

The crying of the whales is instigated by man against the will of nations,
                                 against the attempts at justifying,
                                 against the lies of the necessity for food,
                                 against the pressures of economics,
                                 against the need for research of benefit to
                                                              the whales,
                                 against the slaughter where protection does
                                                 not prevent the will of the few.

The crying of the whales diminishes with the catch,
                                 diminishes with the mothers left to tend their calves,
                                 diminishes with the numbers still left free to roam in
                                                              their inheritance.

The crying of the whales are not heard above the water;
                                 are not heard upon the ships of stealth;
                                 are not heard upon the fleets as gathered;
                                 are not heard,
                                         except within a cabin,
                                         upon the ship charged with the rendering and incisions—
                                         to transform that taken from the seas into the pieces set for
                                                              marketing upon a distant island shore.

The crying of the whales exist upon recordings,
                                 are not popular to hear,
                                 are mournful in their nature,
                                 are sad in their context:
                                         as they spread the news of loss,
                                         as they continue on their journeys related to the seasons,
                                         as they endeavour to avoid the thrashing and the death
                                                           throes they have come to know so well.

The crying of the whales sees the wounded drown within their home,
                                             no longer able to take advantage of being
                                                           nudged to the surface—
                                                where life exists within each breath,
                                             no longer to be seen in majesty upon the seas
                               where they both spout and submerge as their will decides.

The crying of the whales is attributed to man,
            is attributed to the oil lamps of the past,
            is attributed as a curse around the current neck of man—
                for his needless killing of the beauty of the sees,
                for his hunting and destroying of the survivors from the past,
                from his uncaring attitude of the fragility of life
                      when hunted without respite,
                      when hunted without a sanctuary,
                      when hunted as a delicacy which a nation can well
                                            do without.

The crying of the whales is resultant on the exercising of the dominion of man,
            where accountability for a lack of wisdom in the courts of God
                                  exists unto eternity,
            where the scenes of slaughter are not shown unto an island nation,
            where the need to stop the slaughter falls upon the deafest ears,
            where the selfishness of greed should take away the pride:
                  in hunting and in capturing that no longer required
                              to meet the needs of man."

My Content Study Aid

The Fields of Wonder

"The fields of wonder on The Earth of mortality are multi-shades of green.

The fields of wonder in the Heaven of eternity are multi-shades of blue:
>> are seen with different eyes,
>> are seen with a different light source,
>> are seen from within a wider spectrum of
>>>> emitted light.

The fields of wonder within My garden express the grounding of design on a
>>>> different basis,
>> on much greater perception with extension
>>> of the colour wheel as known to man,
>> on much greater awareness of the shadings
>>> as they separate and merge,
>> on much greater control of artistry
>>>> and scenery,
>>> as described upon a palette,
>>> as committed to expression,
>>> as applied to the clouds of variance
>>> throughout the lighting of The Heavens:
>>> accompanied even so by the salutations
>>>> birthed within the heart of man.

The fields of wonder in Heaven see everything initially with the eyesight of familiarity,
>>> where colours are unchanged until
>>>> orientation completes:
>>> when colours slowly assume the palettes
>>>> of The Lord.

The fields of wonder within My garden vary with location,
>> vary with the settings,
>> vary with objectives,
>> vary both with input and with output from and
>>>> to The Stars.

The fields of wonder within My garden vary with the contrast,
>> vary with the brightness,
>> vary with the content of the eye-scape,
>> vary with the colour density,
>> vary with the thought patterns designed
>>>> to modify the fields of view.

The fields of wonder in the residence of The Saints have highlights
                        worthy of closeup examination,
                        worthy of inspection so movement can be explained,
                        worthy of the intent of tuning of the ear so sounds
                                      may be discovered with their meanings—
                                                and conversations thereby begun.

The fields of wonder can be viewed with the colour of dominance,
                        with the colour of default,
                        with the colour of preference,
                        with the colour of familiarity,
                        with the colour of The Lord:
                                  can be reset with a change of thought.

The fields of wonder within My garden are tempered and sustained,
                        are fitted for display with support,
                        are prepared for the scheduled flashover for new
                              scenes to be promoted so interest is maintained.

The fields of wonder give access to trial visits,
                give access to experience a differing reality,
                give access within the safety of the oversight of God.

The fields of wonder may be personalized to the preferences of a visitor,
                            to the preferences of a resident,
                            to the combined preferences of a gathering,
                            to the preferences as set and used by God.

The fields of wonder are areas of special interest within the scoping of the eyes—
                                    which are selected and prepared
                                                      by God—
                                for the enjoyment of The Residents
                                                        at large.

The fields of wonder know the sourcing of vitality,
                know the importance of composition,
                know the profoundness of the decorator's touch.

The fields of wonder know the layouts of the archipelagoes.

The fields of wonder submit willingly to inspection,
                submit willingly to exploration,
                submit willingly in aiding the resolving of many questions,
                submit willingly to welcoming the approaches of The Saints.

The fields of wonder exist and are,
                experience and learn,
                do not come and go.

The fields of wonder uplift and hold in thrall,
> surprise and shatter pre-conceptions,
> exhibit and instruct,
> disclose and encourage
> frequent and modify the attributes of both the visitors and residents.

The fields of wonder are many and abound;
> have many who are inbound,
> have some who come to stay,
> have farewells oft bordering on regrets,
> have farewells which speak of a return,
> have farewells set upon a continuum where time is not a guest.

The fields of wonder witness amazement on the faces,
> impress their properties on the senses,
> imprint their impressions on the memory banks attached to all the
>> senses of The Family of God."

My Content Study Aid

The End-time Psalms of God
or as The End-time Homilies of God

"The End-time Psalms of God are majestic in their construction,
        are precise in their definitions,
        are conveying their simplicity of intent.

The End-time Psalms of God reach out to the populace of God as screened by Grace,
        reach out to the assigned to the destiny of default with
                denial of their God,
        reach out to The Multitudes of uncertainty where Grace
                presently abounds:
        yet Mercy prepares to spread her wings for the
                future needs of man.

The End-time Psalms of God are for the cultures of today:
        so today may impart knowledge of the future realities
                of man,
        so tomorrow may express the start of a new beginning,
        so the past with its hypocrisy may be left upon the dust
                of yesteryears.

The End-time Psalms of God are The End-time backstops to the populators of Heaven:
        to the encouragers to participate
                in a destiny of choice;
        to the markers—
                in desperate need of removal:
                as placed and leading to the
                      destiny of default;
        to the witnesses of Freewill
                declarations of freedom
                and of Truth—
        which will attach to the sacrifice
                as witnessed on The Cross.

The End-time Psalms of God are My love notes to My people,
        are My love notes of reminders,
        are My love notes of encouragement,
        are My love notes from the ages,
        are My love notes born of sacrifice,
        are My love notes building in support,
        are My love notes offering companionship,
        are My love notes stemming from My Creation of the
                spirits of man.

The End-time Psalms of God are invitations to participate in The Offerings of God:
>> in The Blessings of life-changing testimonies,
>> in The Inheritance of The Cross of Grace,
>> in The Immersion of The Bride of The Lamb,
> in the place prepared in readiness for a Temple,
> in joining through adoption The Family of God,
> in dwelling in The Presence of The Living Loving God,
> in the nurturing and discipling by The Good Shepherd
>> as a lamb and sheep within My fold,
> in the answering of The Call to Communion which puts
>> a seal upon the lips.

The End-time Psalms of God are crafted by The Master Potter to be presented as bowls
>> of incense,
>> enveloping and overflowing,
> in this—
>> The End-time of preparation where the sands of time are running through the hour-glass of Heaven and The Earth.

The End-time Psalms of God are the sequences of applicability of relevance to a journey.
The End-time Psalms of God are the contextual references brought to the notice of man.
The End-time Psalms of God are the dictated indicatives of the desires of God.

The End-time Psalms of God address the issues of the day,
> address the issues of the night,
> address the issues of sin,
> address the issues of the body of man,
> address the issues of the soul of man,
> address the issues of the spirit of man,
> address the issues of The Blessings of God.

The End-time Psalms of God reach out to proclaim,
> reach out to draw to attention,
> reach out to bring The Truth,
> reach out to circumvent the lies,
> reach out to refute the multiplicity of religions,
> reach out for the benefit of My Disciples with their
>> Inheritance of The Cross.

The End-time Psalms of God are addressed to The Multitudes across all cultures
>> and divides,
> are addressed to all who would present as The Bride of Christ,
> are addressed to those who would procrastinate:
>> to so risk jeopardizing their well-being
>> from their loss of the benefit of Grace.

The End-time Psalms of God are composed in The Heavens,
        are dictated to The Earth,
        are entered as the records of Divinity—
            placed on screen and on paper—
                for the eyes and ears and hands of man:
                    for The Counselling of man's Freewill as he lives
                            within mortality.

The End-time Psalms of God come from a setting of enormous size and grandeur—
                the throne room of God backed by the whole of
                    creation from every aspect of eternity.

The End-time Psalms of God do not vie with the opinions of man,
        do not vie with the arguments of man,
        do not vie with the explanations of man,
        do not vie with the wisdom of man,
        do not vie with the knowledge of man,
        do not vie with the longevity of man as seated in his
                              timed mortality.

The End-time Psalms of God are correct and stand in their finality in
                          The English Tongue:
            except for translation and spelling and punctuation
                by which all three originate with man."

My Content Study Aid

Missing From My Garden

"Missing from My garden is the linkage of the ages applicable to man.

Missing from My garden is the linkage inherent in The Freewill of man,
                      inherent in the life of man,
                      inherent in the nature of man.

Missing from My garden is that which was removed from the character of man,
                            from the soul of man,
                            from the heart of man.

Missing from My garden are the reminders of the past,
                the invitations of the past,
                the welcomes of the past,
                the behaviour of the past,
                the collections of the past,
                the images of the past—
                          all which restricted honour,
                          all which expanded the scoping of respect.

Missing from My garden are the offerings of the night,
                the installations built on secrets,
                the confusion which abounded,
                the emphasis on wealth casually collected.

Missing from My garden are the archetypes of the weakness of the will,
                are the prototypes of experimentation,
                are the choices leading to the trials,
                are the funds found necessary to continue,
                are the words which strayed from the opened mouth,
                are the sequences of succumbing to the daze within the days.

Missing from My garden are the hesitations on decisions,
                are the hesitations built on lingering,
                are the hesitations surrounding access to a spiral,
                are the hesitations in the breeding of a habit,
                are the hesitations from the joining of a group,
                are the hesitations prior to the untruths deemed necessary for
                                  attending to survival.

Missing from My garden are those who cannot change,
                those who will not change,
                those who see no need to change,
                those yet to encounter the see-saw of despair.

Missing from My garden are those who are content with a lifestyle as encountered,
> who 'pooh-pooh' the testimonies of others,
> who listen but do not hear,
> who look but do not see,
> who touch but do not feel,
> who read but fail to understand the import laid
>> before them.

Missing from My garden are the disguises used by man,
> is the fancy dress used by man,
> are the methods of control used by man,
> are the weapons used by man,
> are the threats and curses used by man,
> is the seeking of vengeance being used by man.

Missing from My garden are partnerships of exploitation which continue past the grave:
> where no-one benefits except the twosome of
>> the 'self'.

Missing from My garden are those who would hide their heart's desire.

Missing from My garden are segments of a populace who follow other gods.

Missing from My garden are those beset on violence.

Missing from My garden is the sin of man when in mortality.

Missing from My garden are the unrepentant sinners of The Earth:
> who stare out upon the world with no shame issuing
>> from their eyes,
> who have worn their consciences into a state of
>> silent uselessness,
> who are strangers to sensations in the spirit and the
>> soul when 'Righteousness with Faith'
>> is mentioned in their presence.

Missing from My garden are all who require their Freewill to be respected—
> all who adopted the destiny of default;
> who never made a choice of that which was within
>> their grasp:
> when Grace and Faith were present for the acceptance
>> of man.

Missing from My garden are those bound to Hell through the respect demanded by their
> Freewill actions.

Missing from My garden in the absence of time speaks of eternity being spent within the
> destiny of default."

My Light Within My Garden

"My light within My garden is the establishment of presence.

My light within My garden is the dwelling place of My Knowledge Base and Wisdom,
>> My sharing and companionship,
>> My Creation with My records.

My light within My garden is My presence awaiting the encounters with those who
>> choose to join in the experience of God.

My light within My garden vibrates with expectancy at the fulfilment of a goal:
>> experienced and carried out;
>> fulfilled and magnified with the task of reconciliation;
> with the day of graduation from the best to the superlative;
>> from the choice to the result;
>> from the past into the future;
>> from the physical into the spiritual;
>> from the mortal into the eternal;
>> from dismissal into reinstatement;
>> from the sin fields of man into the shining of creation;
>> from the loss of status to positions of great honour,
>> from the traps of Satan to the tugs and hugs of God—
>> for such can be the journey and the travelling of man.

My light within My garden knows all the books and letters of man,
>> knows all the books and letters of God—
>>> ones lost in times of strife,
>>> ones written in times of inspiration,
>>> ones containing the wisdom of the generations:
>> with the appearance of the books and the arrival of the letters.

My light within My garden has all the books available,
>> has all the letters placed in the care of families.

My light within My garden no longer holds as sacred the secrets of the past,
>>> the embarrassments of the past,
>>> the mistakes of the past,
>>> the recriminations of the past,
>>> the successes of the past,
>>> the rewards of the past,
>>> the achievements of the past,
>>> the decisions of the past—
>> the records of the lives of man lived under the spotlight
>> of Freewill abilities within the limitations of the times.

My light within My garden includes all the libraries of man before their ends were met,
                includes the library of God where survival was never
                                              in doubt.

My light within My garden is not possible to be either dimmed or extinguished,
                is related to eternity,
                is searchable and true,
                is compiled from the records of each day in each life upon
                                                    The Earth.

My light within My garden is not the lighting of a set,
                is not the lighting of a vista,
                is not the lighting of a dwelling place,
                is not the lighting of existence:
for the lighting of existence has all the reactors of God in place and operational;
                set and trimmed for life;
                set and trimmed for creation;
                set and trimmed where Time is not required,
                            where Time—
                            through need or necessity—
                            is yet to have the requirement to be measured.

My light within My garden is not all shared with man:
                has points of non-disclosure;
                are not part of The Inheritance of The Cross;
                form parts of The Mystery of Creation—
                            as protected from Man for his long term benefit.

My light within My garden has no shadows in its sight,
                has no ripples on the covers,
                has no shivers or shudders anywhere within.

My light within My garden burns very brightly and cleanly,
                leaves neither smoke nor residue,
                is neither destructive nor a palliative,
                is neither incomplete nor edited since the days of compilation.

My light within My garden includes The Lamb's Book of Life—
                        together with all the recorded aspects kept of man—
                                      each in his individuality.

My light within My garden has The Father's oversight,
                has My Spirit's assistance,
                has My angels hovering in attendance,
                has the ways and means to operate to The Satisfaction
                                            of God."

The Maestro of The Intellect

"The maestro of the intellect wears out the debates of man,
        wears out the theories of man,
        wears out the positing of man.

The maestro of the intellect turns the tables on the ill-prepared,
        on the ill-informed,
        on the ill-in-deed.

The maestro of the intellect silences the argument brought without due thought,
        brought without the testimony of
            the simulation,
        brought without the grounding
            required for a theory.

The maestro of the intellect harnesses a theory to seek its basis on The Truth,
        to discover the flights of fancy which may
            bring it crashing down,
        to discover test and witness the strength of
            the foundations.

The maestro of the intellect studies and evaluates the extent of the assumptions,
        searches for the breaches of the protocols,
        expands on a reversion dependent on a unique location.

The maestro of the intellect constructs a timeline recording measured change with the
            willingness to revert,
        searches for consistency of approach within
            the methodology,
        finds the flaws of entrapment hidden in the presentations.

The maestro of the intellect examines the fineness of the detail,
        the practicality of the measurements,
        the quantity and quality of the sampling in the
            supporting of the numbers.

The maestro of the intellect evaluates and proposes,
        starts from the known and verifies the steps for validity—
            with probability for the ownership
                of function and the
                change within design.

The maestro of the intellect surveys and quantifies the keys to definitions,
            the partaking scholarship involved,
            the level of the qualified who would
                contribute to the points of view.

The maestro of the intellect shuns the presentations repeating those of yesterday,
    shuns the footsteps which follow in the mud,
    shuns the grandstanders who want to make a name,
    shuns the thoughtless and the prideful who would seek a platform:
        built by others—
         on which to stand with their
         proclamations full of holes.

The maestro of the intellect will not be shouted down by the impostors,
    will not be dethroned by the immature or deceitful,
      by the selective data gatherers at large,
      by assumptions born of fallacy which
      should not have seen the light of day.

The maestro of the intellect can silence his inquisitors as fixed in their stances,
    can silence the shallowness of arguments in pots which will
        not carry water,
    can silence the hangers-on dependent on the works of others:
      without the first-hand knowledge or experience,
    can silence the regurgitators of the dismissals known
        to yesterday,
    can silence the time-wasters and the charlatans in love with
      their own voices—
        regardless of the content.

The maestro of the intellect knows the exceptions which break the consistency bred
      of selection,
    knows the verifiers of the intricacies of design,
    knows the testifiers who live within their requirements of design:
      the requirements of inter-dependency;
      the requirements for simultaneous development
        as specialists;
      within the skeins of life so both can interlink.

The maestro of the intellect knows the answer to the questioning of man:
      of which came first 'the chicken or the egg';
      of significance and relevance to all external eggs
        upon The Earth.

The maestro of the intellect has practical experience in the fields in which he operates,
    has membership within the triumvirate of God,
    has an assistant he knows well as reliable and trustworthy—
      who assists and is accurate in the
      transmitting of instructions,
      who is a specialist in installing the
      viability of proposals into
      The Light of reality.

The maestro of the intellect sees The End-time spread of 'flat earth' beliefs:
> wherein The Truth is not supportive of the claims;
> wherein The Truth is not supportive of the evidence.

The maestro of the intellect sees the theory of evolution being taught to,
> and proclaimed by,
> the intellectually insecure,
> while discrepancies of life associated with design
> are not addressed,
> so the shell continues to have life while the internal
> is hollowed out and readied for decay.

The maestro of the intellect knows the theory of evolution awaits the cry that
> 'the emperor has no clothes' when all will be
> revealed and embarrassingly dismissed."

My Content Study Aid

The Arrowheads of God

"The arrowheads of God are the means of sending messages to the hearts of man.

The arrowheads of God accompany the rider on the white horse equipped with his bow.

The arrowheads of God fulfil their destiny in The Company of God,
        fulfil their destiny with fluency of preparation,
        fulfil their destiny with their inheritance assured.

The arrowheads of God are charged with Faith and Righteousness,
        are charged with declarations and the words of prophecy,
        are charged with testimonies born from the experiences of
                        attending God.

The arrowheads of God are recycled indefinitely,
        are recycled with recuperation,
        are recycled with a new target:
                with the message loaded for delivery.

The arrowheads of God are as busy as they want to be,
        are used as often as they offer,
        are rewarded with the hugs from the targets where delivery
                        is completed.

The arrowheads of God know the impact on the target,
        the wonder of delivery,
        the surprise at the word of knowledge,
        the attention to the word of wisdom,
        the acceptance and the gratitude for The Words of God
                        made known:
        The Divine appointment where a life is changed for ever,
                where a destiny is averted for
                        the better,
                where a testimony develops as
                the living water is absorbed
                and the dirt is shed.

The arrowheads of God bring The Wisdom of God,
        bring The Tongues of God,
        bring The Promises of God.

The arrowheads of God seek to install the foundations of a temple,
        seek to ensure man is aware of his choice of destiny,
        seek to enable The Inheritance of God.

The arrowheads of God bring healing in their flight paths from The Throne Rooms
                        of God.

The arrowheads of God are steadied on the rock of revelation,
        are steadied by the stability of the fletching,
        are steadied by the flight path set by the rider on the white horse
                in the moment of release.

The arrowheads of God fly straight and true,
        do not forget their messages,
        do not mumble in delivery.

The arrowheads of God do not damage what they strike,
        do not embed within an organ,
        cause no pain to be experienced by man,
        bring pain to the rider when he witnesses the arrow head being
                brushed aside and left behind:
                      without attention to the message of new life.

The arrowheads of God are joyous in assembly,
        are joyous in reporting,
        are joyous in the horseback ride as gathered for the quiver,
        are joyous in fulfilling the taskings of the rider on the white
                horse of revelation,
        are joyous for the target where the message is adopted and a life
                is changed as to the goal within a new found destiny.

The arrowheads of God are The Stars of God,
        are the populators of Heaven,
        are the synchronizers of where the needs of man are married to
                the solutions of God.

The arrowheads of God are the answers to a prayer uttered in despair;
        are the answerers awaiting questions:
            to initiate due diligence with the kings- and queens-in-waiting,
                in bearing an eternal introduction to The Living Loving God.

The arrowheads of God are the multipliers of the harvest,
        are the kernels of the outreach of God,
        are The Blessings of God moving in the disguise of man until the
                mouth is opened for delivery of the message
                whereby God reveals Himself.

The arrowheads of God are loved and rewarded as they serve—
                experience The Favour of The Lord,
                      The Blessings of The Father,
                          The Counselling of The Holy Spirit
                              with His Gifts in tow:
        so bodies of the past may become The Temples of the future;
        so a journey of wonders and of miracles may commence
                which has no end;
        so adoptions may occur into The Family of God;

so knowledge and wisdom may be acquired from God along
the pathway leading home.

The arrowheads of God are The Miracles of God in action,
are The End-time Marvels of the age,
are The Master-strokes of The Lord:
who moves and lives within the commitment to their Faith."

My Content Study Aid

The Wishing of Man

"The wishing of man is not a prayer to God.

The wishing of man is a desire that is not of God,
    is a desire tabled on the altars of idolatry,
    is a desire of coveting that has no claim to ownership,
        that has no life within reality,
        that has no summary that falls within the
            bounds of an agreement.

The wishing of man is based on flights of fancy,
    can be on the basis of a lie,
    can be born of exaggeration,
    can be birthed through misadventure,
    can open up a portal for the crowding in of the demonic,
        for their crowing of success,
        for the onset of the pain and the discomfort of the body.

The wishing of man greets the day with disappointment,
    greets the night with dissatisfaction,
    greets the morrow with an endless supply of wants as if laid before
        a witch.

The wishing of man is not helped by a coin dropped in a well,
    by a coin thrown in a fountain,
    by a coin pushed in a slot.

The wishing of man is destructive to his Faith,
    is hypocritical of his prayer life,
    is thankless to his God who cares for and watches over all his child
        both says and does.

The wishing of man is recognition of the dreams of man remaining out of reach,
    spurs selfishness to override a life of common sense,
    spurs the will of man to concentrate on the ingrain searching for
        wish fulfilment.

The wishing of man places man in a hunt for the inane,
    for the ridiculous,
    for the suggestions of satanic forces:
        from the reading of the stars;
        from the made up stories from the psalmists
            and false psychics who fill
            the columns of the day—
        worded so that 'Truths' can be detected for
            application from within the nonsense.

The wishing of man leads to a disconnect from reality,
        to a disconnect from life,
        to a disconnect from Faith,
            from commitment,
                from walking in The Truth which would lead
                      such safely home.

The wishing of man creates worthless comparisons which feed upon themselves,
            which are given credence as they are
                given dominance,
            which are difficult to delete once the
                habit is established and
                counsel is foregone.

The wishing of man is without achievement,
        lays a bedding of frustration,
        encourages a living in the past where the chorus of 'what ifs' fill all
                the days of sanity and longing.

The wishing of man are the daydreams of man:
            when his thinking is not governed by direction;
            when his spirit is silenced by the soul;
            when he gravitates towards demonic invitations;
            when he dwells on the 'unfairness' of his position;
            when he decides he has been 'hard done by';
            when he becomes convinced he is 'owed' within 'a right'—
                to possess that seen to be so coveted yet remains
                      beyond his reach.

The wishing of man surfaces amidst the turmoil of the mind,
        surfaces within the turmoil of expression,
        surfaces within the network of desires as birthed and spread—
            by a waywardness of application—
            by thoughts without either perception or control.

The wishing of man should be stamped on at the outset,
        should be banned as a verb within a vocabulary when used in the
                      first person,
        should not come forth as a profanity from the lips of man:
            in expressing dissatisfaction for all the gifts of God—
            where the heart is not impressed by gratitude—
                is without a list of all which is received.

The wishing of man has no promises of supply,
        no promises of provisioning;
            becomes strengthened with the lengthening into a satanic list,
            becomes a burden on a back not easily dislodged.

The wishing of man is neither a vision nor a dream as brought by God,
    is the encroaching of sin into an opened field of play:
        where dangers lurk for both 'Faith' and 'Righteousness'.

The wishing of man brings restrictions to the field of endeavour,
    brings attributes from different sources encouraged to feel at home,
    brings acceptance of dispersion for the hunt of 'like with like':
        as the attack proceeds with the search for reinforcements
            which fester on agreement.

The wishing of man separates man from his God,
    widens a hollow:
        into a ditch,
        into a moat,
        into a crevasse—
    where a bridge is then required to overcome the
            built-in difficulty:
    of access to a body soul and spirit now in need of rescue—
        prior to darkness completing its descent."

My Content Study Aid

The Whistler in The Wind

"The whistler in the wind requires a lot of practice.

The whistler in the wind achieves very little unless guided by the will to set up signalling
                                                                to the barkers of the flocks.

The whistler in the wind of God sends a signal of contentment,
                       a signal of partial loneliness,
                  a signal where the content is often copied,
                                is oft repeated,
                                is oft disjointed in fits
                                        and starts,
                                is oft tuneless in the
                                    absence of a skill,
                                is sometimes tuneful in
                                matching the notes
                                and timbre of a song.

The whistler in the wind sets the self a challenge in establishing a meaning with intent:
                                is not expectant of a reply,
                                can wander back and forth,
                                can cycle up and down,
                                as the mind strays without direction
                                    while the lips are far from clear.

The whistler in the wind is not seeking understanding,
                is filling in the silence with activity and sound,
                is within a loop which is difficult to stop,
                is stuck in repetition where the notes are very limited,
                          where the key is unimportant,
                          where the level of the skill is not
                                              in question,
                          where the birds fail to recognize a chortle
                                        from a chuckle.

The whistler in the wind is happy in his whistle,
                does not seek attention,
                does not seek an interruption which terminates the whistle.

The whistler in the wind sometimes needs to whet his whistle,
                              finds it difficult when the mouth is dry,
                              finds improvement with concentration,
                              is immaterial when calling for attention,
                              when seeking the lost or the
                                                  mislaid companion.

The whistler in the wind is not frustrated by the effort,
>	is not discouraged by a request to stop,
>	is not disconcerted by a lack of appreciation.

The whistler in the wind speaks of a soul within an environment waiting
>	>	for completeness;
>	of a soul waiting in expectation for an intrusion to the
>	>	thought pattern;
>	of a soul waiting for the time piece of man to separate
>	>	the divisions within a life.

The whistler in the wind drifts into silence with the attention-getter of the moment,
>	with the bird in flight across the sight lines,
>	with an insect intruding on the peace of mind.

The whistler in the wind restores the lips in readiness to resume from where the whistle
>	dwindled to a stop in midpoint of the breath.

The whistler in the wind mixes patience with concentration,
>	with mixed success at producing:
>	>	the whistle going forth,
>	>	the constancy of the whistle as emitted,
>	>	the whistle without improvement of
>	>	>	the fingers,
>	>	the whistle without an accessory in
>	>	>	the mouth.

The whistler in the wind is relaxed in stance,
>	is relaxed in putting a foot into the wind,
>	is relaxed with the tethering of a kite within the sky.

The whistler in the wind watches the drifting of balloons with the baskets hanging under
>	the canopies catching the residues of fire.

The whistler in the wind watches the yachts scudding on their way with helmsmen
>	>	in delight,
>	leaning overboard with ropes at the point
>	>	of balance.

The whistler in the wind retreats lower in the hide as the guns are pointed;
>	as ducks or geese take avoidance action,
>	as the shot is thrown into the air,
>	as the dead and dying are returned
>	>	promptly to The Earth,
>	as the fortunate continue on their way.

The whistler in the wind is not an innocent bystander,
           shares a common goal with the victims—
           in seeking to feed the mouths at home;
           so seeks his pounds of flesh,
           as gathered from the marsh lands—
           which survivors know as a waypoint on a journey.

The whistler in the wind knows the days of wind,
           knows the reading of the clouds,
           knows the smell of rain,
           knows the activity selected for the day and the resultant need
                            for preparation.

The whistler in the wind knows little of The God within eternity:
           of the opportunities being allowed to go to waste;
           of the opportunities not being uplifted in fulfilment
                of The Offerings of God;
           of the opportunities which can change a destiny
                from one set as default to
                the one in Freewill choice.

The whistler in the wind can develop a thankful heart—
           with understanding of the need for The Blessings of Grace—
              accompanying the development of Faith—
           all enabling access to an eternal destiny of renown."

My Content Study Aid

The Temperature of The Day

"The temperature of the day is destined for new highs and lows in the recorded
                                    experience of man.

The temperature of the day is a function of location on The Earth,
        of atmospheric movements on the surface of
                The Earth,
        of the energy within surrounding seas as the
                blanket of The Earth,
        of the movement and the fullness of the sun in
                beaming energy to The Earth,
        of the terrain and covering encountered on
                The Earth,
        of the purity and changes imposed by man—
        upon that which undertakes the support of life:
        in the compiling of the building of man's breath
                upon The Earth.

The temperature of the day should be within a cycle of stability,
        a cycle of predictability,
        a cycle of responsibility.

The temperature of the day should be within a cycle of sustainability for the dressage of
                The Earth:
        to be dressed as intended for security of tenure.

The temperature of the day recovers from its loading in the nightly period of rest,
                when activity is at a minimum and
                dissipation of the heat load
                seeks restoring of the norm.

The temperature of the day fluctuates with the direction of the wind,
        with the intensity of the wind,
        with the timing of the wind.

The temperature of the day fluctuates with the likelihood of rain,
        of ice,
        of snow,
        accompanied by the onset of the frosts:
        as The Earth prepares for the springing of new birth.

The temperature of the day is a result of the setting of the scene,
        of the variables in play with the lifetimes allocated,
        of the topography at home within the bounds of measurement,
        of the degrees of accuracy inherent in the reported
                measurements of man.

The temperature of the day cycles the clothing of man,
                cycles the diet of man,
                cycles the cooling and the heating in comforting the
                              dwellings of man.

The temperature of the day in excess upsets the stability of the ice fields of The Earth,
                promises a rise in the water levels of The Earth,
                indicates an increase in humidity which speaks to
                              the cloud formations:
                threatening to unleash increasing rain
                              and snow storms;
                        on the flood lines of The Earth;
                        on the snow fields out of time.

The temperature of the day grows into a much watched indicator fuelling the
                              expectations for the day,
                accumulating a positioning in the increased
                            watering of The Earth,
                for the buildings presently residing on areas
                        soon subject to the flooding
                        of the plains and shores.

The temperature of the day witnesses changes to the vegetation and to the tree lines of
                                            The Earth.

The temperature of the day resets the climate mode,
                with the attaining of further stability—
                where the data re-intersects at a higher level.

The temperature of the day chases and imprisons,
                captures and puts in chains,
                grasps and won't release.

The temperature of the day is now an instrument of change,
                may no longer be a friend of man,
                has yielded up the data so checks and balances may
                              be instigated,
                as a long term reversal becomes more urgent by the day.

The temperature of the day becomes able to imperil or destroy the lives and livelihood
                                            of man,
                to dismay or threaten the achievements of man,
                to contaminate or make useless the efforts
                              of man,
                to forsake and so desert the habitations of man:
                      as the living space comes under both threat
                      and fear of destruction and of a likely loss.

The temperature of the day should be placed within the hands of God by The Freewill
of man,
should be the subject of much earnest prayer based on
filtering and subtraction,
should be for the urgent attention from those who made it so
and placed no care upon the treating of the waste.
The temperature of the day has accountability falling on those:
who knew the effect and preferred the
dumping of the gases
regardless of the future,
who preferred to fill their purses at the
expense of mortgaging the future,
who preferred the silence of the guilty to the
curtailment of the spewing without
control or due consideration.
Such as they will answer as The Divine courts of justice so decree the contamination
of The Earth to have been both avoidable and wise."

My Content Study Aid

_____
_____
_____
_____
_____
_____
_____
_____
_____
_____
_____
_____
_____
_____
_____

The Withering of The Vine

"The withering of the vine should not be a sight of presentation before either the eyes of man or of God.

The withering of the vine can be as a result of damage to the roots,
    of the lack of water,
    of the influx of disease,
    of excessive heat,
    of the approach of death,
    of the drifting of the sprays of man.

The withering of the vine can be as a result of a curse,
    of a loss of Faith,
    of a lack of communication,
    of a feeding on the fruit as gathering in the bunches,
    of an infestation weakening the bearing of the branches,
    of the evidence of a lack of care,
    of the absence of a need for cultivation,
    of the absence of a pruning knife charged with the season for new life.

The withering of the vine can be revitalised with life,
    can have the yield restored,
    can repay the owner of the vineyard for the space so occupied.

The withering of the vine demands attention from the viticulturist,
    the expert of experience,
    the carrier of responsibility for:
    the health within the vineyard,
    the fruitfulness of the vineyard,
    the preparation for the harvesting to new wineskins:
        to be so filled with more than expectations,
        to be so filled with acceptance to the palate,
        to be so filled with colour and with flavour
            which speaks of the potential value of the vine,
        to be so filled with storage capabilities
            which protect and honour the inputs of the past,
        to be so filled by knowledge:
            as juice which spoils becomes
            the wine of purity in fulfilment
            of the harvester's intent.

The withering of the vine yields below that for what it has been trained,
        for what has been expensed,
        for what has been expected,
        for what the dresser of the vineyard both
                required and needed in
                repayment of the effort.

The withering of the vine is not an example worthy of praise,
        worthy of duplication,
        worthy of an example to be followed,
      worthy of the bother to recall a past performance,
      worthy to assess the likelihood of success when the rot sets in.

The withering of the vine disgraces all the vineyard,
      does not bring honour to the ground wherein it roots,
      does not bring envy from the surrounding relatives,
      does not bring satisfaction of performance when comparing
                the results,
      does not bring certainty of tenure if the present indicates
                the future,
              if bitterness is permitted to
                overwrite a
                grateful heart,
            if the effort of man is not
                linked to the effort
                made by God.

The withering of the vine speaks of a weakness in meeting the needs of the vine,
        speaks of a lack of understanding from one charged with the
                upkeep of the vine,
      speaks of ignorance not replaced with knowledge from one
            failing in the meeting of obligations.

The withering of the vine can be halted by putting it under the care of God,
    can be healed by The Blessings of God,
    can be reinvigorated with the learning of a destiny where life
            is freed from disease and worry:
            to be filled with The Promises of God
            birthed from the sojourn on a cross.

The withering of the vine can be halted by being rooted in The Truth,
        by bearing the fruits of love,
        by seeding The Faith of Righteousness,
        by following in the footsteps of The Master with
                the vineyard who gathers and collects:
                all who would be a vine and so learn to
                    stretch their arms.

The withering of the vine can be halted by discarding all which causes rot,
      which carries dissatisfaction to the core of belief,
     which leaves open the doorways inviting
        unwelcome guests who will not leave,
      who invite others to join them as malfeasants,
      who neither love nor care for the host who fills
        the day with groans and
         moans and travels in the night.

The withering of the vine can be prevented by a change of heart—
     by a change from:
       The Spirit banished and sent to Earth:
      to The Spirit at home within The Heavens;
     by a change from:
       the paucity of the company of man
        to The Glory of The Company of God;
      from hearing the monologues from the
        voices within the vineyard:
      to the amazing authority as the vine
        begins to hear the uplifting
         voice of God.

The withering of the vine does not occur when the vine is truly adopted into the vineyard
           of God,
      is truly bound by a commitment,
      is truly established in a new
        beginning sealed as a new
         vine within the vineyard:
      with the rosiest of futures now to be experienced
      within the care of The Living Loving God."

My Content Study Aid

_____
_____
_____
_____
_____
_____
_____
_____
_____

The Bleating of My Sheep

"The bleating of My sheep are evidence they do not speak in unison,
        they do not speak with wisdom,
        they do not speak in their tongues
                without encouragement.

The bleating of My sheep are oft within the flock,
        are somewhat rare in seeking God.

The bleating of My sheep are circuitous and repetitive,
        rarely touch on the need for preparation:
        rarely catch the interest of My Bride.

The bleating of My sheep really should know much better,
        should gather in their enthusiasm,
        should be eager for progression,
        should stamp their feet in agreement built on compliance
                and not that of defiance,
        should surround themselves with counsel which will
                lead them home,
        should activate their spirits and their souls to direct their
                bodies while it is today.

The bleating of My sheep are often a chorus of unbelief,
        a chorus of the trivial,
        a chorus of the frivolous,
        a chorus not worth the time of listening,
        a chorus wherein there is a need for exculpation of
                My Bride.

The bleating of My sheep should search and find and do that which they have
                been asked,
        should not debate commandments,
        should not pull down the tent in which they shelter,
        should not damage or defile The Edifice of God.

The bleating of My sheep need to know Me better,
        need to have more frequent conversations,
        need to acquire the entrée to the hearing of My voice.

The bleating of My sheep rarely contain a testimony of the activities of God within a life:
        thereby will such fail to qualify to be included in The Bride;
        thereby will such fail to generate the reason for the
                testimony of The Lord before The Father;
        thereby will such fail to have security in the bridging of
                the gap,

                    until such is not the case,
              when and as My Spirit so records in
                              The Lamb's Book of Life.

The bleating of My sheep show little dissatisfaction,
        are more about family history and intent
            as filtered through the 'busyness'—
            with time so wasted by the encroachment of TV,
            where semi-vacant eyes regard matters not worthy of
                      remembering even 'til the morrow,
            where repetition catches all with the polished hook—
            there to be beached within a chair and found not even
                            struggling to be free.

The bleating of My sheep need targeting with arrowheads—
            further to transform hearts of satisfaction—
            unto completion under wisdom based on knowledge:
            so expectations soar for the hungry and the feeding.

The bleating of My sheep speaks of not settling where the pasture is lean
                            and unappetizing,
            where the hay is dry without
                    many nutrients,
            where the evening meal is bypassed to
              be left unscheduled for some future day,
            where water is served instead of milk,
            where meat rarely appears among
                    the fare,
            where the meals are lacking both in
                content and in failing to
                locate the eager appetites.

The bleating of My sheep are suffering stunting of their growth,
            are not likely to retire to a new plateau where the fare is better,
            cannot be heard while ears are not tuned to that which should
                            be heard,
            cannot be subject to change while the rocks remain beached
                          upon the shore:
                where new waves are rushing to surround,
                only to be ignored and beaten by withdrawal.

The bleating of My sheep will encounter The End-time Bag of opportunities,
            opened with the contents scattered,
                with the options there to be selected,
                with the tools renewed and working,
                with the pasture recharged and replenished on a
                            different scale,

with the fare both of interest and nutritious there
for growth within the flock,
for the fattening of the flock,
for the energizing of the flock,
for the excitement of the flock,
for the chartering of the flock,
for the new found testimonies within
the flock—
for enabling The Onward Psalms of God."

My Content Study Aid

The Reins of Power

"The reins of power should be held very lightly.

The reins of power should not be adjusted as if to hold a bucking horse,
                       as if to subdue the spreading of dissent,
                          as if to conquer and divide in the strength
                                            of domination.

The reins of power should not be confused with the reins of Authority,
                          with the reins of Love,
                          with the reins of Righteousness,
                          with the reins of Growth,
                          with the reins of Governance,
                          with the reins of Nation Building,
                          with the reins of Kingship.

The reins of power speak of insecurity,
              speak of a power base which is restricted,
                          which is not well developed,
                          which is not to be envied,
                          which imposes stress,
                          which breeds determination on both sides
                                          of divides,
                          which introduces weapons to the scenes
                                      within humanity—
                  as all are put at risk of both life and limb.

The reins of power cannot be held for ever,
                  cause shadows to be examined:
                  bring grief unto the populace,
                  bring shame upon the instigators of injustice,
                  bring force into equations of subservience as the gaols are filled
                                                     to overflowing,
                  bring hospitals to a standstill,
                  bring shops to the inability to restock the empty shelves,
                  bring the roar of engines in introduction of the missiles,
                  bring crowds into the streets with defiance as their call,
                  bring the flourishing of a city to a standstill—
                          as the homes of yesterday become the sniper posts of the
                                                     coming dawn.

The reins of power struggle to prevent the new beginnings,
    struggle to maintain the status quo,
    struggle to retain the flow of funds to offshore accounts,
    struggle to overcome the sanctions of distrust arising from the
        broken promises,
    struggle to succeed by turning forces of protection into forces
        imposing injury and death,
    struggle bringing wastelands to where stood the crops of life.

The reins of power in the challenge to control see the streaming of the refugees,
    see the searching for the sanctuaries,
    see the harassments as the members of
        each family flee a homeland
        no longer safe or welcoming.

The reins of power are neither the reins of Grace nor of forgiveness,
    are neither the reins of Mercy nor of gratitude,
    are neither the reins of acceptance nor of vision.

The reins of power are the reins grasped firmly,
    are the reins not to be relaxed,
    are the reins which tie the people into knots,
    are the reins which are the robbers of hope from a despairing soul.

The reins of power stifle development as investment flees,
    stifle education as the schoolyard remains empty,
    stifle health and well being as funds are siphoned off,
    stifle freedom of the press as inspecting eyes know to fear The Truth,
    stifle The Fear of God as Faith is lined up before the barrel of a gun,
    stifle information as the instigator of The Call to freedom.

The reins of power strengthen and restrain while suspicions generate the 'evidence',
    subdue and beat until all movement ceases in a huddle,
    torture and murder until sated by the blood.

The reins of power know the grimness of the unsmiling face,
    know the self-promotion of lies which masquerade as The Truth,
    know the regime determined to hold onto power at any cost,
    know the banishment of heroes across a line of demarcation,
    know the imprisonment of the silent in cells of noise and pain where
        suffering is endemic,
    know the mistreatment which speaks of the forsaking of humanity
        where 'justice' is neither spoken nor expected.

The reins of power think there is immunity from accountability,
> think there is no greater power able to usurp,
> think their secrets are secure,
> think their futures can be maintained,
> think all is well within their world of power,
> think the daily paydays transfer only what is theirs by right and by deed.

The reins of power despise The God of others who are more informed,
> despise the beliefs of others leading to eventual downfall,
> despise the prayers of many with a cumulative effect.

The reins of power discount the possibility of a culmination,
> discount the possibility of the need to flee,
> discount the possibility of a new season bringing change,
> discount the possibility that their lives may be under threat—
>> yet keep the birds of prey primed and ready to depart.

The reins of power cannot outlast the reins of God,
> cannot replace the reins of God,
> cannot surpass the reins of God.

The reins of power are the reins of Satan and not the reins of good intent.

The reins of power fall for the love of money and so become corrupt.

The reins of power fail the test of Righteousness and so breed the nests of evil.

The reins of power fail to have a vision and so watch the people perish.

The reins of power are the reins of man in his iniquity who so fails to support or nourish.

The reins of power will be consigned to history:
> to be covered by the dust—
>> within the view of God."

My Content Study Aid

The Beauty of My Garden

"The beauty of My garden has the fragrance of delight,
        has the fragrance of the morning dew,
        has the fragrance of the evening dusk.

The beauty of My garden has the scent of My Spirit,
        has the movement of the zephyrs,
        has the spell-bound immobile where there is no spell.

The beauty of My garden reflects the rays of gold,
        reflects the iridescent and the sheens,
        reflects the colours of the cut where sparkle is expected,
        reflects the colour of the variant where marvelling breaks out.

The beauty of My garden is enhanced by the waterfalls of majesty,
        the cascades of many tiers,
        the falls of many ribbons,
        the rushing of the torrents,
        the crashing to the pools,
        the whispering of the trickle as if a finger with
                the gentlest touch.

The beauty of My garden magnifies the journeying of a brook,
        the tumbling of a stream,
        the swirling of a river,
        the boiling of a cataract,
        the whitewater of the rapids.

The beauty of My garden rests upon the time of man,
    rests upon access to the havens,
    rests upon the failing or the birthing of the light as the clouds are caught in fire,
where the shepherds were warned or delighted at the arrival or the leaving of the day.

The beauty of My garden knows the areas of both peace and of tranquility,
        of both quiet and of silence,
        of both raucousness and of joviality,
        of happiness and contentment,
        of both blooming and of scent.

The beauty of My garden is the ongoing highlight of a life,
        the target of redemption,
        the objective of a journey,
        the rewarding of salvation,
        the functioning of the sacrifice of God,
        the plan for each spirit birthed within creation before time
                had begun.

The beauty of My garden is the achievement of God,
        is the wonder stemming from creation,
        is the bounty of the worship,
        is the reward of Faith,
        is the safe harbouring of God,
        is the destiny of honouring,
        is The Inheritance of adoption,
        is the dwelling place set apart for The Saints of God.

The beauty of My garden is unique in the setting,
        is unique in the fulfilment,
        is unique in the presentation,
        is unique in the ease of access,
        is unique in the depth of design,
        is unique in the singularity of intent,
        is unique in the backing and creation.

The beauty of My garden reaches in all the directions known to man,
        reaches to all the locations known to God,
        reaches to all the access points as needed for the graves of man,
        reaches to all the portals where appropriate which are installed
                              by God,
        reaches to the depths and heights,
            to the marked and the unmarked,
            to the reserved and the preserved of God.

The beauty of My garden extends throughout eternity,
        does not experience an 'off' season,
        does not close either for repairs or maintenance,
        does not close for time divisions familiar to man,
        does not close for a purpose of exclusion of those who
                              so belong.

The beauty of My garden is a wonder to behold,
        extends in all directions the eyes of man can see,
        contains the minutest detail,
        contains the grandest of the grand:
        contains all occurring within the two extremes.

The beauty of My garden contains all the wonders of God set for the eyes of man,
        from the largest to the smallest,
        from the furthest to the nearest,
        from the most embellished to the plainest,
        from the functioning to the static,
        where travelling is not a difficulty as experienced within the
                              history of man.

The beauty of My garden includes the various dimensions:
> where controls prevent the fiddling alterations born
>> of curiosity,
> where substance may be difficult to verify,
> where intent is always constant within the nature of
>> The Loving Living God,
> where Faith with belief are the forerunners:
>> of the disclosures of the realities for the senses
>>> to perceive.

The beauty of My garden requires intensity of description,
> requires understanding of the categories,
> requires knowledge of the localities and the specialists
>> in occupation,
> requires a willingness to expand the mindset of man,
> requires a willingness to reach out to an appreciation of The
>> Mindset of God.

The beauty of My garden is a triumphant declaration to all who become adopted into The Family of God."

My Content Study Aid

_____
_____
_____
_____
_____
_____
_____
_____
_____
_____
_____
_____
_____
_____
_____
_____

The Lining of Peru (Nazca Lines)

"The lines upon the slopes and plains of the land of Peru were a long time in discovery,
>were a longtime in the absence of scholarship,
>were a long time in requesting The Counselling of God.

The lining of Peru is a puzzle as laid before the intellect of man,
>fails man's understanding of the purpose,
>>understanding of the means,
>>understanding of the view best seen from above the
>>>topography of the land,
>>understanding of the vastness of the scope with the
>>>reasoning leading to existence:
>>>of the residues within the here and now.

The lining of Peru restores the knowledge base of man,
>from that which has been lost within man's history,
>from that which was dramatic,
>from that wherein only partial residues remain,
>from that which holds no promise for the future,
>>hides no threat from the past,
>>has no benefit within the present.

The lining of Peru dates from many centuries,
>dates from a time of habitation,
>a time of population,
>a time of high activity,
>a time of high belief,
>a time of motivation,
>a time of illness and decline.

The lining of Peru is not recorded within the history books of man,
>is not perceived of being of much value,
>is but a curiosity spread upon a landscape in the past.

The lining of Peru took some effort in installing,
>took some effort in aligning,
>took some effort in resolving the intricacies displayed,
>>within an inspection,
>forming as a result of additions by the later over those of the earlier.

The lining of Peru occurred in layers as the later generations built upon the efforts of
>the earlier:
>occurred as the straight lines occupied the space;
>occurred with the new layer enforced to become diagonals to
>>distinguish from the previous;

occurred as the further layer so filled its layer—
                              which were inscribed as circles,
            still claiming such uniqueness within the patterning of man;
                      finally came the constructs of uniqueness,
            still identifying the families of participation in the claims
                                                      to ownership,
                  together with the records of the earlier generations as they
                                                      came and went;
                        now presenting an intermixed conformity—
                        from which is hard for man to fathom the 'how',
                                                            the 'when',
                                                            the 'why.'
The lining of Peru are the family histories recorded for posterity on their land
                                                      of inheritance:
                        with the length of line determining the extent
                              of the family within a generation—
                        which is intended to be sized by the variability
                              in the steps involved in the
                              totality of the walking of the line;
                        with the size of circles and the size of
                              glyphs within the ownership of
                                    the land concerned;
                        with the later spread of new glyphs based on
                              perceptions from the lives—
                  as families extended their possession of
                                                the land;
                                          and even later,
                  as time erased land-based relationships,
                  as the land became a drawing board,
                        for those without an interest
                                                in inheritance,
                        for those driven to leave their mark upon
                                                the scene—
                              as do the graffiti artists of today.
The lining of Peru in other areas,
            where depressed circles show the residues of surrounding mounds:
                  are the result of the harvesting of salt pans via the salt ponds—
            where water with its contents was concentrated by the evaporation of
                                                            the days—
                        when this was practical and practised in the inhospitableness
                                                            of surroundings—
                  prior to the event and onset of sickness and disease brought
                                          from afar in the trading of the salt.

The lining of Peru was not intended to be viewed from space:
> had no concept of the vertical appearance from a height;
> had no idea of the puzzle so presented—
>> by The End-time Capabilities to view and
>> to wonder—
>> by the source of the intentions as
>> displayed from such a view.

The lining of Peru is a record of the etchings and the scratchings of man over time upon
> The Earth:
>> in an endeavour to proclaim an ongoing entitlement
>> to occupy the space so claimed—
>> by the families in existence within mortality,
>>> yet but for a blink within eternity,
>>> yet without knowledge of The Loving God
>>> who witnessed it with understanding—
>>> of the driving motivation of man for man's
>>> security of tenure—
>>> within an environment of peace."

Scribal Note:
In answer to a scribal query concerning the origin of the 'Nazca Lines' in Peru.

My Content Study Aid

Visiting My Garden (2)

"Visiting My garden is dependent on the circumstances.

Visiting My garden is dependent on man's age within mortality,
        is dependent on man's proximity to death,
        is dependent on man's willingness to testify,
        is dependent on man's willingness to return unto his glove,
        is dependent on man's willingness to forsake his glove—
                in travelling to a destiny with an invitation based on Grace.

Visiting My garden opens eyes to see,
        opens tongues to question,
        opens all the senses deeper than before as they visit the festival of
                sight and sound.

Visiting My garden leaves impressions not forgotten.

Visiting My garden creates substance to The Faith.

Visiting My garden leaves a trail of tales to tell.

Visiting My garden is as a recurring dream where details are exact,
        is as a support of testimonies where Truth is to the fore,
        is as an affirmation of the leading of mortality to find and to prepare,
        is as a confirmation of the destiny as sought within The Promises
                of God,
        is as a continuation where Grace creates the staircase to and for
                The Stars of God.

Visiting My garden starts the eyes to darting,
        puts awe upon a face,
        surrounds with sounds of might and majesty not yet heard upon
                The Earth.

Visiting My garden is not for all to attend,
        is selective and precise,
        is filled with witnessing both to the spirit and the soul of man.

Visiting My garden oft changes the previous goals within mortality,
        oft changes the belief systems of the guests,
        oft changes the mind sets of the attitudes which redirect the effort.

Visiting My garden is not an end unto itself.

Visiting My garden exhibits an open door to surroundings wherein My Saints can dwell.

Visiting My garden brings the future for recall to the present,
        brings the concurrency of events,
        brings the clients to view the effort of the architect on their behalves.

Visiting My garden sheds light upon the coming dawn:
                as the patterning of raindrops will eventually wet The Earth
                                                in completeness—
                when they fall within persistence of concurrency.

Visiting My garden is not born of a waywardness of extremity,
                is not born of a necessity of shoring up,
                is not born of any need to lend a hand to Truth.

Visiting My garden is to encourage the fence sitters to land on the side of evidence,
                to encourage the atheists and agnostics to examine:
                              the witness of the eyes,
                              the circumstances surrounding
                                                  each visit,
                              The End-time witnessing born both
                                      of desperation and of hope.

Visiting My garden is an offering of assistance in support,
                is of much avail through trials and tribulation,
                is the instigator of the tales of triumph,
                            of the achievement of success in the answering of
                                                  the suppositions.

Visiting My garden is a snapshot of existence beyond the reins of mortality.

Visiting My garden is an experience within the reality of existence:
                with ramifications from the selecting of a destiny,
                        from making a commitment,
                        from seeking an adoption,
                        from crying out the despairs within a soul,
                        from accepting a dependency for forgiveness
                                            on The Son of God,
                        from the gratitude within a heart at the
                                        sacrifice established,
                        from the flood of Grace which opens wide the
                                        pathways of The Law:
                previously too difficult for man to walk successfully.

Visiting My garden can be examined for the annotations as recorded by each visit,
                can reveal the similarities,
                can compare the experiences,
                can compare the likelihood of Truth as the backdrop to each theme,
                can assess in the light of the descriptive texts that which:
                                                has been,
                                                is,
                                                shall continue,
                            in The Presence of The Living Loving God.

Visiting My garden occurs in the desperation of a momentary invitation,
    is neither to be envied nor sought in duplication.

Visiting My garden makes possible the ability to reflect on an occurrence outside the
    normality of the life of man:
    that which is reserved unto the future life of man,
    that which expresses the confirmation due The Faith
    of man,
    that which shouts from the past into the present so
    the future may not go unrewarded,
    that which requires the presence of Grace to envelop
    a contrite heart while it is today."

Scribal Note:
Refer: 'The Visitors to The Garden', Bk1, 'GOD Speaks of Return and Bannered'.

My Content Study Aid

Vacancies Within My Garden

"Vacancies within My garden are not known as such.

Vacancies within My garden do not occur as per mortality,
        have no death event to create a vacancy,
        have no transfer to a colony to be regarded as a vacancy,
        have no vacancy at all waiting to be filled.

Vacancies within My garden do not have a queue waiting to be satisfied,
        do not have an emptiness waiting to be matched,
        do not have an absence of entity in expectation of return.

Vacancies within My garden are prepared and readied in a different sense:
        can be completed and located within an instant build
                      in time;
            within an instantaneous light flash
            of intent in the absence of time;
            within an eye blink,
                if there were one,
        where change occurs faster than can be measured;
            faster than perception;
            faster than the reactions of those
                who witness such and know.

Vacancies within My garden is a useful metaphor to enhance the understanding
        of The Saints of God,
        of The Bride of Christ:
            to the capacity for adoption,
            to the capacity of Heaven,
            to the capacity of Hell.

'Vacancies' within My garden can not be filled by any ordering of man,
        by any prioritizing by man—
        neither by deposit,
        nor by payment,
        neither by presentation,
        nor that by way of reservation.

'Vacancies' within My garden are not determined by the prayers of man,
        by the order of the filling of the graves,
        by the stilling of the heart beats,
        by reference to the wills of man or:
        by whatever is decreed;
        by wherever such is stored;
        by however great or low is the inheritance so treated.

'Vacancies' within My garden are governed by My Spirit,
        are governed by the actions of Freewill,
        are governed by the master entries in
                The Lamb's Book of Life,
        are governed by the closeness of the relationships
                with God.

'Vacancies' within My garden reach out and absorb knowledge with the wisdom;
        reach out and fulfil The Promises of God;
        reach out and uphold the rewards for servanthood both
           established and verified in the absence of exaggeration.

'Vacancies' within My garden are refused with good cause,
        are delayed with an appeal of fact,
        are delayed when the record is disjointed with Freewill
                activities changing by the day,
        are delayed when subject to appeal from an appellant with
            a claim worthy of resolution,
        are delayed when a plaintiff seeks redress from what has
                gone before."

My Content Study Aid

Snowfields in My Garden

"Snowfields in My garden have an existence there on which to play and frolic,
                         on which to traverse at speed,
                         on which to venture up and down,
                         on which to skim the tops,
                         on which to plumb the depths,
                         on which to be enchanted by the views
                                     with enjoyment of the scenes.

Snowfields in My garden are exotic and spectacular,
           know no injuries occurring in the falls,
           know no difficulties of achieving:
                  the targets of the hearts;
                  the abilities of the bodies;
                  the speed within the reckless;
                  the slowness within the cautious;
                  the satisfaction of the climber who summits to regard the
                                 vista as laid before his eyes.

Snowfields in My garden have no threats:
                     either from the avalanche or the crevasse—
           have no threats of their intrusion on the pathways set for fun;
           have no threats which would threaten or injure life.

Snowfields in My garden have no need of dressing,
           have no need of grooming,
           have no need to have the presentation improved
                                   after inspection,
           have no need to have the snow—
                  because of scarcity—
                  augmented under the guidance of a supervisor.

Snowfields in My garden have a variety of perceptions,
           are not the cause of frostbite from the cold,
           are not the sites with sunburn from the rays,
           are not a cause of danger to the body soul or spirit.

Snowfields in My garden have all the thrills and spills as expertise is gained,
                         as familiarity is attained,
                         as practice so demands,
                         as the beauty of surroundings
                                   so distracts.

Snowfields in My garden are within an easy reach,
          require no commitment to an extended journey to the placement,
      can be explored at leisure,
      can be reached with a decision to make a visit—
                or for a longer stay in time.

Snowfields in My garden arise and shine where they are needed:
      can be sculptured as required;
      can be laid out for the level of expected expertise;
      can be monitored for compliance to the settings of experience;
            the settings of convenience;
             the settings for beginners;
             the settings for the mature:
          all of which are met in deed,
              in action,
              and in capability.

Snowfields in My garden will test the abilities of the experts:
             in thought;
             in perception;
             in experience;
             in self-control—
        as control of the ski field is assumed by the skier
        which locks the field to the settings of his thoughts:
        which also control the setting of the obstacles which
                can bring about a fall.

Snowfields in My garden are popular and enjoyable,
      are tailored to demand,
      are installed with runs where timing is recorded,
      are installed with runs where enjoyment overrides the
                importance of the time:
      allowing stops to enjoy surroundings,
          to enjoy companionship,
          to enjoy the experience of the downhill run with
                its twists and turns:
      as if a graded slalom course set for competition resulting
                in awards.

Snowfields in My garden have plenty of snow to throw,
      have plenty of snow to duck,
      have plenty of snow to return from whence it came.

Snowfields in My garden are fun places to discover,
      are fun places with which to become familiar,
      are fun places with testing accesses not spoilt by the threat of
                injury or pain.

Snowfields in My garden are enjoyed by the young at heart,
                are popular for extended family outings,
                are not beset by costs.

Snowfields in My garden can be flat for towing,
                can undulate with the ups and downs,
                can be slopes galore with varieties in steepness and of length
                              of runs,
                can be started from the mountaintops where speed is
                              all important,
                        where abilities are stretched in
                            the retaining of control,
                        where reaction is the key to a
                              successful run.

Snowfields in My garden are for the enjoyment of My Bride,
                for the dwellers in My garden,
                for those who are expected to reside in the places
                              so prepared."

My Content Study Aid

_____
_____
_____
_____
_____
_____
_____
_____
_____
_____
_____
_____
_____
_____
_____
_____
_____

Food Source of My Garden

"The food source on The Earth within mortality is one of digestion and of replenishment,
        is one of growth and of development,
        is one of nourishment and sustenance,
        is one with balancing the food with
                the drink,
        is one requiring the continuance of the
            life within the body until
            death brings termination with
            the decaying of the flesh.

The food sources of The Earth are familiar to all who search and find,
        to all who strike and kill,
        to all who plant and reap,
        to all who await the harvesting of their labours.

The food source of My garden is unfamiliar to The Saints of God,
        to My Bride-in-waiting,
        to My Father's flock within mortality.

The food source of My garden is contained within My garden,
        is surrounded by My garden,
        spreads out from the centre of My garden.

The food source of My garden neither shrinks nor fades away,
        neither touches nor encroaches,
        neither relaxes nor retreats,
        neither expands nor circumvents,
        neither releases nor constricts,
        neither spits nor spurts,
        neither crushes nor stirs,
        neither visits nor ignores.

The food source of My garden emits yet does not bake,
        charges yet does not move,
        feeds yet does not grow,
        supplies yet does not starve,
        exceeds yet does not restrict,
        thirsts yet does not drink,
        settles yet does not complain,
        links yet does not retract.

The food source of My garden is efficient and responsible,
        is quiet and peaceful,
        is productive and restful,

     is saving and sharing,
     is familiar and a stranger,
     is lighting and delivering,
     is frequenting and mature,
     is signalling and developing.

The food source of My garden is as a beehive of activity,
     is compatible with the functioning of state,
         of a kingdom,
         of the demands of governance,
         of the feeding of The Multitudes,
         of the restoration of a home,
     of a replevin busied in repossession of
         all which has been taken.

The food source of My garden is ample in supply,
     has a surplus to requirements,
     has provisioning as needed.

The food source of My garden yields according to equations,
     according to the numbers,
     according to projections which are both accurate
              and true.

The food source of My garden does not shrivel the produce of the schedule,
     does not distort the viewing and the listening,
     does not interfere with clarity of thought,
     does not mislay the relays for the senses,
     does not manipulate the demand or smooth the
             excess down,
     does not succumb to short cuts,
     does not blow a fuse.

The food source of My garden does not deliver mass.

The food source of My garden is not an entity under stress.

The food source of My garden messages and receives,
     tunes and adjusts,
     measures and records.

The food source of My garden is not a pressure cooker,
     is not a fence sitter awaiting instructions,
     is not a call to arms so every hand is busy.

The food source of My garden is filling and satisfying,
     is ongoing and enduring,
     is refreshing and replenishing.

The food source of My garden yields and yields and yields,
                leaves no dishes to be washed,
                requires no utensils of conveyance as to the mouth
                              within mortality.

The food source of My garden is not born from fertilizer,
                is not born from earth,
                is not born from life.

The food source of My garden serves neither milk nor meat,
                serves neither fish nor fowl,
                serves neither plant nor weed:
                        as known either upon The Earth or within the seas.

The food source of My garden has stability and definition,
                has logistics of approval,
                has freighting still unknown.

The food source of My garden is the first within My garden—
                    as feeding establishes for the entities of being
                              with acceptance:
                    prior to an arising from the graves of man.

The food source of My garden is under the oversight of The Loving Living God.

Let those with understanding—
        know.

Let those with wisdom—
        expect.

Let those with the abundant life—
        accept."

My Content Study Aid

_____
_____
_____
_____
_____
_____
_____
_____

The Sourcing of Evil

"The sourcing of evil is never for the benefit of man,
        is the multiple acts of vengeance usurped by Satan against God,
        is the attacks on man deployed as the living tools of Satan in his
                          hitting out at God.

The sourcing of evil will have his day in court,
        will have a charge sheet almost without end,
        will have every one addressed in the twilight of his freedom.

The sourcing of evil will see his ruptured plans dealt with by The Cross of
                            The Living Christ.

The sourcing of evil who laughed and danced a jig when viewing a body on the cross.

The sourcing of evil is the scourge of man,
        is the promiser of fulfilment of the pride of man,
        is the generator of the hate crimes paraded before the face of man
                          within their livelihoods with God.

The sourcing of evil is the throttler at the neck of man,
        is the appointment driver of sexual interference under The Freewill
                              of man,
        is the generator of pornography within the lusts of man.

The sourcing of evil is the breeder of iniquity in all its many guises—
                      to satisfy the quests of man for more,
        is the breeder of the bugs and germs which put man into a bed of
                          sickness and disease,
        is the institutor of pain upon and in the body as the tormentor of the
                      waves designated so to fall on man.

The sourcing of evil spreads the lies for man to utter on his highway to join The Lost,
        spreads the blasphemy upon the tongue of man where the tongues of
                      Heaven are unknown,
        spreads the mattress on the bed:
        where misconduct between the consenting parties who reject the better,
                have witnesses to their habits and their lusts;
        where the vows are neither valid nor approved within the sight of God.

The sourcing of evil is as a vampire from a nightmare at the throat of man,
        is the chief overseer of the bloodletting of man,
        is the instigator of the 'accidents' which result in the death of man
                              in innocence,
        is the harvester of The Lost gathered for companionship in Hell.

The sourcing of evil sets a downhill slide in place,
            trips the feet,
            binds the hands,
            blinds the eyes,
            deafens the ears,
            destroys the touch,
            primes the mouth,
            loads the habits,
            cheers as the addictions take hold,
            supervises the obtaining of the funds so such may feed,
            turns out the light so darkness may prevail.

The sourcing of evil giggles with delight at the crop which has since spread—
                                      from an apple in a garden,
            giggles with delight at the ease in having man succumb to become
                                            a follower,
            giggles with delight at all his lies believed and enacted in the lives
                                            of man.

The sourcing of evil is not short of assistants,
            is not short of helpers,
            is not short of hangers-on,
            is not short of servants,
            is not short of slaves,
            is not short of supporters enlisted from the would-be rank and vile
                                            of man.

The sourcing of evil is everywhere abounding,
            is neither scarce nor difficult to find,
            is in the hands of encouragers who seek converts to their cause,
            is bereft of sympathy for the young and the naïve,
            is the funding source of proliferation—
                    which feeds on the contents of the tablets vials and needles—
            where questions are not asked and help is far away.

The sourcing of evil is in his heyday of success.
The sourcing of evil is fast running out of time.
The sourcing of evil will soon meet with his chief opponent head-on in a battle.

The sourcing of evil mounts a throne he cannot hold,
            sits in a high place from which he will again be thrown down,
            will be forced to discard his fancy dress in readiness to assume the
                                            garb of prisoners.

The sourcing of evil uses knowledge without wisdom,
            acquires consensus built on needs,
            achieves allegiance from the believers of the malicious falsehoods.

The sourcing of evil will not repent before The Great White Throne,
        will not offer recompense for what has gone before,
        will not relinquish willingly the clandestine numbered gains
                amongst The Endangered and The Lost.

The sourcing of evil is on a countdown of the numbered days ahead,
        has accountability looming to the fore,
        wears the vagrancy of man as a feather in his cap.

The sourcing of evil is as a burlesque show running at an end-time speed,
        is the paraphernalia of a wayward kingdom
                about to meet The Fire of Righteousness,
                about to have replaced the tendrils of evolution,
                about to have rescinded a visitation of The Earth,
                about to have fitted the leg-irons of restriction.

The sourcing of evil is soon to encounter the longterm cramping of his style,
            in the presence of accountability,
            within the courts of The Living Loving God."

My Content Study Aid

The Visions for The Future

"The visions for the future are to be carried by the visionaries of God,
        by those He has entrusted,
        by those who value accuracy,
        by those who stand fast within The Fear
                of God.

The visions for the future are brought forth by My prophets whom I know,
        are brought forth with earnestness and fervour,
        are brought forth in the written and the spoken,
        are brought forth in The Tongues of Heaven and with
                interpretation by one with like standing before
                The Throne of Grace.

The visions for the future are brought forth in Truth and Righteousness,
        will not fade away,
        will find the heralds to so broadcast around The Earth,
        will speak to the spirits of My children when all is well within
                the bringing forth of My prophetic word
                from My prophets whom I know.

The visions for the future will build upon the past,
        do not discard as rubbish that which was once valued by the
                attentive and the wise,
        do not shrink from proclaiming the words as issued and
                attended by My prophets whom I know:
        My prophets who speak in Truth and in integrity of spirit,
                who honour and uphold the callings from God
                      as made known to man.

Be aware of the prophets who self-proclaim their assumed titles from afar,
        yet bring no honour to their cause with money as its base,
        yet bring no resolution as to how or when they
                were established,
        yet have a flourished document with very little value in the
                presence of My Spirit.

For even so does My prophet hear and know My voice.

For even so will My prophet serve in Righteousness.

For even so will The Word of God ring out with clarity and understanding,
        with integrity and purpose,
        with honouring and Truth unto the
                intended audience:
        where My Word will carry meaning beyond the wisdom of man.

For even so will the false be discerned from the true with penalties involved.

For even so will My Spirit affirm My prophets' conveying of My Word on My behalf.

The visions for the future will impart The Mysteries of God,
    will transfer knowledge and wisdom on request,
    will interpret and convey the understanding of the tongues
        of Heaven—
        so thoughts may be transitioned from one entity to another
           without delay.

The visions for the future are far reaching yet contained,
    are practical yet reliant,
    are conducive yet disclosing in the fullness.

The visions for the future are stepwise yet consistent,
    are detailed yet complete,
    are incredible yet verified within the reins of Truth.

The visions for the future are majestic yet confirmed,
    are magnificent yet plausible,
    are powerful yet restrained by each Freewill.

The visions for the future are oft placements from the past:
    may have their origins from another time and place,
        from originating as a mention in
           My Word,
        from developing in their scope for The
           End-time Bride of Christ.

The visions for the future grow and develop for disclosure within My Spirit of revelation:
    do not involve the imagination of man;
    are not thrown down upon The Earth as a challenge to man.

The visions for the future are there to confirm:
    the way of preparation of My Bride;
    the way of a decisive walk with Me;
    the way of Righteousness with peace in tow;
    the way of life eternal with a destiny of choice;
    the way of Freewill achievements which tip the scales of man;
    the way of My two commandments within My people's souls
        of love.

The visions for the future declares what is to be encountered in the ways of man,
    declares the furnishing of Heaven and The Earth,
    declares the integrity of the many ways of God:
        as applicable to man within His umbrella of protection and
           of love.

The visions for the future are carried by The Promises of God:
> by the partial revelations of the past;
> by the present activities of My Spirit in interacting
>> with My people as they attend their calls,
> by the decreasing numbering of days as the sands of
>> time run through the hourglass of mortality.

The visions for the future are secure within the oversight of God,
> are secure for the attention of The Multitudes,
> are secure in the guidance to completion of each
>> journey home."

My Content Study Aid

_____
_____
_____
_____
_____
_____
_____
_____
_____
_____
_____
_____
_____
_____
_____
_____
_____
_____
_____
_____
_____
_____
_____

The Pathway of The Stars of God

"The pathway of The Stars of God is both signposted and directive.

The pathway of The Stars of God starts as a funnel in a tunnel,
      ends with wide open vistas fit for the kings and queens
                 of God.

The pathway of The Stars of God leads all who tread it home to God,
      home to The King of kings,
      home to the place prepared,
      home to My garden for The
          Family of God.

The pathway of The Stars of God leads into a new beginning
      with eternity's open door in front with a banded
          hand of welcome,
      with mortality behind and buried in the past by
          the filling of the grave.

The pathway of The Stars of God is as the highway to Heaven which bespeaks a destiny
          of favour,
      is as a walkway freed from encumbrances,
      is as a sealed footpath on which the pedestrians
          are welcomed,
      is as a level playing field bereft of steps and ramps,
      is as the displayer of areas of much interest where ups
         and downs go completely unnoticed by the feet.

The pathway of The Stars of God is the 'be all' and the 'end-all' of
      the achievement of a transfer,
      the achievement of a relocation,
      the achievement of the finality of adoption into
         an ever-lasting living family,
      the achievement of a goal in fulfilment
          of commitment,
      the achievement of a new found status within
         The Family of God,
      the achievement of a destiny chosen in Freewill,
      the achievement of a goal with the requirement
         of Faith.

The pathway of The Stars of God is confirmation of the finding of the elixir of eternal
life which transfer man from his mortality into
eternal life within The Grace of God,
is the recipe which restores the borrowed gold of man
back into the eternal gold of God,
is the fulfilment of the recipe of salvation as birthed
upon the cross in death with the renting of the
curtain and as witnessed by the empty tomb with
The Risen Lord.

The pathway of The Stars of God salutes The Living Loving God in homage and in love.

The pathway of The Stars of God is the way and the means from the stepping-stones in
mortality unto the birthplace of the manna for
the feeding of My people in the wilderness.

The pathway of The Stars of God has no turnstile with a counter,
has no means of verification of a right to travel on
the pathway,
has already approved The Stars of God access to their
promised places as so prepared and readied.

The pathway of The Stars of God is sacrosanct and holy,
is polished and well trod,
is recommended and approved by God.

The pathway of The Stars of God is frequented by the angels as they try to glimpse their
charges coming home.

The pathway of The Stars of God leads to the preparations for the coronations
where each crown is placed upon a head;
where a bridal feast prepares within a close proximity,
where the rewards of persevering are counted as
to gain.

The pathway of The Stars of God does not have a reversal of procedures,
a reversal of the movement of
My People,
a reversal of a benediction into
a valediction.

The pathway of The Stars of God is a welcome sight to God when the path is
fully loaded,
is a welcome sight to God when The Stars are at
their brightest,
is a welcome sight to God when prior arrivals gather to
greet the newcomers within
the new found family of God."

The Days of Thunder (2)

"The days of thunder are approaching as an express train travelling at speed.
The days of thunder are the follow-ups to the onset of The End-time troubling of man.
The days of thunder announce the rebellion of creation against the jurisdiction of man.
The days of thunder cascade from Heaven without a let-up or a respite.

The days of thunder shake and vibrate the structures of man,
        lay waste all the shelters of the iniquities of man,
        set to nought the evil plans of man,
        brings to accountability The Freewill of man as it runs amok with
                harm and injury and death.

The days of thunder test the very foundations of The Integrity of man,
            of The Righteousness of man,
            of The Truthfulness of man,
            of The Hypocrisy of man,
            of The Altruism of man,
            of The Character of man.

The days of thunder bring the tempest with the rain,
        bring the quagmires with the barriers to movement,
        bring the penitent to prayer upon their knees,
        bring the obnoxious to flee from where they stand to the imagined
                shelter of resources,
        bring The Multitudes of hate,
            of force,
            of violence and of death—
        the bearers of the weaponry of man—
        the conquistadores of today who harry as they chase,
              who cast to the ground
                with the chop and slice
                  regardless of the
                  victim's pleas,
        where Mercy is out of reach,
        where Grace no longer is sought to dwell nor made
                to feel at home.

The days of thunder fix the record of the beastliness of man,
            of the call to ride roughshod over all that man has valued,
            of the destruction wrought upon the safe havens of man,
            of the laying waste of the lands of man.

The days of thunder are not many in their number,
              are extensive in their reach,
              are vicious in their coming,
              are exhausted in retreat.

The days of thunder witness the broken glass,
              witness the fires of man,
              witness the dragging and the screaming,
              witness the failed attempts to flee.

The days of thunder see the upraised hands which do not encounter Mercy,
              see the calls to war as hostilities prevail,
              see the foes at loggerheads as one strikes down the other,
              see the crippled and the maimed as they assume their roles of
                                                  begging for relief.

The days of thunder do not share,
              do not befriend,
              do not assist a neighbour in his plight,
              do neither shepherd nor protect the mothers with the children under
                                                    stress and loss.

The days of thunder measure The Multitudes at risk of life and limb,
              measure the inclement weather as it beats upon the skin,
              measure the destructive forces where prayer does not exist,
              measure the soup bowls of the hungry and forlorn.

The days of thunder leave scenes of desolation:
                    of death and of destruction,
                    of selfishness and of cruelty,
                    of lies and of pillaging,
                    of abuse and of desertion.

The days of thunder open doors to the escape of many,
                    to the escape of those with the promise of inheritance,
                    to the escape of those who know and are prepared:
                    to the preservation of the loved and found,
                    to the preservation of the loving and the righteous,
                    to the preservation of the families with their Kings and
                                                  Queens of Faith.

The days of thunder end with a great cleansing of The Earth,
>   of the washing of the shorelines,
>   of the shaking of the structures of man,
>   of the deluges bringing flooding,
>   of the storms of fire engulfing,
>   of the raging of the vengeance of God
>   >   clashing head on—
>   with the wrath of man under the
>   >   control of Satan.

The days of thunder ease into the recent memories of man,
>   usher in a new beginning of man within the mortality of The Multitudes:
>   welcome in The Coming of The King of kings with The Hosts of Heaven;
>   welcome in the changes in lifestyles about to become evident;
>   welcome in The Edifice of God in its fullness of application and of being;
>   welcome in a new government on Earth as His Kingdom comes and
>   >   His Will is done."

My Content Study Aid

The Tin-lizzies of The Skies

"The tin-lizzies of the skies are the primitive airborne ships of the seas.

The tin-lizzies of the skies are the people movers of The Earth,
                are the work horses of the travellers,
                are the spreaders of pollution,
                are the mixers of the germs and bugs and The End-time
                                              viruses of man.

The tin-lizzies of the skies know the points of departure,
                know the points of arrival,
                know the circling of The Earth.

The tin-lizzies of the skies do not care what they leave behind:
                        what once used is left to form a trail,
                        what once discarded is not intended for recovery,
                        what once done and dumped is not set
                                              for retrieval.

The tin-lizzies of the skies fly higher than before,
                fly faster than before,
                fly larger than before,
                fly heavier than before,
                fly more powerful than before,
                fly more loaded than before.

The tin-lizzies of the skies partner with the spewing of the steel mills of The Earth,
                partner with the causes of congestion as they crawl upon
                                              the highways,
                are the setters of the hothouse for the coming emissions—
                        from all which has been sealed in place by the ice and
                                            snow and rock.

The tin-lizzies of the skies are deemed to be acceptable as they plough their furrows in
                                                                  the sky.

The tin-lizzies of the skies crisscross above the sight of man,
                above the hearing of man,
                above the impressions of man,
                above the sanctions of man,
                above the wisdom of man,
                above the common sense of man—
                as the once stopped bottle is uncorked to release the
                        contents into the breathing environment of man.

The tin-lizzies of the skies need to be restrained,
        need to have the access limited–
                from the frivolous who want to go and stare,
        need to give priority to that of economic worth,
        need to increase the cost of travel for The Multitudes so they
            choose to stay at home within their lands of birth.

The tin-lizzies of the skies should have their services controlled by governments
                      gifting access,
        should have an impost levied on the seating,
        should have an impost which ensures the decline in numbers
            of the touring travellers to the lands of choice.

The tin-lizzies of the skies are as the cigarettes of the mouth:
        whereat the wise of government ensure the abstentions
            from The Freewill of man.

The tin-lizzies of the skies need to have their frequency of flights reduced to the
            bare necessities,
        need to have the rivers in the skies cleaned and dredged from
            the contaminants born of overuse,
        need to have the vapour trails become a rarity to the eyes
            of man,
        need to have the numbers such that build-ups can reduce,
            such that heating is reduced,
                stalls,
                is reversed,
            such that life may continue in its
                Glory on The Earth.

The tin-lizzies of the skies together with the potential cellmates:
        are set to incinerate The Earth,
        are set to destroy the habitat of man,
        are set to impair the food chains of The Earth.

The tin-lizzies of the skies are the smokers of the bacon,
        are the drip feeders of destruction,
        are the slow cookers of man as he waits below for the
                temperatures to rise.

The tin-lizzies of the skies causes man to shake his head and utter words without effect,
            utter words without the intent to stop the
                stewing of man,
            utter words in denial to placate The Multitudes,
            utter the call for others to fix the mess they
                have created on the home of man.

The tin-lizzies of the skies require men of resoluteness,
            require men of state,
            require men who agitate and multiply,
            require men who seize the moment prior to the tipping of
                                      the scales,
            require men of vision who can see the cost of doing nothing,
            require men of action who can reverse the laissez–faire with
                                      its journey to despair,
            require men of determination that The End-time shall not be
                                      one of doom,
            require men of Righteousness to persevere in overcoming the
                        cartels of the skies and of The Earth
                        that the changes may be wrought—
        so not to dwell in a bakehouse of the devil where the
                        temperature is slowly rising:
        in what can be an inevitable conclusion in the
                        absence of reversal.
The tin-lizzies of the skies should be the setting of a standard of enforcement
                                      for a fresh beginning:
                    for an urgent call to arms to fight the residues
                              of a past century:
                    where foresight was not present and profit
                            prevailed at any cost to man."

My Content Study Aid

The Relationships Within My Garden

"The relationships within My garden are of love and tribute.

The relationships within My garden are fully rounded and sincere,
                are of praise and worship,
                are exuberant and welcoming,
                are inquisitive and learning.

The relationships within My garden are refreshing and restoring,
                are determining and linking,
                are accepting and mind filling.

The relationships within My garden explore and reunite,
                discuss and are attentive,
                greet surprises with a smile and laughter to the fore.

The relationships within My garden are one with the heroes of the past,
                the heroes with a cause,
                the heroes with a history built on
                            their achievements,
                the heroes with biographies well
                            worth assimilation.

The relationships within My garden are studies in consent,
                are studies in awareness,
                are studies in circumspection,
                are studies in the scope and scale of life.

The relationships within My garden build both on knowledge and on wisdom,
                build with the sought discovered,
                build with a greeting declared in certainty,
                build with an understanding of the circumstances
                            resulting in a presence.

The relationships within My garden are both just and honest,
                have integrity of purpose,
                have the ability to function without discrimination,
                        without impairment of
                              the body,
                        without the muzzling of
                              the mind.

The relationships within My garden are thorough and sustained,
                are interesting and considerate,
                are magnified and mighty both in thoughts
                              and deeds.

The relationships within My garden come to know the visited,
    come to know the distant,
    come to know the majestic and imposing:
        all of which impact on life within My garden.

The relationships within My garden impose responsibilities,
    impose a choice of action,
    impose selections which have to do with governance:
        within the field of injustice,
        within the field of reparations,
        within the field of abuse,
        within the field of desertion,
        within the field of addiction,
        within the field of injury,

        within the field of violence,
        within the field of prematurity,
        within the field of abortion,
        within the field of torture,
        within the field of neglect,
        within the field of penury,

        within the field of replevins,
        within the field of promises,
        within the field of theft,
        within the field of care,
        within the field of medicine,
        within the field of misfeasance,

        within the field of malfeasance,
        within the field of imprisonment,
        within the field of the armed forces,
        within the field of lies,
        within the field of death,
        within the field of the Commandments,

        within the field of immorality,
        within the field of idolatry,
        within the field of temptations,
        within the field of martyrdom,
        within the field of church and state,
        within the field of war,

        within the field of crimes committed against
            both the living and the dead,
        within the field of accountability for the
            actions of Freewill.

The relationships within My garden are active and restorative,
                are honouring and sustaining,
                are dependent and increasing.

The relationships within My garden are reflected on The Multitudes at large,
                The Multitudes who managed to
                      survive the troubling of man,
                The Multitudes without a
                      relationship with God.

The relationships within My garden are far reaching and amending,
                are discerning and evaluating,
                are selective yet non-discriminatory,
                are the determinants of justice reborn in the fullness
                      of The Truth.

The relationships within My garden have access to the unknown,
                have access to all The Stars of God,
                have access to the knowledge base of God—
                      so judgment is neither trivial nor wrong as it
                            issues from a throne."

My Content Study Aid

The Meeting of The Minds

"The meeting of the minds speaks of a time of savouring.

The meeting of the minds speaks of a discussion group in earnest,
                speaks of a mortal throwback,
                speaks of the intensity of follow-ups,
                speaks of a commitment to partake,
                speaks of the bombardment from the thoughts.

The meeting of the minds does not reflect a shallow pond of intellect,
                does not reflect a harvesting of ineptitude,
                does not reflect the 'um's and 'err's of yesterday,
                does not reflect the opening and shutting of the mouth as if a
                                            goldfish in a bowl.

The meeting of the minds does neither splinter nor frustrate,
                does neither shout nor interrupt,
                does neither cycle nor retire,
                does neither forsake nor condone,
                does neither impose nor vacillate,
                does neither rubbish nor retreat.

The meeting of the minds knows sequences of significance,
                knows harshness is uncalled for,
                knows mysteries should not be challenged,
                knows the imposing and the artful are there for a reason,
                knows the methodical and the artistic have discussions of
                                            their own.

The meeting of the minds can carry and recall,
                can test and reinstate,
                can puzzle and resolve,
                can empty and fill,
                can resolve and depart,
                can leave and return.

The meeting of the minds can examine and verify,
                can enhance and polish,
                can establish and rescind,
                can protect and lay bare,
                can magnify and surround,
                can consider and decide.

The meeting of the minds like the mathematics of the models,
                like the language of conundrums,
                like the existence of enigmas,

            like the plotting of the graphs,
            like the solving of a challenge,
            like the games of puzzlement and of foresight.

The meeting of the minds is not one of confrontation,
            is not one of testing for supremacy,
            is not one of rating the positioning of man.

The meeting of the minds is the sharing of advancement,
            is the witnessing in the field of knowledge,
            in the expansion of the mindset of wisdom.

The meeting of the minds is an expression of enjoyment,
            is a measurement of progress,
            is a contribution to understanding by the soul,
            is a salutation to the teaching in eternity.

The meeting of the minds does not carry the residues of mortality:
            the intenseness of competition,
            the grasping of every opportunity,
            the bringing forth of that which is confounding.

The meeting of the minds is not a race of inequality,
            is not a seizing of position,
            is not a chattering as if among the trees.

The meeting of the minds is at the forefront of progression,
            is the rewarding of fraternity,
            is an objective in the making which has no cause for an appeal.

The meeting of the minds resolves conflicts of understanding,
            clarifies The Truth as the basis of a tenure,
            modifies the stance in the evolvement of inspection,
            circulates the settling of a position when opened for discussion.

The meeting of the minds brings no rancour,
            hears no rancour,
            leaves no rancour.

The meeting of the minds resolves no inequities,
            establishes no infringements,
            transmits no condescensions.

The meeting of the minds does not linger on deception,
            does not linger on the understandings of the past,
            does not linger on the competition once seen at a table.

The meeting of the minds is ready for the concepts,
            is ready for the challenges,
            is ready to resolve such issues as are in The Presence of
                                                                       The Spirit.

The meeting of the minds has no limits on attendance,
    has no qualifying of abilities,
    has no determining of capabilities,
    has no exclusions of those not in immediate agreement,
    has the will to share the enlightening of the minds of
        eternal beings.

The meeting of the minds knows the implications of eternity,
    knows the variability of time as a servant of understanding,
    knows the impressions made by the change in lifestyle,
        by the change in dress code,
        by the facilities now encountered
            in the surroundings
            as encountered.

The meeting of the minds do not encounter superfluities,
    do not arouse feelings of insecurity,
    do not arouse the discontent arising from dissatisfaction.

The meeting of the minds is in the schoolroom of God,
    is the place of contributions,
    is the genesis of thought,
    is the consideration of philosophies,
    is the forum for participation,
    is the governance founded on unity of intent:
        in both love and justness of application.

The meeting of the minds resolves differences of perception,
    differences in approach,
    differences in resolution.

The meeting of the minds verifies and supports The Edifice of God,
    models and thrives on the architecture of God,
    enlists and upholds the companions of God."

My Content Study Aid

_____
_____
_____
_____
_____
_____
_____

The Songsters of God

"The songsters of God enliven the surrounds of God.

The songsters of God bring the voice of man to dominance in the home of God,
                in the company of the loved and loving,
                in the presence of The Multitudes attentive
                          with both ears,
                in the accompaniment of the chosen who
                      play the fingerings in harmony,
                in the gathering of The Saints where reigns
                      both praise and worship.

The songsters of God are assiduous in practice,
        are perfect in renditions,
        are conscious of their contributions,
        are the presenters of the fare as laid upon The Altar of The Lamb.

The songsters of God are not caught out with echoes,
        are not found wanting in their words,
        are not found to be upset by a tonal slip.

The songsters of God carry much within their spirits,
        more within their souls,
        even more so in the lyrics which cascade from the lips.

The songsters of God have an extensive repertoire,
        can match selections to occasions,
        can lead The Saints in song.

The songsters of God know the psalms of David,
        are to encounter the psalms of God.

The songsters of God know not the tunes of David,
        are to encounter the tunes of God.

The songsters of God are a speciality of the house of God.

The songsters of God are vibrant in their approach,
        are clear in their enunciation,
        are in unison of purpose:
                to give voice as the sentinels of praise and worship.

The songsters of God know the hymnals of the past,
        the hymnals of the present,
        await the hymnals still to be.

The songsters of God constrain themselves from laughter,
        restrain themselves from signs of excessive joy,
        present themselves with a smile upon their faces,
              as they witness and observe the countenances
                  of all who stand to sing,
                  of all who praise melodiously,
                  of all who worship in their sox and boots,
                  of all who would partake willingly—
                      in the love-strokes of The Lord.

The songsters of God overflow with enthusiasm,
        walk the walk of jubilation,
        search and find a close relationship with God.

The songsters of God are constant in their adoration,
        are constant in their prayer life,
        are constant in their reading,
        are constant in their quest for knowledge bound in wisdom.

The songsters of God are dressed without embarrassments,
        are garbed to honour God,
        are presented not to be distractions in their callings from God.

The songsters of God are happy in their callings,
        are fulfilled in their callings,
        are excited for their callings,
        are thankful for their callings.

The songsters of God are each filled with gratitude for all that God has done,
              for all that God is doing,
              for all that God has promised to fulfil.

The songsters of God are not hesitant in voicing,
        are confident in where they stand,
        are circumspect when approaching near The Altar,
        are end-time carriers of The Fear of God.

The songsters of God promote the visitations of The Spirit.
The songsters of God promote The End-time sounds of prophecy.
The songsters of God promote The Glory with The Fire of God.

The songsters of God travel on request,
        travel as a guest,
        travel with The Blessings of the best.

The songsters of God have recordings of endeavours,
        have a showcase filled with testimonies of God,
        have a far-flung audience who desire to see and hear,
        have attentive audiences who desire to know more of that for
                which the songs prepare.

The songsters of God receive accolades of appreciation,
        receive the approval of The Spirit,
        receive the tendering of the ministry of God.

The songsters of God do not bow and scrape to man,
        stand erect and bold before the throne of God—
                with a psalm upon their lips.

The songsters of God carry joy within their hearts,
            their spirits and their souls—
        as The Temples of The Living Loving God find rejoicing—
                in the music of the dance.

The songsters of God are the vibrant prongs of God charged with leading the voyages to
                and for The Stars of God."

My Content Study Aid

The Rewards of Faith

"The rewards of Faith can seem to be constantly postponed.

The rewards of Faith are not immediately apparent,
        are not feasting in the exclusion of the hungry,
        are not waking up the neighbourhood,
        are not a song heard in the night.

The rewards of Faith are sincere in their existence,
        are there to be observed by an active spirit,
        are there for participation with The Presence at a divine appointment,
        are there to raise the temperature of each soul,
        are there to establish that a walk with Me is not without adventures,
                is not without the signs,
                      the wonders,
                          the miracles of God.

The rewards of Faith are locked into the reality of man,
        of My Disciples,
        of The Saints of God.

The rewards of Faith are active outside the sphere of Faith,
        beyond the bounds of imagination,
        far beyond the belief patterns of My people.

The rewards of Faith do not accumulate for a rainy day,
        do not build up like books within a bookcase—
                where the dust settles at its pleasure.

The rewards of Faith are triggered in the presence of the insightful,
        are triggered within the talk of a coincidence,
        are missed by the busy and the doubtful.

The rewards of Faith come when unexpected,
        come when the thought patterns permit,
        come when the way is impeded by the thoughtless and profane.

The rewards of Faith multiply with recognition,
        multiply with gratitude,
        multiply when in the fields of boldness,
        multiply when in the active indwelling of My Spirit as He
                              goes before,
        multiply when Grace is appreciated with the willingness to share.

The rewards of Faith despatches unbelief,
        opens up the field to more substantive entries in a diary,
        brings the eyes to attention with the ears spellbound by
                a testimony—
                which has the ring of Truth.

The rewards of Faith build upon the knowledge base,
        expand within the mantel of wisdom,
        Glory in the satisfaction of a soul so won for God.

The rewards of Faith speaks of provisioning,
        speaks to siblings and the off-spring,
        speaks to the in-laws in their chairs,
        speaks to the outlaws as they journey—
                where numbers are much greater,
                where the ears are prone to inattention,
                where the message needs to be both short and sweet.

The rewards of Faith transcend the rewards of man:
        in their presentation with the introductions;
        in their words of God as arrows to the heart,
        in the grasp of wisdom wrapped around the word of knowledge.

The rewards of Faith showcase the giftings of The Spirit,
        showcase The Tongues of Heaven,
        showcase the lifestyle of each Saint in meeting expectations,
        showcase the stand of Faith in The Temple of Faith—
                where Faith proceeds in a Faith-filled stream as Faith
                        and Grace abound.

The rewards of Faith are to receive the hugs,
        to be present at the healings,
        to participate in the pain of a confession,
        to speak the word of God in action as a two-edged sword.

The rewards of Faith are in the field of impartation,
        are in bringing The Reality of God as a personal revelation,
        are in teaching the sanctifying of The Cross with The Promise
                of Inheritance.

The rewards of Faith have times for their delivery,
        have the need for fullness of the armour,
        have the need for company upon the battlefield of life.

The rewards of Faith are not claimed back,
        are not sought out,
        are not decried by attribution to a mortal cause.

The rewards of Faith magnify and glorify The Name above all names,
>> multiply and develop the testimonies of Disciples in the making,
>> graduate and honour the lambs as they grow into His sheep.

The rewards of Faith witness the rising from the grave,
>> witness the adornments on each gown of life,
>> witness the persevering in the race well run,
>> witness the garland for the victor at his journey's end.

The rewards of Faith establish each temple of a new-found child of God—
>> in honoured adoption into The Eternal Family of God."

My Content Study Aid

The Gardens of God (2)

"The garden of eternity is variable and beautiful.

The garden of God is divisible and active,
        is progressive and relaxing,
        is similar yet different,
        is wondrous and exhilarating,
        stretches across divides in reaching out to the spectacular.

The gardens of God are designed—
        distinguished—
        denoted for their quality of thoughtfulness and access.

The gardens of God are the playgrounds of His family,
        are the parks of recreation with the venues,
        are the havens where the viewings are outstanding with the interest levels high.

The gardens of God are built in part:
        upon the themes from the past history of The Earth,
        the themes from the present dispositions of The Earth,
        the themes which are yet to be in the future releasing of The Earth,
        the many themes scattered far and wide within the creativity of God.

The gardens of God have very many facets which appeal to the diverse characters of My people,
        which appeal to memories from childhood,
        which appeal to the times of happiness where contentment reigns supreme.

The gardens of God know neither aches nor pains,
        know neither stumbles nor trips,
        know neither hesitations nor excessive pauses.

The gardens of God assist and revitalise:
        renew at the tables of exhaustion resulting from the unrestrained coming and the going;
        refresh at the tables of the fare where choice abounds aplenty;
        replenish at the tables of recuperation from the exertions of the day;
        recover at the tables of repose from the excitements of the senses;
        reassemble at the tables of discovery where the minds assimilate the input of the visiting.

The gardens of God are the micro- and the macrocosms of creation;
    are the displays of record of the handiworks—
        as prepared by the chief protagonists;
    are the amphitheatres and the auditoriums of the revelation
        of activity—
        on the grandest of the scales—
        with the magnificence of detail.

The gardens of God are teeming with life in all its varied forms,
    in all its various environments,
    in all its various purposes and functionings.

The gardens of God are filled with dioramas where life enacts existence,
    where life can convey understanding
        of the principles,
    where life can mature yet not age on
        the tableau of eternity.

The gardens of God stimulate responses;
    invigorate appreciation of the scope and scale;
    blend the rules of man with the principles of God.

The gardens of God reflect the ideas of the gardener who carried the specifics,
    the motivations which yielded the results,
    The End-time of accord where man is introduced to the
        handshake of creation.

The gardens of God are healthy and alive,
    are mobile and encircling,
    are orbital and returning.

The gardens of God are imposing and sanctified,
    are impressive and amazing,
    are outstanding and enfranchised.

The gardens of God are self-sustaining and reactive,
    are self-contained and isolated,
    are self-assured and insulated.

The gardens of God exchange information,
    issue invitations,
    provide the necessities of life.

The gardens of God are a gardener's dream,
    are a gardener's perfection,
    are a gardener's design:
        which is confirmation of the reality of man's initial
        invitation to partake in a walk of Faith.

The gardens of God lie beyond reach of an attack,
        lie beyond the capabilities resident in the mortalities of the species,
        lie beyond the reach of all but The Family of God and those within
                His kingdom.

The gardens of God deserve the cynosure of man,
        are worth the commitment of man,
        are available with the cost of entry already paid in full.

The gardens of God speak of the lands which lie within eternity:
        all which God has prepared for man;
        all which awaits the acceptance and repentance
                of man—
        while dwelling in Faith with Grace
                within mortality."

My Content Study Aid

The Movement of The Soul

"The movement of the soul is an unreliable bedfellow.

The movement of the soul wants to stray from the spirit,
                wants to follow a line of independence,
                wants to satisfy the desires of the flesh,
                wants to be answerable to no-one,
                wants to be the jockey on the horse,
                wants to encourage the cravings of the body.

The movement of the soul would follow the line of least resistance,
                would follow in the wake of turbulence,
                would follow the scent of immediate reward,
                would follow the highway to gratification of the self.

The movement of the soul is not an exponent of exercise for the sake of exercise,
                is not a warrior looking for a fight,
                is not a worrier looking to the future,
                is not a warrior looking to defend,
                is not a worrier concerned with past deeds,
                is not a warrior looking to overcome,
                is not a worrier about accountability.

The movement of the soul is not a warrior struggling against the current of the river
                                                        of life,
                is not a worrier of what lies ahead as he casually floats
                              downstream in an oarless dinghy.

The movement of the soul stands in need of guidance and direction,
                of supervision and adjustment,
                of responsibility and advancement.

The movement of the soul does not like a straight line,
                prefers to amble and enquire,
                does not mind a stumble,
                does not dodge a trip wire set to harm the body.

The movement of the soul exasperates the spirit,
                exasperates companions with a goal in mind,
                exasperates the souls who have found a better way,
                exasperates the souls who have come to appreciate the
                              functions of the spirit.

The movement of the soul is like a ship without a rudder—
                knows not where it's going nor the path of its return;
                knows not why it is going nor the feelings of dissatisfaction;
                knows not the choice available nor the destiny of default.

The movement of the soul suffers and prolongs,
                bears and complains,
                experiences and enjoys,
                returns and seeks for more.

The movement of the soul drifts within the bounds of drowsiness,
                knows the stupor of both night and day,
                muddles and mystifies observers of the lifestyle of the soul.

The movement of the soul can be aberrant and unfeeling,
                can be trimmed and repositioned.

The movement of the soul is like a joystick in a plane—
                      which is all about the flaps with the ups and downs,
         is not like a steering wheel within a car—
                      which is only concerned with steadiness and the
                                      intentness of approach.

The movement of the soul needs to assess its functioning,
                its wayward dispositions,
                its effects upon its residence,
                its lack of goal with a far-reaching impact on the spirit
                            the body—
                            and the very soul itself.

The movement of the soul needs an awareness of the second death,
                          the loneliness ahead if signposts
                                      are ignored,
                      the inevitability—
                of the ageing of the carrier,
                of the death of the flesh,
                of the onward journey lying in wait
                          for an unsuspecting soul.

The movement of the soul needs to accept correction and subservience,
                needs to follow the example of the spirit in maturity,
                needs to adopt the spirit in its role of the mentor of the soul.

The movement of the soul should correct its figurehead of choice,
                should come to understand the reins of guidance on Freewill,
                        the reins of strategy pointing to the future
                                of the body soul and spirit,
                        the reins of love as built of the threads of
                              gossamer with the lightest of control.

The movement of the soul is designed to have the spirit as its helpmate,
            the spirit as its counsellor,
            the spirit which is aware if its way home:
            the spirit which will ensure a long and
                      happy life together as a
                      threesome of renown.

The movement of the soul seeks leadership and must settle on the best,
            must have certainty of knowledge,
            must have a source of wisdom,
            must ensure the wellness of its being as it
                      functions in a position
                      of great responsibility.

The movement of the soul must be in relationship with God,
        must set the goals accordingly,
        must look to the spirit's leading as the spirit itself is led with
                                        unity achieved."

My Content Study Aid

The Coming of The Tulips

"The coming of the tulips have a season in their sights.

The coming of the tulips have colour in their midst,
        have a time span for a vase.

The coming of the tulips have viral attacks which spoil the dressings of the uniforms,
        which mess-up and confuse that which
                was intended.

The coming of the tulips aggregate the songs of spring,
        aggregate the songs of festivities,
        aggregate the songs of happiness and joy,
        aggregate the songs of life and the gardener's delight.

The coming of the tulips have companionships galore:
        are not lonely in their bed,
        are not short of friendships,
        are surrounded by the scents of new birth.

The coming of the tulips speak of the lengthening of days,
        the contractions of the nights.

The coming of the tulips are regular and timely,
        are annual and perennial,
        are valued and commercial.

The coming of the tulips are a source of inspiration,
        are a measure of man's caring,
        have a history all their own.

The coming of the tulips vie for space within the fields,
        vie for space within a garden,
        vie for shelter and protection from the winds of change.

The coming of the tulips are silent in their approach,
        wait until the days have warmth,
        raise and flourish the single child of birth.

The coming of the tulips do not hang their heads in shame,
        raise their cups up to the sun in pride,
        showcase their finery and colour for appreciation by the loved.

The coming of the tulips are events of grandeur,
        are events of livelihood,
        are events of gathering within the marketplace of man.

The coming of the tulips have a destiny in vases,
> have a destiny in bunches,
> have a destiny of cheer,
> have a destiny with beauty,
> have a destiny with bouquets,
> have a destiny with the floral and the greenery.

The coming of the tulips encourages decoration and adornment,
> placement and critiquing,
> blending and reviews—
>> arrangements with the praises due effect."

My Content Study Aid

I, The Lord Jesus (3)

"I,
    The Lord Jesus,
        would speak this day to all who would dwell within My garden.

"I,
    The Lord Jesus,
        would encourage all to learn and understand
                the pre-requisites of entry,
                the pre-requisites of citizenship,
                the pre-requisites of adoption by The Father,
                the pre-requisites of guidance and of counselling
                            by My Spirit.

For these are the days of the preparation of My Bride,
    these are the days approaching the tribulation of The Earth,
    these are the days just prior to My return,
    these are the days when My prophets find their voices,
    these are the days when the witnesses visit Heaven and return to testify of all
                            which they have learnt.

For these are the days when The Earth does tremble;
    these are the days when the shores of man are washed by the seas of God;
    these are the days when the stripping of The Earth by man brings the torrents
                          with the mud slides—
                which inundate the mistakes of man;
    these are the days when mayhem expands its reach,
            when misery approaches the woebegone,
            when life is threatened by the miscreants,
            when pillaging follows in the wake of destruction,
            when victims are molested by the sons of Satan,
            when the times of lightning and of thunder cause all to run to
                            shelter from the storms.

For these are the days when life will be held in low esteem,
        when plunder and robbery are the seizers of both the day
                            and night,
        when despair and mourning fill the eyes,
            the ears,
                the faces of The Lost and The Unforgiving,
    when the child is separated from a parent,
    when a marriage and a family are beset by fear,
    when a home is razed to the ground,
when survivors stumble on their way in attempts to flee what follows in their tracks.

"I,
    The Lord Jesus,
        cry out to The Lost:
            to put each house in order;
            to prepare to overcome;
            to store in safety that which will be needed in a maelstrom of iniquity;
                  that which will be unavailable to purchase with the
                            monies born of man;
            to acquire the gold of God;
            to acquire value which will last,
                which will not fade away with the coming of the dawn,
                which will bring penury when inflation becomes a curse.

"I,
    The Lord Jesus,
        call out to My People,
            The Makeup of My Bride,
            The Gathered of The Cross,
            The Recognisers of The Messiah,
            The Lovers of The Father,
            The Saved and The Committed of God—
                so these may focus on survival,
                    may focus on The Will of God,
                    may hark to—
                so to hear and follow—
                    The Counselling of God.

    My People,
        shift and move from your homes on the floodplains of the rivers,
        shift from the homes within the reach of the seas which come to wash
                                                    and launder,
        shift out of reach from the down-side of the candles of The Lord,
        shift from where the tremblings of The Earth are likely to be evident.

    My People,
        shift from the buildings of man reaching to the skies,
        shift from the homes built in the shadows of the buildings reaching to
                                                      the skies—
                            which will need a place to fall,
        shift from the surroundings where bush and brush fires can rampage—
                                    in seeking the proximity of fuel.

My People,
    remove yourselves from slopes where rock falls and avalanches can sweep
                              all before them,
    remove yourselves from homes upon the cliff edges—
                    with a precipice at hand,
    remove yourselves from viewing positions—
                    selected for the eyes—
                    which may be the cause of untimely death.

My People,
    do not dwell where access can be easily denied,
        where threats to life are evident,
        where injury is possible,
        where shortages can accrue,
        where household services may be broken for an extended time.

My People,
    do not dwell without protection from the wind shear,
            the whirlwind,
            the cyclone,
        which will carve a home to pieces,
        which will scatter and destroy;
select your homes for this their time of safety—
            as your sanctuaries of shelter—
for in these times those with wisdom will seek the assent of My Spirit—
                    in all they decide to do.

"I,
    The Lord Jesus,
        reach out to My People so they may be prepared:
        for the storms about to assail the homes of man who have:
                turned from,
                denied,
                ignored,
                sinned,
                blasphemed—
                thereby affirming by deed or action the
                    non-relevance of God within a life;
        who have dishonoured their souls and spirits,
        who have condemned their bodies as unfit for further use,
        who have expressed their Freewill choice—
                by attitude or stipulation—
            of any further interest of ever being in
                    The Company of God.

"I,
   The Lord Jesus,
      care for My sheep,
      love My sheep,
      call and shepherd My sheep—
      that My sheep may dwell in safety in The End-time of My Church:
         so they may not be dispossessed by the cleansing of The Earth;
         so they may not be caused to flinch as the angels spread their wings of fury
                              over the encountered sin;
         so the angels will have marked the sanctuaries of The Lord for the passover
                              of the vengeance of The Lord—
      so to fall on those still practising their iniquities at large."

My Content Study Aid

My Sheep within The Saleyards

"My sheep within the saleyards break the heart of God.

My sheep within the saleyards dismay the heart of God,
                embed the heart of God,
                direct the heart of God.

My sheep within the saleyards include the lambs of blessing,
                include the hoggets with their outlooks on life,
                include the sheep of substance with time still left to serve.

My sheep within the saleyards have been stolen from the shepherd,
                have been stolen by the wolves,
                have been stolen to fill an order,
                have been stolen to be matched with the highest bidder.

My sheep within the saleyards are terrified and filled with dread,
                are dismayed and concerned for others,
                are separated and strive to find their lambs.

My sheep within the saleyards are not free to move,
                are constricted and held in check,
              are supervised and marshalled both on age and
                              on appearance.

My sheep within the saleyards are awaiting an auction,
                an auction where the rams of Satan
                    descend into the pits as animals at large,
                    descend below the lower ebbing
                              of immorality—
              as rams do mount the rams both night and day,
              as rams do mount and move on to the next,
              as rams do mount until exhausted by their urges.

My sheep within the saleyards have their future limited as the shepherds seek and search:
            in an endeavour to recover both the stolen and the invited;
                      the trapped and the imprisoned;
                      the sought and the ransomed;
                      the victims and the immature;
                      the frightened and the terrified;
                      the wounded and the dazed.

My sheep within the saleyards await the calls of animals,
        see the gathering of the packs of wolves
              as they slobber at the gates,
              as they enter to feel and touch,
              as they evaluate for the filling of the orders.

My sheep within the saleyards mill about in anguish,
        attempt to comfort one another,
        pray for their release.

My sheep within the saleyards note the wolves in control,
        hear the gavel fall upon a shout,
        see the drafting for a destination within a dark interior,
        feel the heat and the exhaustion stemming from the lack
                of care.

My sheep within the saleyards are blindfolded and restrained,
        are silenced with a gag,
        are threatened into silence as their legs are trussed.

My sheep no longer in the saleyards suffer,
        are distraught,
        cry within their fears,
        are scared of all they witness since the timing of
                their capture.

My sheep no longer in the saleyards are sent as freight to their destinations,
        are sent in trucked containers or on the ships at sea,
        are sent according to the bidding and the lust
                of wolves—
        pretending to be righteous and fitted out with means.

My sheep no longer in the saleyards know not where they're going,
        know not where they've been,
        know not what awaits them on arrival at the scene.

My sheep no longer in the saleyards are accustomed to the darkness,
        are accustomed to being trundled,
        are accustomed to encountering the ructions and
                the waits.

My sheep no longer in the saleyards hear the bolts withdrawn,
        the creaking accompanying the opening of the doors,
        the surprised expressions of the men in uniform,
        the assistance and the aid with the helping down,
        the assurances that their journeying is over and all is
                well as freedom is regained.

My sheep no longer in the saleyards are reunited after feeding and a rest,
                          are reunited with familiar faces,
                          are the fortunate and blest,
                          are the rescued in recovery,
                          are secure in their safety,
                          are now valued much more highly than they
                                                                        were before.

My sheep no longer in the saleyards are now out upon the pasture,
                          see the flowing of the brooks of living water as
                                          testimonies are heard,
                          as counselling is received,
                          as the welfare of My sheep is attended to with
                                                        loving care.

    Woe to those who mistreat My sheep.

    Woe to those who prefer My lambs.

    Woe to those who feed their depravities from among the stolen and the innocent,
                                  the beautiful and the lovely,
                                  the immature and the young—
                                            both in body and in heart.

For on such surely will The Wrath of God fall in might and majesty—
                on the exercised Freewill with the latter serving of accountability."

My Content Study Aid

The Settlers within My Garden

"The settlers within My garden are from another time and space.

The settlers within My garden are external to the time sphere of man,
>are beyond the beck and call of man,
>are not within the knowledge base of man,
>are mentioned in My Word° in passing—
>>which were not intended to be applied with certainty:
>>>by every then current generation who brought opinions
>>>>to the fore.

The settlers within My garden are misinterpreted by man:
>are claimed to be what they are not;
>are claimed by man as being validated by future events as
>>timed within the past;
>>>as bringing to present situations of the day—
>>>that which could only thrive—
>>>when standing in the shadow of Biblical authority*.

The settlers within My garden do not speak the tongues of man,
>do speak the tongues of Heaven.

The settlers within My garden are also still having some with time within mortality;
>are also transitioning with their bodies souls and spirits
>>into eternity with God.

The settlers within My garden have also had a place prepared:
>where they too will feel at home in surroundings
>>of familiarity.

The settlers within My garden do not bring a clash of cultures,
>are accepting of the changes,
>are accepting of their rebirths from their graves,
>are accepting of the need for thought transference and the
>>achieving of fluency of expression.

The settlers within My garden are not set in their ways with troublesome priorities,
>know the same commandments,
>have also tried life under the seasons
>>of covenantal law with sacrifice;
>>of covenantal Faith with Grace;
>and soon to become aware of governance of Truth in
>>wisdom with Mercy pled at The Bema.

The settlers within My garden are jocular and friendly,
              love the jokes and jests,
              explore and understand,
              seek and do not query,
              are amused when struck by puzzlement,
              are awestruck by a new idea,
              have understanding serviced by the centuries—
              as 'Truth' gradually became the basic structure of societies.

The settlers within My garden are winsome and popular,
              are respected and honoured,
              are inviting and responsive.

The settlers within My garden are identified and recognized,
              are welcomed and befriended,
              are generous and likeable.

The settlers within My garden have stories of much interest:
              have histories with generational accuracy;
              have the scope and experience to enthral their new found
                            thought-recipients;
              have the ability to listen to the concerts in
                            quadrophonic sound.

The settlers within My garden love to talk on their four feats;
              rest with hems tucked tidily beneath:
              can jump and run and leave a kangaroo behind;
              can play and dart and check and run—
                    which leaves others standing still while watching
                                  in amazement.

The settlers within My garden are there for the enjoyment of their achievements
                                      of conviction:
              of the souls they won
                        and welcomed;
              of their sight lines of success
                    in applying their
                      telescopic "eyes".

The settlers within My garden have qualified as children of God,
              for entry to eternity,
              as overcomers of all which has been set
                          before them—
              in a lifestyle of great hardship—
              where the rewards are also great.

The settlers within My garden are welcomed by My people to eternity:
> are welcomed by My people to My garden;
> are welcomed by My people into The Family of God;
> are welcomed by My people to their places as prepared;
> are welcomed by My people as their fellow travellers in My Gospel;
> are welcomed by acclamation for all they have achieved and done—
> within the sight and tasking of God down through their ages of existence."

Biblical authority* 1 Peter 3:18-20 (NKJV) Abridged ...

... [19] **by whom also He went and preached to the spirits in prison,** [20] **who formerly were disobedient,** when once the Divine longsuffering waited in the days of Noah, while the ark was being prepared, ...

Luke 23:50-53 (NKJV) *All verse references abridged for reasons of space.*

[52] This man went to Pilate and asked for the body of Jesus. [53] **Then he took it down, wrapped it in linen, and laid it in a tomb that was hewn out of the rock**, ...

Scribal Note: The KJV and NKJV both say that Jesus "preached" to the spirits in prison (verse 19). However, the Greek word used is not the usual New Testament word for preaching the gospel. It simply means "to herald a message"; the NIV translates it as "made proclamation." Jesus suffered and died on the cross, His body being put to death. But His spirit was made alive, and He yielded it to The Father (Luke 23:46). According to Peter, sometime between Jesus' death and His resurrection (The Spirit of) Jesus made a special proclamation to "the spirits in prison."

Genesis 6:1-3 (NKJV) *Abridged ...*

... that **the sons of God saw the daughters of men, that they were beautiful; and they took wives for themselves of all whom they chose.** And the Lord said, "My Spirit shall not strive *(abide, in other Bible variants)* with man forever, for he *is* indeed flesh; yet his days shall be one hundred and twenty years." ...

These "sons of God" appear to be the "spirits in prison" who had earlier been "disobedient". **Emphasis is Scribal.**

My Content Study Aid

_____
_____
_____
_____
_____

The Apocrypha of Man

"The apocrypha* of man are widespread and carry stories.

The apocrypha of man are not worth the summing up,
                are not worth the fall of favour,
                are not worth the reading time of man.

The apocrypha of man illustrate the many roads to Hell,
                      the many roads of falsity and misbelief,
                      the many roads leading to idolatry and satanism.

The apocrypha of man fail to establish Truth and Love in action,
                fail to establish the quest for peace and happiness,
                fail to affirm the safety of the soul,
                      the future of the soul,
                      the companionship of God.

The apocrypha of man fails in expressing The Love of God for His Creation,
                            The Love of God for the structure within
                                        His planning—
                            the forward destiny of man,
                    The Love of God substantiated and upheld—
                      by His sacrifice of self upon The Cross of sin,
                          upon The Cross of paganism,
                          upon The Cross of excruciating pain
                                and suffering for an innocent.

The apocrypha of man talk of misplaced trust,
                talk of the battlefields arising from exclusion,
                talk of the spilling of the blood for neither rhyme nor reason:
                              but to satisfy the will of man.

The apocrypha of man can be gathered all together,
                can fill a library with nothingness except the jottings of
                                    wishful thinking,
            can fill a head with nonsense straight from the mystagogies**:
                    concerned only with creating an unending flow of wealth.

The apocrypha of man target man for captivity of his spirit soul and body,
                for his standings before false altars,
                for his offerings to fund to feed the unemployable
                                          by God—
                          in all their shapes and forms,
                          in all their robes and dressings,
                          in all their mantras of repetition,
                          in all their falseness behind the calls to prayer,

in all their inaugurations of the rites of passage—
to only God knows where.

The apocrypha of man stand in testimony of the way in which the misogynists of Hell
choose to treat their womenfolk—
in levels of dishonour and of "non-existence",
in levels of retraction and of non-involvement,
in levels of social mores where treatment and
respect speak of the hypocrisy—
so evident in the apocryphal-based soul of man.

The apocrypha of man are not pathways to general social development,
feature only the desires of the elite,
ensure subjugation of The Multitudes where they are not taught
to think.

The apocrypha of man speak of travesties of cultural order,
speak of the containment of wealth within hierarchies
of privilege,
speak of a lack of skills as leading to inventions.

The apocrypha of man are salads of mismatched ingredients,
are blendings of the moderate and insincere,
leave superlatives alone,
are unfamiliar either with The Truth or The Wisdom of God,
propound the agendas of the lost in time,
the concepts arising from the stirring of the pots,
the imagining of minds within drugdoms of release,
in the spiritual molestings of man,
in the claimed be-all and catch-all of belief:
as imposed upon his fellow man.

The apocrypha of man are bred in a quest for status,
are bred in a walk of justification,
are bred from minds who mistreat,
rape and desert:
the women recorded in their lives.

The apocrypha of man have histories of success in the absence of The Truth,
have followers who resort to violence when threatened by
The Truth,
have teachings which cannot stand in the presence of The Truth.

The apocrypha of man will fail when faced with The Truth,
when tested by The Truth,
when surrounded by The Truth.

The apocrypha of man will be discarded for The Truth,
        will be impotent before The Truth,
        will be immolated because of Truth,
        will be ignored for The Truth,
        will be searched and found wanting for The Truth of God.

The apocrypha of man are but shells without the kernels,
        are but gloves without their forms,
        are but mysteries without the knowledge,
        are but unsatisfactory mistakes of history as written to
                            ensure conformity:
        in the retaining of control over the reliant and believing.

The apocrypha of man are not worth the study;
        are not worth the retention in a library;
        are not worth the widow's mite.

The apocrypha of man is superseded by,
        is supplanted by,
        is overcome by:
                The Good News of The Bible.

For the Bible with its message of uniqueness—
                the testimonies of miracles;
                    of signs;
                    of wonders,
                        of prophecies upheld fulfilled and waiting—
    witnesses as Jesus,
        The Messiah,
        comes and loves and leads His People—
        from the shadows of The Cross of Glory unto the promise of return.

For Jesus,
    The Loving Living God,
        as declared within The Bible,
is affirmed as alive and well in this day and age—
        with His Spirit's gifts all seen in action—
        for the benefit of man and The Faith within His followers."

Scribal Note:
    *apocrypha: writings or reports not considered genuine.
    **mystagogies: teachers or propounders of mystical doctrines.

The Passing of a Cloud

"The passing of a cloud is not a major event in the life of man.

The passing of a cloud can go completely unnoticed,
    can be completely non-remarkable,
        completely unhindered by the wind,
            unchecked as it climbs and unfurls in the cumulus
                of majesty,
        as it dissipates and slowly vanishes before the
            eyes of man.

The passing of a cloud can be violent with the lightning and the rolls of thunder:
            as it exists both to threaten and to lash;
    can upset the crops of man with hailstones:
            as the triggers of destruction;
    can be far reaching across The Heavens as snow blankets all:
        over which it spreads in the mantling of The Earth;
    can be shaped as funnels which trap and seize to so break
            into pieces:
        that as driven by the winds;
    can be the answering of prayer as the carriers of the watering of
        The Earth:
        in giving of themselves without complaint.

The passing of a cloud can be silent and in a hurry as it competes with nearby
            fellow travellers:
        the dust brooms of the skies;
    can be stationery and resting prior to receiving the
            next commission:
        to attend elsewhere in bringing the
            requirements of The Earth;
    can be secretive and bashful to only work at night:
        so to greet the freshly awakened with
            the surprises of the morn.

The passing of a cloud leaves its impressions on all that it surveys:
        whether as little as the shadowing of shade;
        or the shearing of the ways and means:
            as scheduled for performance;
        or a presence with The Blessings which precede:
            the sign of the promise from the past.

The passing of a cloud can be business personified as each is tolled and troubled:
        by a land mass in the way,
    can be greeted and appreciated as each dumps upon demand:
        in a downpour of delight and satisfaction,
    can be welcomed with much joy as each comes to stay awhile
        with steadiness of purpose:
        for the soaking of the seams and streams of life.

The passing of a soul is the major Faith event in the life of man.

The passing of a soul is accompanied by the spirit and the body of the flesh,
    is accompanied by the sighing and the tears,
    is accompanied by the grief within the present and the joys
        within remembrance.

The passing of a soul can leave an echo of existence or the imprint of a walk;
        a history difficult to place or a book of memories filled
        with doings and achievements;
        a trail of dissolution or a pathway to the stars.

The passing of a soul attempts to shelter from the storm with the dressings of distress;
        or sings a song of triumph in arriving at the destiny of delight.

The passing of a soul may need to accept the hindrances besetting of the body,
        to accept the pain arising from an onslaught of attacks;
        to accept the rites of passage with all which is intended.

The passing of a soul may be peaceful and sublime,
    may be sudden and surprising,
    may be when at rest within the folds of sleep,
    may be violent and disturbing at the hands of another:
    yet as The Cross of Sacrifice so ensures the honouring of Freewill.

The passing of a soul may be unexpected with the soul still unprepared,
        with the commitment still lacking
        from postponement,
        with the chalk still un-erased and present on the
        slate of life.

The passing of a soul may be caught up in a struggle,
    may be fixated on a wrong belief,
    may express uncertainty within the dilemma of determining the
        rights and wrongs,
    may be a candidate for the destiny of default:
    with The Freewill earning of respect brought to the fore.

The passing of a soul opens either the doorway or the gateway to where life is
        still continuing.

The passing of a soul witnesses the stillness of the sands of life within the hourglass:
        in completion of the timing as set for preparation.

The passing of a soul travels from its birthday to its day of death:
        with the latter undeclared.

The passing of a soul should not approach the pending day of death with trepidation or
        with unbelief:
        when preparations are in place,
        are completed,
        are absorbed.

The passing of a soul sends the accompaniments by the couriers of God."

My Content Study Aid

The Sustaining of a Vision

"The sustaining of a vision requires a relationship with God.

The sustaining of a vision requires The Call of God,
        requires consistency of application,
        requires the applying of a goal.

The sustaining of a vision sweeps away distractions,
        sweeps away the other visions which would seek to encroach,
        sweeps away the vision which is not relevant to The Call.

The sustaining of a vision in The End-time of God requires the motivation implicit in
        The Call,
        requires the attention to the detail with
            clarity of focus,
        requires the time of man as a
            component within the
            coming Psalms of God.

The sustaining of a vision requires the provisioning of God within the timing of God,
        requires the two way conversations which strengthen the will
            of His servant,
            which support His servant
        with the opening of doors,
        with the preparing of the way,
        with the access to the hands of skills,
        with access to the hands of expertise,
        with access to the two hands of
            knowledge bound with wisdom.

The sustaining of a vision has integrity within the scope and scale,
        has integrity within the process and the effort leading to fruition,
        has integrity for sharing within the minds of assistance and the
            means of completion,
        has integrity so functioning is imparted to The Glory of The Son
            and hence The Glory of The Father.

The sustaining of a vision may be short or long in the life of a chosen servant,
        a servant who is willing,
        a servant with The Faith,
        a servant who can catch the vision from The
        Heavens and call such down upon The Earth.

The sustaining of a vision offers what may be a prospect for reality into the likelihood of
        an on-going presence accompanying man.

The sustaining of a vision has the potential often unrealised by the holder
        until completion,
    joins in the potentials of visions waiting in alignment to
        be birthed,
    has the potential of the magnitudes associated with the will
        of God.

The sustaining of a vision should not be subject to interruption,
    should not be upset in the planning,
    should not be brought to no avail by the actions of
        satanic forces.

The sustaining of a vision stands in need of perseverance,
    stands in need of witnessing the "hows" and "whens" of God,
    stands in need of consultations between the two participants.

The sustaining of a vision is to the benefit of man,
    is to the benefit befitting of embrace,
        befitting of the assembling of resources which
        enhances the ease of progress.

The sustaining of a vision can last for the many years of man,
    can grow and develop within the pace as set by God,
    can be in the time frame of acceptance when such are practical
        and permitted by the governance of man.

The sustaining of a vision can yield effects of benefit to nations;
    can impress the leaders and the rulers,
    can be seen as worthy of support,
    can be witnessed for evaluation as Righteousness overcomes
        the residues of evil:
    in the populations based on past ignorance of Truth.

The sustaining of a vision leads into the lands of gratitude,
    into the lands of appreciation for the effort,
    into the lands of change resulting from the delivery of
        The Truth.

The sustaining of a vision maintains the relationship with The Son,
    maintains the direction of The Spirit,
    maintains the oversight of The Father,
    maintains the compliance of the servant within the unity
        of God.

The sustaining of a vision moves the heart of the servant,
    moves the hearts of the helpers,
    moves the hearts of all those working to achieve the will of
        God declared.

The sustaining of a vision carries rewards along the way:
> the rewards of relationships established,
>> of prayers promptly answered,
>>> of the presence of the healings of the
>>>> miracles and wonder
>>>> as the signs proceed,
>>> of the discussions of amazement at all
>>>> which God brings to pass within His
>>>> timing set for both man and His servants.

The sustaining of a vision is a mighty work of God with His servants who participate."

My Content Study Aid

The Management of God

"The management of God carries responsibility for the oversight of The Earth.

The management of God knows and knows and knows all there is to know.

The management of God puts every bump and nook and cranny into every cloud which
    passes on His palette of the skies.

The management of God establishes the order of every leaf to fall from the bounty of
    a tree.

The management of God has in mind the particles of sand on the foreshores of the
    beaches of The Earth,
    the particles of sand between the toes of all who
    play upon the beaches—
    and remove them to join the count elsewhere.

The management of God supervises the building of the foreshores with the ballast of
    the seas.

The management of God supervises the erosion of the foreshores in the absence
    of the prayers of His people;
    of the prayers of The Multitudes of
    man who dwell outside idolatry.

The management of God is yielded to the management of His people who know both
    what to bind* and what to loose*:
    so the desires resident on locations on The Earth
    become the desires resident within The Heavens:
    so the binding and the loosing within the souls upon
    The Earth are instituted as the binding and the
    loosing of control from within The Heavens.

The management of God awaits the increase in the knowledge base of man:
    for The God of all creation knows the degrees of His
    sharing of authority—
    that which He has shared with The End-time Faith of man;
    where His sharing arising from the binding and the
    loosing on locations on The Earth—
    have empowered the enduring will of man:
    as evident in the behaviour resulting from
    the modifying—
    as sought with the passing of the time clock
    dwelling in each man.

The management of God shares the entrusted management of man with Faith
    and Wisdom—
  to all aspects of the weather where sufficiency of knowledge abounds:
    where flooding is prevented,
    where the wind velocity is set where
      damage does not occur,
    where the ice the snow the frosts will not
      become the harbingers of death—
  to the life on which they fall;
  to all aspects of the weather in meeting the needs of
    the growers of the food chains,
    the fishers of the seas,
    the harvesters of the skies—
  so droughts are avoided,
  so rain is redirected,
    is not started without the end-point
      being set,
  so storms of destruction can be redirected to
    avoid the seat of value:
  to both the labourer due his wages for
    the day,
  and the owner who planted or
    established his visions for the future.

The management of God has established the landing fields of rain,
  has established the rivers to drain the run-off—
    from what has been deforested by man,
  has established the waves upon the seas—
    as they beat upon the shores bringing
      erosion as a threat.

The management of God is not foresworn within His Will by imprudent directions
    lacking wisdom:
  in arising from the inept will of man;
  the inept will of man beset by a heart of meddling,
  by a heart of vengeance,
  by a heart of playing "what if's" with the plans of God;
  by a heart without any semblance of gratitude,
  by a heart intent on the love of money,
  by a heart without respect for the laws of man—
    yet would seek to control the laws of God.

The management of God allows for resolution of clashes of direction:
  where locations with the times are neither
    accurately nor sufficiently identified:
  in being just and fair to all.

The management of God has his sharing of authority active in respect to the above:
    since the day of Pentecost which dwells within My Word;
    since the time of man where loosing and binding was
        decreed as a resource of My Spirit:
    since being made available to man within his giftings as
        received from God.

The management of God advances the livelihood of man,
    advances the welfare of man,
    advances the efforts of man,
    advances His relationships with man:
 so all may come to know Jesus—
    The Living Loving God who died upon the cross of sacrifice for each soul
        who now is dwelling on The Earth."

Scribal Note:
*Refer Mat 16:19
 "And I will give you the keys of the kingdom of heaven, and whatever you bind on earth will be bound in heaven, and whatever you loose on earth will be loosed in heaven."

*Refer Mat 18:18
 "Assuredly, I say to you, whatever you bind on earth will be bound in heaven, and whatever you loose on earth will be loosed in heaven.
        The Bible, NKJV. Used by Permission

My Content Study Aid

_____
_____
_____
_____
_____
_____
_____
_____
_____
_____
_____
_____
_____
_____
_____

The Gardening of Man

"The gardening of man is determined by his knowledge.

The gardening of man is restrained by his lack of knowledge,
        by his lack of acumen,
        by his lack of passion,
        by his lack of commitment to the chores of the day,
        by his tendency to procrastinate that which he deems
                can wait for another day.

The gardening of man can observe the plantings thrive when placed under the specifics
        of the care of God,
        of the care for His Creation,
        of the care for the nurturing of nature and of
        life with the gift to both "visit" and "return".

The gardening of man demonstrates the pride of conquest in reaping the harvest
        of bounty,
        in picking the blooms
        of largesse,
        in wafting the scents of beauty,
        in viewing the endeavours of a
        task well done.

The gardening of man has charge over all which dwell above and below the surface of
        The Earth,
        which dwell upon the leaves,
        which dwell upon the stems,
        which dwell within cocoons as transitions are
        scheduled to take place,
        which come as visitors to partake of all which
        is on offer.

The gardening of man has a time of preparation,
        has a time of planting,
        has a time of reaping,
        has a time of cleaning and maintaining—
        all according to the seasons which befall with the installing
        of the relevance—
        as each brings impact to the cycling of life upon The Earth.

The gardening of man can be a form of recreation,
        can be a form of livelihood,
        can be a form of enhancing a desert in a wasteland,
                a desert in demand of water,
                a desert with more than its fair share of
                      the sunlight of the day,
                a desert with too much cold with frost
                      and snow.

The gardening of man can be done with enthusiasm in presenting in abundance,
        can be done half-heartedly with little to be gleaned or shared,
        can be ignored where the weeds and thorns are given permission
                to promote themselves undeserving of reward.

The gardening of man centres on his preferences,
        reflects the tastes he savours,
        responds to the likes and dislikes of his palette.

The gardening of man protects his efforts from the mites and frosts,
                from the viruses and moulds,
        invites the friendly insects of the butterflies and bees.

The gardening of man has an eye for the colour of the seasons
            arising from the bulbs and tubers,
                from the corms and plantings,
                from the perennials and seeds of the latest generation.

The gardening of man has flowers to go to visitors,
        has flowers readied for the picking,
        has flowers designed to stand within a vase,
        has flowers in abundance which bring their scent indoors.

The gardening of man sees fruit trees of his choice,
                of favour granted to the few,
                of selections based upon location in recognition of
                        their preferences,
                of cropping seen to be plentiful for both the birds
                      and man.

The gardening of man speaks of an attitude displayed,
            speaks of the emphasis intended,
            speaks of favouritism brought to the fore.

The gardening of man speaks of the wild stocks of God being tamed by man.

The gardening of man speaks of the variety of preferences as exposed by man.

The gardening of man speaks of colours loved unto selection within the scenes of man.

The gardening of man selects and prunes and weeds the discards from the garden,
                        the dead and dying from the seasons
                                  of the garden,
                        the end of fulfilment of the beauty of
                                  the planted—
            as they travel to the albums to be trapped within the memories:
            in their images of wonder with admiration for the delicacy—
                of such designs of grandeur as laid before the eyes of man.

The gardening of man without a vision neither lasts nor lingers in the absence of
                                  the gardener,
                      neither recalls nor revisits what has been
                                  and gone,
                    neither speaks of expended effort nor the
                                  results obtained.

The gardening of man with a vision can last for the centuries,
              can impress on a landscape,
              can imprint on a desert of the sands,
              can speak of past glories with a valuing of history.

The gardening of God can speak of His efforts on The Earth as modified by man,
              will speak of His efforts in eternity with His Will established
                                  and upheld,
              will speak to the spirit soul and body in the rewarding of
                                  their Faith."

My Content Study Aid

_____
_____
_____
_____
_____
_____
_____
_____
_____
_____
_____
_____
_____

The Tableting of Man

"The tableting of man is either a curse of excess or a blessing of functioning within the life of man.

The tableting of man rings the production tills of man,
    rings as the entrees to a meal,
    rings the need to count,
        to verify,
            the tablets of the day.

The tableting of man is widespread and excessive,
    is set up to compensate for the "deficient" diet of man,
    is the process where the supplements are taken with hope
        and expectation.

The tableting of man controls the serving of the supplements,
    the serving of the anxious and the imaginative,
    the serving of the pills deemed to fill the unconfirmed
        shortages of "essential" vitamins:
        in the diets of the gullible and the fearing;
    to fill the "vacancies" of minerals and leaves,
    to fill the "vacancies" of roots and seeds,
    to fill the "vacancies" of the sea-borne and the sea-swept:
    so all may be addressed in appealing to the nervous and
        the paranoid who suspect and believe,
    without the presenting of the evidence of confirmation,
    the efficacy of each tablet prepared for entry to the mouth.

The tableting of man is dependent on the selling of "beliefs" without a firm foundation,
    on the selling of recurrent treatments without a cure,
    on the patterning that the demand confirms conviction
        of acceptance,
    on the supposition that the diet of man is deficient and
        in need of augmentation,
    on the ingestion in the multiples where more is seen
        as better,
    on the self-help market where purchases are not
        subject to an oversight with knowledge.

The tableting of man can be the source of death,
    can be the source of lumps and bumps where allergies
        are suspected,
    can be the source of excess which the body cannot handle,
        which the body cannot evacuate,
        which the body cannot counter.

The tableting of man can be the superimposing of that for which the body has
                                        no defences,
                    for which the body is not deficient,
                    for which the surplus cannot
                                  be excreted.

The tableting of man imposes storage problems for the excess,
        imposes symptoms calling out for wisdom,
        imposes effects upon the body not easily traceable to the source:
                where Truth is being stupidly withheld.

The tableting of man should befriend the testing of the blood,
        the analysing of the blood,
        the close examination of the blood:
so both the mouth and heart know what they are doing;
        know the goal in mind;
        know the sufficiency of the day;
        have a common objective where neither harms the other.

The tableting of man is a blessing with control,
        is a curse when not accountable—
        is able to assist in the running of a factory where the need
                            is genuine,
        is able to be overcome when pride and recommends in ignorance
                            are the guardians of the day.

The tableting of man is not a hit or miss affair which can be stoked with impunity,
        is not a situation where the excess can be burnt and emitted from
                            a smokestack,
        is not a functioning at risk with "choice" alone as the only player at
                            the table,
        is not the measuring of surplus where tolerance is seen to be
                            on leave,
        is not the "cure-all" for the imagination,
        is not wisdom where garnered from the advertising
                            promoting availability:
                yet without an oversight,
                speaking with much caution,
                into a situation.

The tableting of man carries responsibility to do no harm when within the framework of
                            insistence such is so:
        ensures most are harmless and without effect as the placebos
                            of man.

The tableting of man oft ignores the problems of recurrently enlarging of the dosage
						without the supervision,
				ignores the problems of the imported where quality controls
						are missing,
				ignores the problems of subversive manufacture in the homes of
						the depraved and greedy.
The tableting of man oft ignores the mixing of toxicity—
					the downing of a tablet with a swill of alcohol,
					the party mode oft to be filled with regret,
							with ignorance abroad,
							with implications unexpected,
							with the memory impaired and
									needing help.
The tableting of man should be limited by wisdom to the confines of a consultation:
					within the medical profession who
							know "What is" and
							"What is not",
					of what is beneficial with the reasons
							for the "Why?" and the
							"How" and "When".
The tableting of man is seen by God who knows the rights and wrongs of admittances
						granted to the body—
				with security for the functioning of the three in unity:
						the body soul and spirit."

My Content Study Aid

_____
_____
_____
_____
_____
_____
_____
_____
_____
_____

The Bow of a Ship

"The bow of a ship overcomes the inertia of the medium in which it thrives,
                                  for which it was designed,
                                  for which it has the engines to
                                  thrust its load to the destination
                                  beneath The Stars of God.

The bow of a ship prepares the way for the rest to follow,
                prepares the way so effort is reduced,
                prepares the way so speed is not sacrificed to the onslaught of
                                                            the waves.

The bow of a ship accepts the buffeting as a way of life,
                accepts ice layers are there to be shattered for the passage,
                accepts the winds as obstacles in the building of the waves,
                              in the surges of the tide,
                              in the swirling of the mists,
                              in the safety of the souls at home upon
                                                the ship.

The bow of a ship points the way so the bulk must follow,
                so the bulk will not fracture to break free,
                so the bulk will answer to the leading of the bow,
                so the bulk will follow meekly to where the
                                                bow intends.

The bow of a ship can guess the coming port of record,
                has assumed this stance before,
                is familiar with the seesaw of the waves,
                is cognizant of the rocks which hide their own agendas,
                recognizes the land masses in passing serenely by.

The bow of a ship is loaded with an anchor,
                is inclusive of the chain at home within the depths,
                is tethered by such when within the confines of a harbour,
                is running free before the guidance of the rudder:
                        when the chain is lifted up to be claimed at home within the hold.

The bow of a ship visits and protests,
                buckles and gives way,
                is inspected and repaired.

The bow of a ship is painted and named,
                is proud and stately in its stature,
                is subtle and quietly pleased at the surrounding fuss.

The bow of a ship does not like the splashes of champagne,
        does not like the inept who do not help in the breaking of a bottle,
        does not like to feel the bouncing of a bottle after attending
                nervous hands.

The bow of a ship is glad when the fuss is finally over,
        when the ship is launched and foreign ports await,
        when the engines growl and ropes are loosed:
                and creeping movement is observed.

The bow of a ship is dismayed at casual engagements,
        does not like poking in to where it is not wanted,
        does not like being scraped and bent,
        does not like the sound of hammers bent on the removal of the dents,
        does not like the crowding of the shipyard where ownership is known
                to be at risk,
        does not like adjusting to a repaint nor to a change of name.

The bow of a ship is not often visited by strangers,
        is more at home in the shearing of the waves,
        is most secure in the automation of the functions:
                as built within thereby to present a timed report.

The bow of a ship can be a pretty sight,
        can portray a lack of care.

The bow of a ship can be fastidious in the presentation,
        or battle-scarred and tide worn resulting from the
        length of service: where refits are very scarce.

The bow of a ship does not speak of home,
        speaks of the merchant adventurers from times past,
        speak of the growth in size and speed as cargoes have enlarged,
                as wages have increased,
                as port fees have so threatened,
                as fuel intends to confirm:
                the difficulty to trade successfully—
                in the face of supples requested for
                bulk delivery.

The bow of a ship has witnessed the presence of harpoons as fired and fired again,
        has witnessed the nets and pots as lifted with much care,
        has witnessed the intensity of lights focused on the seas for the
                hooking of the squid,
        has witnessed the on-board waste as species are discarded which do
                not serve the purse of man.

The bow of a ship has attributes similar to those employed of man,
        has capabilities not unknown to man,
        has activities not strangers to man,
        has appearances recognizable by man,
        has properties similar to man,
        has counting of the waste as furnished by man with a heart
                              to misreport.

The bow of a ship tells a story of dwelling alongside the presence of man,
        of transporting and of carrying,
        of success and of disaster,
        of freedom on the seas and of captivity when tied up in
                              a dock.

The bow of a ship denotes the arrival of the expected,
        the arrival of the promised,
        the arrival of the loved and laughing,
        the arrival of the shattered and imprisoned —
all are known and loved with their imperfections:
in dwelling within the sight and sound of The Living Loving God."

My Content Study Aid

_____
_____
_____
_____
_____
_____
_____
_____
_____
_____
_____
_____
_____
_____
_____
_____
_____
_____

The Dressing of My Garden

"The dressing of My garden is incomplete without the presence of My people.

The dressing of My garden is in need of My spirits,
> My souls,
> My bodies of renown.

The dressing of My garden awaits the rewarding of the beauty of My three in ones.

The dressing of My garden is not a place for statues,
> is not a place where semblances stagnate,
> is not a place where images dictate impressions on the souls:
>> those who dwell within eternity in The Family of God.

The dressing of My garden gives attention to much detail,
> pays attention to much activity,
> calls attention to those who may be ignored or considered
>> out-of-step.

The dressing of My garden stretches far and wide,
> has no equivalent on Earth where the purity is
>> somewhat lacking,
> has no adjunct fit for partying which can be used instead.

The dressing of My garden has multiple environments,
> has multiple sources of the testimonies,
> has multiple real-life stories where the recent immigrants are
>> intrigued by the past retelling of mortality.

The dressing of My garden has the seekers of the best,
> those who passed the test,
> those who travelled from the west,
> those who succeeded in their quest,
> those who visited as a guest,
> those who sought it as a homing nest,
> those who knew it would have freedom from the pest.

The dressing of My garden is built for The Saints of God,
> is built for the people of The Lord who struggled with the law,
> is built for the followers of The Christ who revel in the sanctity
>> of Grace.

The dressing of My garden is progress seen in action;
> is progress marked by Multitudes in their coming to Faith—
>> with commitment very strong and certain;
> is progress marked by The Martyrs of The Cross
>> with their sacrifice in Faith.

The dressing of My garden garners My apostles standing strong and tall,
>> My prophets with their families,
>> My evangelists with their travels of commitment,
>> My shepherds of the proxy who fulfilled their call
>>>> to service,
>> My teachers of My Word to the young,
>>>> the married,
>>> and the mature of both thought and deed,
>> My people of the law,
>> My people of the covenants
>>> as under both the old and the new,
>> My people under Grace.

The dressing of My garden places the greeted within a throne room.

The dressing of My garden is determined by the qualities of the characters—
>> The Faith-based Righteousness of man;
> the commitments of the souls—
>>> the application of Faith
>>> within Freewill in the
>>> relationships with God;
> the abilities of the spirits—
>>> the structures established for
>>> the leading of each soul;
> the resurgences of the bodies—
>>> in accepting a new beginning
>>> with the refit due each body.

The dressing of My garden justifies existence within the sight of God,
> justifies the inscriptions on white stones,
> justifies the extent—
>> the intent—
> within the honouring by God of His participants in eternity—
> with all which is implied,
> with all which is inherited,
> with all to be granted arising from The Promises of God.

The dressing of My garden is not a rough-hewn rockery,
> is not a polished slope,
> is not a trip and stumble,
> is not a bang upon the head.

Anthony A Eddy (Scribe)

The dressing of My garden is one of skill and forethought,
> is one of planning and design,
>> is one requiring acceptance both of beauty and of concept,
>> is one requiring knowledge sustained by wisdom so
>>> enjoyment may be complete,
>> is one where the word "impossible" no longer has existence
>>> within the thought patterning of eternity.

The dressing of My garden welcomes all in their completing the cycle of life:
> of returning to the origin with the spirit unimpaired,
> of existing through transitions where the outcome is unknown,
> of surviving all the difficulties encountered from the evil and the helpful
>> where Truth is a little hazed by mist,
> of repelling the attacks of demonic forces where illness and disease are
>> the bedfellows of ill-health,
> of the seeking and the finding of the pathway as set for The Stars of God,
> of the trumpet call of God which sounds throughout The Earth.

The dressing of My garden is filled with eternal overtones with meanings of significance:
> for the welcomed and sustained within The Family of God."

My Content Study Aid

_____
_____
_____
_____
_____
_____
_____
_____
_____
_____
_____
_____
_____
_____
_____
_____

The Requiem of Man

"The requiem of man has repercussions on a life.

The requiem of man recalls the deeds of yesterday,
        recalls the deeds of shame,
        recalls the deeds of pride,
        recalls the deeds where anger reigned supreme,
        recalls the deeds which cannot be reversed,
        recalls the deeds which haunt and harry the consciousness of man.

The requiem of man recalls the secrets of a heart,
        recalls the crimes and passions of the past,
        recalls the distant back into the present,
        recalls what was thought to be lost and buried yet rises again
                      continually to confront.

The requiem of man turns the inside out upon a scene,
        churns the soul within a fear field of discovery,
        freezes the heart to a moment set in time.

The requiem of man is but a token of remembrance,
        is but an act where contrition is yet to dawn,
            where understanding is out of reach,
            where acknowledgement is still on a bed made
                      within denial,
            where recovery relapses into a call for help.

The requiem of man lies heavily on a damaged soul,
        on a spirit filled with horror,
        on a voice which cannot utter,
        on a tongue now forced to lie.

The requiem of man is sinister and polished,
        is hidden and a secret,
        is forbidden yet enacted,
        is lodged yet not ready for removal,
        is buried deep yet surfaces in the nightmares of the nights,
        is pushed back down yet refuses there to stay.

The requiem of man brings the soul calling for release,
        brings the spirit seeking much forgiveness,
        brings the body still in no fit state to face the consequences.

The requiem of man seeks retribution for the wrong inflicted,
        seeks justice for the wrong escaped,
        seeks accountability for The Freewill act which brought an
                          unruly ending.

The requiem of man is not a song of peace,
        is not a tranquillizer for the night,
        is not an escape hatch for the invaded and the lost.

The requiem of man sings of remembrance of past deeds,
        sings of the wrongs inflicted,
        sings of the pain and suffering,
        sings of the dead and wounded,
        sings of the frightened and the terrified,
        sings of the deadly and deserted.

The requiem of man hears the static within the noise,
        hears the screams and shouts,
        hears the silence of the damned and the relief of the monsters
                              of destruction,
        hears the fetus call for Mercy from the womb,
        hears no response from ears deafened to such calls,
        hears the walls of witness with their ears attuned to hear the
                              shaming of man.

The requiem of man is a marker of behaviour,
        is a disaster in the making,
        is an entry for the loss of innocence,
        is an entry requiring accountability,
        is an entry which cannot be overlooked,
        is an entry in The Lamb's Book of Life.

The requiem of man is not a swansong on a stage,
        is not a swansong of performance,
        is not a swansong calling for forgiveness,
        is not a swansong of restitution,
        is not a swansong of rebuttal,
        is not a swansong from the monied and the mean,
                from the corrupt and greedy,
                from the godforsaken in their livelihoods of
                          procuring death upon a table—
    where death is already booked with reservations for their souls.

The requiem of man is a swansong for the very young and helpless—
                in a vulnerable position.

The requiem of man is a testing field with many angels in attendance,
            with many angels attending the transportation of the
                    innocent denied life within mortality,
            with many angels bringing the spirits into The
                    Presence of God,
            with many spirits rescuing the bodily remains now
                assembled in perfection of completion,

with many angels now victorious in achieving The
Perfect Will of God.

The requiem of man has many sights of wonder,
    has many sights of signs,
    has many sights of miracles near the hands of man;
    has many sights of rescues from the hands of man;
    has many sights of marvelling performed by the hands of man.

The requiem of man is overseen by God,
    knows the records of deliverance,
    knows the records of destruction,
    knows the records of the righteous,
    know the records of the weaponized and wicked.

The requiem of man speaks woe to those who attend at the creation of a single record
    of destruction:
    for they shall be judged with the utmost of severity."

My Content Study Aid

The Garden of The Cross

"The garden of The Cross is evident to all,
>> is the symbol of The Saviour as set for the targeting of man,
>> is the symbol of The Father in a sacrifice of love,
>> is the symbol of The Holy Spirit with His free gifts for man
>>>> at Pentecost:
>> man who dwells within his many temples of The Lord.

The garden of The Cross is where the loving gather,
>> is where the hurt and the incomplete are repaired and
>>>> made whole,
>> is where the Holy Spirit greets The Temples in which He dwelt
>>>> within the mortality of the committed.

The garden of The Cross is of special significance to the gentiles,
>> is the goal set to be achieved within their lives,
>> is the target described within the arrowhead of Truth,
>> is the blessing of the rider of the white horse at large—
>>> He who holds the bow—
>>> He who gathers the arrows on His ride—
>>> He who has released them,
>>>> and does release them still,
>>> to impart the knowledge of the garden filled with life.

The garden of The Cross knows the sepulchre of burial,
>> knows the residues left there with no further need for use,
>> knows the glad tidings of great joy when the angel spoke.

The garden of The Cross is a true wonder to behold:
>>> when displayed in all fullness before the senses of the being
>>>> with a history of mortality.

The garden of The Cross will be of significance to My people of the law,
>>>> to My people still awaiting understanding:
>>>> to be without the benefit of hindsight;
>>>> to be gathered:
>>>> they who knew and know their scriptures
>>>>> given for their guidance:
>>>> via the Good News⁰ of their time—
>>>> as completed within their covenant of
>>>> preparation with a foretold change in pace.

The garden of The Cross beckons understanding,
>> beckons wisdom,
>> beckons love,

      beckons Righteousness,
      beckons participation born of Faith,
      beckons man determined on joining The Family of God.

The garden of The Cross has memories galore,
      has memories requiring forgiveness,
      has memories requiring an adjustment of an attitude,
      has memories forsaken in consignment to the past,
      has memories of hope amplified by Grace,
      has memories of joy built upon The Love of God.

The garden of The Cross holds an extravagance of adventures,
      holds an extravagance of discoveries,
      holds an extravagance to attend the senses of the body soul
              and spirit—
        each deemed to be of interest to all coming from mortality—
          into a new location with The Stars of God.

The garden of The Cross does not dwell unduly on the past,
      does not dwell unduly in the present,
      does not dwell unduly in the present speeded up.

The garden of The Cross has an inherent equilibrium where stress is no longer present,
          where hope and Truth prevail to
            overcome the bandwidth
            of anxiety,
          where expectations co-exist to serve
            the cherished with their
            spirits and their souls.

The garden of The Cross speaks of victory over sin,
      speaks of a troublemaker well imprisoned,
      speaks of an outcome to be repeated in the days of Armageddon.

The garden of The Cross has sinew within its bones,
      has strength within its majesty,
      has Truth within the actions of governance with justice,
      has outcomes arising from injustice where the faces of the
         plaintiffs now have smiles upon the faces—
        no longer shadowed by the past within mortality—
        as such has now been well and truly put to bed.

The garden of The Cross supports and carries life indefinitely,
      supports and carries life eternally,
      supports and carries life without an ending ever seen in sight.

The garden of The Cross has the highest standards of performance,
      has the morality of God,
      has the attributes of purity as achieved by the participants,

> has the fulfilment of inheritance,
> has the rewards which travelled through The Refiner's Fire.

The garden of The Cross is the epitome of creation in completion of the circle:
> in all aspects,
> but one,
> once available within the garden known as Eden."

Scribal Note: *Good News⁰ Refer* Isaiah 52:13 - 53:12, *'Behold My Servant'.*
The Bible, NKJV. Used by Permission
This text is also included in His Bk3, refer: 'The Livery of God',
'GOD Speaks as His Spirit Empowers'

Isa 52:13 Behold, My Servant shall deal prudently; He shall be exalted and extolled and be very high.

Isa 52:14 Just as many were astonished at you, So His visage was marred more than any man, And His form more than the sons of men;

Isa 52:15 So shall He sprinkle many nations. Kings shall shut their mouths at Him; For what had not been told them they shall see, And what they had not heard they shall consider.

Isa 53:1 Who has believed our report? And to whom has the arm of the LORD been revealed?

Isa 53:2 For He shall grow up before Him as a tender plant, And as a root out of dry ground. He has no form or comeliness; And when we see Him, There is no beauty that we should desire Him.

Isa 53:3 He is despised and rejected by men, A Man of sorrows and acquainted with grief. And we hid, as it were, our faces from Him; He was despised, and we did not esteem Him.

Isa 53:4 Surely He has borne our griefs And carried our sorrows; Yet we esteemed Him stricken, Smitten by God, and afflicted.

Isa 53:5 But He was wounded for our transgressions, He was bruised for our iniquities; The chastisement for our peace was upon Him, And by His stripes we are healed.

Isa 53:6 All we like sheep have gone astray; We have turned, every one, to his own way; And the LORD has laid on Him the iniquity of us all.

Isa 53:7 He was oppressed and He was afflicted, Yet He opened not His mouth; He was led as a lamb to the slaughter, And as a sheep before its shearers is silent, So He opened not His mouth.

Isa 53:8 He was taken from prison and from judgment, And who will declare His generation? For He was cut off from the land of the living; For the transgressions of My people He was stricken.

Isa 53:9 And they made His grave with the wicked—But with the rich at His death, Because He had done no violence, Nor was any deceit in His mouth.

Isa 53:10 Yet it pleased the LORD to bruise Him; He has put Him to grief. When You make His soul an offering for sin, He shall see His seed, He shall prolong His days, And the pleasure of the LORD shall prosper in His hand.

Isa 53:11 He shall see the labor of His soul, and be satisfied. By His knowledge My righteous Servant shall justify many, For He shall bear their iniquities.

Isa 53:12 Therefore I will divide Him a portion with the great, And He shall divide the spoil with the strong, Because He poured out His soul unto death, And He was numbered with the transgressors, And He bore the sin of many, And made intercession for the transgressors.

Bible Commentary: *New Spirit Filled Life Bible, NKJV Variant, 52:13-53:12. Behold My Servant: This is the final servant Song. It is one of the greatest passages in the Bible, the mountain peak of Isaiah's book, the most sublime messianic prophecy in the OT, relating so many features of Jesus Christ's redemptive work. The song concerns the enemies' killing of the Servant (Messiah) (53:4, 5), who astonishingly is restored to life by Yahweh (53:10. All His suffering and His death are for others' sins (53:5).*

The Glory of My Garden

"The Glory of My garden is difficult to communicate when still unseen.

The Glory of My garden is difficult to imagine when expectations are not visualised,
                         when the reality is not yet open for
                                       an entry,
                         when the visitors have observations being
                                 far from complete yet
                                 still are lost for words.

The Glory of My garden witnesses the form of man in exaltation—
                         in The Presence of his God:
                               exalted before his God,
                               exalted by his God,
                               exalted for his God.

The Glory of My garden hosts for all eternity My people triumphant and rejoicing
                                                     in exultation:
               with the receiving of their inheritance—
                         their existence with The Lord;
                         their first sighting of The Jewels of God
                                 which were stored beyond the reach of man,
                                 which were not razed by fire,
                                 which were not placed within the reach of
                                           rust and thieves to appropriate,
                                 which are emblazoned on their garments as
                                           statements of their love—
                             for their fellow man and for their God.

The Glory of My garden is truly fit for Kings and Queens,
                 matches up to promises,
                 achieves and surpasses all the expectations and the wondering.

The Glory of My garden is the setting which enhances The Glory of My People,
                 My People in their purity of thought and of expression,
                 My People in their gratitude which makes their wait worth while,
                 My People coated with amazement at the fitments and fittings,
                                 the furnishings and finishings,
                                 the fragile and fastidious,
                 all which prevail upon the senses for use and honouring in their
                                       new found freedom for activities.

The Glory of My garden showcases the beautiful and the lovely,
                         the wonderful and marvellous,
                         the glorified and stately.

The Glory of My garden exhibits the designs of God,
                portrays the designs of God,
                subscribes to the designs of God,
                appreciates the designs of God,
                revels in the designs of God,
                reflects the designs of God.

The Glory of My garden is surrounded by the designs of God,
                is enhanced with the designs of God,
                          exists within and for and through the designs of God.

The Glory of My garden has no need of the future.

The Glory of My garden is and is and is and forever shall be.

The Glory of My garden continues on and on and on in Glory without end.

The Glory of My garden has no comparison,
                has no other lifeboat self-contained and independent,
                has no predilection to travel a preferential pathway:
                            other than did and shall and does exist already.

The Glory of My garden is a startling proposition,
                is an affirmed outreach among humanity,
                is a fresh call to man within the bounding of reality,
                is a fresh response in terms of The Living Water,
                            in terms of meeting the requirements for life
                                        after death within mortality,
                            in terms of evidence put before the eyes
                                        of man—
                of signs wonders and miracles giving credence to The Faith
                which reasons for such existence within the real-time
                            testimonies of man.

The Glory of My garden achieves all the objectives set by God,
                achieves all the rationales of theory and explanations,
                achieves all the considerations both relevant and real,
                achieves all the installations considered delightful and distinct,
                achieves all the comforts seen as wise and useful,
                achieves all the essentials for the ultimate and ubiquitous
                                        longevity of man:
                            beyond the grave of his transition.

The Glory of My garden is the opening venue for the grand finale of man:
                is there for those who commit to a berth of honour which
                                          ensures an arrival;
                is not a promoter of another line carrying respect into the stigma
                                          of the ultimate default.

The Glory of My garden is offered freely to man who has The Faith with
>   The Love declared,
>   for the way prepared,
>   in the setting when compared:
>   his future home within The Family of God."

My Content Study Aid

The Sea of Faces

"The sea of faces is the sea of the lost.

The sea of faces is the sea who gather so to listen,
        is the sea without a name,
        is the sea of humanity crying out to be saved.

The sea of faces is the sea which welcomes My evangelists.

The sea of faces is the sea which stands upon its feet,
        which listens with both ears,
        which participates with attentiveness and keenness.

The sea of faces is the sea which walks,
    is the sea which talks,
    is the sea which hawks—
        the "Good News" of The Kingdom.

The sea of faces have smiles upon their faces,
    have joy within their hearts,
    have the message of The Kingdom ready on their lips.

The sea of faces are upturned and excited,
    are receiving knowledge based on wisdom,
    are preparing for a journey:
        into the very presence of The God of Love.

The sea of faces number past a million souls where the teaching is quite rare,
        where the teaching is much sought after,
        where the teaching is believed.

The sea of faces hear The Call which builds a wave moving to the front,
    which builds a wave of expectation,
    which builds a wave awaiting the gifts of God upon
        each soul.

The sea of faces express the intensity of commitment,
    are there in the assertion of belief,
    are there to become a part of The Family of God.

The sea of faces receive with joy and gladness within much gratitude—
        for the move of God within their ranks,
    where they stand as witnesses,
    where understanding is readied for a new day with the
        coming dawn,
    where their return to home is lightened by the gifts they bear.

The sea of faces dwell within the torrent of living water which soaks and cleanses;
    dwell within the land as set aside for miracles,
        for signs,
        for wonders,
        for deliverance,
        for healings;
    dwell within The Presence of My Spirit—
      who brought the gifts to all who sought the creation of The Temple
          from the glove—
    as carried at the starting out upon a journey to find the source of Truth.

The sea of faces are uplifted to The Son,
    are uplifted to fresh hope,
    are uplifted to a new beginning,
    are uplifted to the starting point,
      where the default is vanquished,
      where the garden of The Lord awaits,
      where eternity is Christened and opens wide its doors.

The sea of faces is a semblance of mankind,
    is a gathering in a land where The Truth is hard to find,
      where restrictions are imposed by man,
      where attacks can quell and silence the seeking from their quest.

The sea of faces are a measure of the need of man to worship and belong,
        to understand and to partake,
        to remember eat and drink under the
          new found Grace.

The sea of faces is enlivened by The Fire of My Spirit going forth from My servants,
      going forth to reach out to
        The Multitudes,
      going forth to bring salvation to the
        querying and the lost.

The sea of faces are far from disappointed,
    are far from the gateway of rejection,
    are far from the beliefs of the recent past which now fail the test
        of Truth.

The sea of faces will depart with much more than they brought,
      with their lives now exchanged for light,
      with their tongues now chattering in the tongues of man and
        the tongues of Heaven,
      with their families now knowing the reality of their God in
        action in their lives.

The sea of faces saturate their neighbourhoods,
    speak to neighbours in a witness—
        as if a bell in clarity,
        with inbuilt purity of tone,
        which summons all to hear and do and act.

The sea of faces have masks no longer intended to be worn,
    have masks destined for disposal,
    have masks constructed for a wayward past
        which are no longer relevant,
        are no longer valued,
        are no longer sought to fill the stage of life with evil.

The sea of faces recognize the stage of jubilation,
    recognize the new found promises of God,
    recognize the beauty of their Temples with The Presence of My Spirit.

The sea of faces remember well the face of the evangelist:
    he who comes to declare the wonder of The Will of God;
    as a willing servant of The Most High God who lives and loves—
        His people now found within The New Covenant of Grace."

My Content Study Aid

The Scream of Agony

"The scream of agony is heard within the gates of Hell.

The scream of agony surfaces each time the gates of Hell are opened,
                is silenced each time the gates of Hell are shut.

The scream of agony is vocal and is real,
                is concerted and intense,
                is primitive and basic.

The scream of agony carries all through the bounds of Hell,
                carries all through the rooms of Hell,
                carries all through the corridors of Hell,
                carries all across the lakes of fire,
                carries all across the lakes of molten sulphur where the blue flame
                              of eternity sputters as it burns.

The scream of agony from within the throat of man is worse than that of any animal,
                is worse than that of any bird,
                is worse than that of any fish,
                is worse than that of any other
                            mammal known to man.

The scream of agony is the scream of ages:
                is the scream of both the anger and the terror;
                is the scream of excruciating pain as if nailed upon the cross,
                is the scream building from summation of the sensing by all the
                          nerve endings as they transmit in bulk;
                is the scream of loneliness with frustration built upon the lies with
                              none found to be true.

The scream of agony is magnified by the participation of the inmates who have inherited
                          justly all which was previously denied,
                by the participation of the enforcers as inflicters of the
                          suffering on the victims—
                of both their play and of their choice,
                by the participation of the onlookers who stood back
                          inspecting all they had invoked upon the
                          innocent of years and the innocent of heart,
                by the participation of the liars and false prophets
                          where morality deserted them
                          and ethics were rejected,
                by participation of Satan and his cronies who had him
                          as their figurehead despite the
                          warning signs made known.

The scream of agony builds in disillusion,
>> builds in desperation,
>> builds in realization of all that is entailed in the second death.

The scream of agony builds as understanding dawns on the reality of their surroundings:
>> now within the practical of the fear-filled life within eternity.

The scream of agony builds to a crescendo which neither ends nor diminishes,
>> has silence descending as the gates of hell are finally locked
>>>> and barred,
>> when justice has been served as Truth and reparations
>>>> complete upon the iniquity of man,
>> of both animal and beast,
>> of the dragon in all his many forms and instances
>>>> and his servants which did his will.

The scream of agony is not a song of repentance,
>> is the roar of evil now caged and out of action,
>> is the scream of doom which is falling on the bound,
>> is the scream of substance where the soul of man is subject to the
>>>> justice now brought to the actions of Freewill.

The scream of agony verifies the punishment previously declared,
>> verifies the actions previously not believed,
>> verifies the place the lies said did not exist,
>> verifies the destiny of default when joking was alive and well as
>>>> Freewill ran amok,
>> verifies the field of blasphemy which warranted the respecting of
>>>> Freewill when the scales were tipped.

The scream of agony does not fade away,
>> is imperative and active,
>> is frightening and forlorn,
>> is collective and continuous within the gates of Hell.

The scream of agony is a cacophony of despair,
>> is a cacophony without a pause,
>> is a cacophony where headphone are neither required nor wanted.

The scream of agony is like a search light in the sky,
>> where the origin is obvious but the target is missing from the beam:
>>>> as the beam just wanders back and forth.

The scream of agony is not heard in Heaven,
>> is not heard within My garden,
>> is not heard by My people in the garden of their goals.

The scream of agony is real with the souls of the imprisoned,
        is real for the receivers of Freewill respect,
           is real for those who walk past the open gates of Hell:
                as they 'escape as through the flames.'"

Scribal Note: "If anyone's work is burned, he will suffer loss; but he himself will be saved, yet so as through fire."

                1 Corinthians 3:15, The Bible, NKJV.

My Content Study Aid

The Example of The Philistines

"The example of The Philistines is not to be followed by My people,
    for the Philistines' place in history is both invasive
            and obstructive,
    for they knew the wording of the law but not The
       Wisdom required within the application.

The example of The Philistines is as a culture set apart,
    a culture not able to be blended,
    a culture not familiar with
     the beauty and the style within the potter's hands;
     the usefulness,
     the application,
       of the weaving the dyeing the assembling of
          the cloth;
     the attraction and enjoyment of the song and dance.

The example of The Philistines is one of austerity and criticism,
    is one of separateness and comparison,
    is one where the supercilious attained long noses to
           look down.

The example of The Philistines does not speak of companionship and friendship,
    does not speak of sharing and laughter,
    does not speak of relaxation in the evening of a sunset.

The example of The Philistines did not grant reasons for delay,
    were addicted to the law,
    took pride from within their capabilities and learning,
    remained a disparate people even in their presence.

The example of The Philistines was not a powerhouse of achievement,
    was one of presenting in the background,
      of inspecting what "was" and what "was not
          to be":
    but not with the "how" and "when and "why".

The example of The Philistines was one of severity within the law,
    of a non-appreciation of the finer things in life,
    of the practicality and observance linked to the
        functioning and purpose.

The example of The Philistines was not one of decoration,
    was not one of forbearance,
    was not one where children were running free.

The example of The Philistines was not one of love displayed,
        was not one of a greeting with a smile,
        was not one of humility but of excessive pride,
        was not one of friendship bespoke with honour—
                but rather at a distance with respect.

The example of The Philistines was as the wearing of a veneer
        of self-assertiveness,
        a veneer of self-aggrandisement,
        a veneer of self-assuredness,
        a veneer of self-selection:
            where opinions of others carry
            no need for consideration.

The example of The Philistines was hatched in times of need,
        in times of deprivation,
        in times of settlement:
            within a culture spreading from a shoreline
            where familiarity was missing from the
                conditions as encountered.

The example of The Philistines was honed and tightened on the back of necessity,
        was bred and spread upon the quest for survival,
        was generated by the spirit of independence in a setting
            of non-reliance on the unreliable.

The example of The Philistines is not of traits to be copied,
        is not of traits deserving of adoption,
        is not of traits which should be seen to surface in
                My people.

For My people are highly valued:
        have histories of interest,
        have histories of escapes,
        have histories associated with the overcoming,
        have histories associated with the persevering.

For My people with the precious souls are the spillover from tanks already full
                and overflowing,
        are the excess without a home looking for a place to settle,
        are the inhabitants under law of restrictions and conditions,
        are the squabblers and the bickerers going round and round
                and round,
        are the nitpickers of both a childish and a childless generation,
        are composed of the unqualified the disqualified the rejects of life.

For such as these seek the shelter of the secure,
>   express no gratitude for assistance,
>   confirm the worst in life each time their mouths are opened,
>   blame a lack of understanding,
>   retreat on an offering of indifference,
>   have difficulty with communication of their needs,
>   have surrendered all hope born of experience with the out-turn of
>> the days."

For such as these are the new found stars of God,
>   the uncut gems of God,
>   the diamonds in the rough with the sparkle still inside,
>   the diamonds waiting to be cut so purity can surface in release:
>> with a temple of assembly from the workshop of The Lord.

For such as these are the precious lambs of God destined for success:
>   where My garden awaits the entrance of the pearls of God as sheep
>> within My flock.

For My people seek and find.

> My people knock,
>> the door opens.

> My people accept and rejoice.

For My people have an ability to recognize The Truth,
>   to speak The Truth,
>   to extol The Truth,
>   to process The Truth,
>   to restore The Truth,
>   to keep The Truth within their hearts,
>> their spirits and their souls;
>> so bodies are not sacrificed in vain,
>   with the destiny of choice espousing The Truth
>   in its fullness of belonging,
>   in its fullness of expression,
>   in its fullness of the exhalation of the hidden
>> and absurd—
>   with the recovery of the purity so valued and re-acquired.

For My people should not be able to be confused with The Philistines of old.

For My people answer to a different call,
>   know a different walk,
>   have a different destination—
> which speaks of a royal prerogative due The Kings and Queens within The Royalty
>> of God:
> with The Kingdoms of The Crown under the auspices of The Living Loving God."

The Superintendency of God

"The superintendency of God is actioned through My Spirit,
>The Holy Spirit of God.

The superintendency of God is the overseer of God,
>is the manager of activity,
>is the observer who reports,
>is the bearer of the gifts,
>is the healer of the nations,
>is the activist at large,
>is the dweller in The Temples,
>is the counsellor of My people,
>is the assessor of the thought patterning of man.

The superintendency of God is the conveyor of instructions,
>is the measurer of souls,
>is the reader of the scales before and after tipping.

The superintendency of God is the surveyor of the particulars of man,
>is the composer of the entries for The Lamb's Book of Life,
>is the guardian who commands the scribes who write within
>The Lamb's Book of Life in all its awesome detail,
>>in all its cross-filed data,
>>in all its cross-linked
>reconstructions when requested by a judge.

The superintendency of God goes before in planning,
>opens doors that were shut,
>closes down the threats to life,
>sends the guardians for the valued and the critical.

The superintendency of God records the clandestine among the secrets,
>records the actions of the secretive,
>records the acts of violence,
>records the acts of war,
>records the acts within the presence of injustice,
>records the acts within relationships as their interaction,
>records the activities of man as the testimonies of Truth.

The superintendency of God is far reaching and precise,
>is accurate and all-encompassing,
>is kept until sealed as no longer relevant.

Beware the sealed of God where conflicting testimonies appear to touch.

The superintendency of God prevents clashes on the camera of time,
                ensures an ordered sequence,
                follows step by step.

The superintendency of God is the archivist of the past,
                is the harbinger of the present,
                is the script-holder of the future scenes of relevance—
                              with guests as played upon requests.

The superintendency of God is the overseer of Kings and Queens in governance,
                of Kings and Queens with edicts,
                of Kings and Queens among the rules
                              and reigns.

The superintendency of God has no sands running through an hour glass,
                has no appointments which are not kept,
                has no conversations forgotten or overlooked,
                has no promises not destined for fulfilment,
                has no secrets birthed in man which remain unknown,
                has no protagonists who can maintain dissent,
                has no authorities to which the knee is bowed.

The superintendency of God gives confidence of access,
                gives confidence of response,
                gives confidence of Truth.

The superintendency of God was,
                is,
                and shall be the only worthy God for man.

The superintendency of God was,
                is,
                and shall be the only good and just God for man.

The superintendency of God was,
                is,
                and shall be the only living loving God for man.

The superintendency of God is the functionary of The Son,
                is the Holy Spirit of the Trinity,
                is the architect instructed with the oversight of the needs
                              of man.

The superintendency of God knows the intimacy of man,
                knows the thoughts of man,
                knows all which is within The Temple of The Spirit:
                      the home of God within the heart of man in his mortality.

The superintendency of God knows The Cross of man which killed The Christ of God.

The superintendency of God is present at the birth of The Messiah,
> is present at the return of The King of kings,
> is present at the closing of His residence within The Temples,
> is present at the closing of the age of Grace,
> is present at the timing for the pleading of the calls for Mercy.

The superintendency of God is active and progressive in the life of man,
> is prompting and counselling within the guidance set
>> for man,
> is continual and conscientious in His relationship with
>> The Christ of His people,
>> The Saviour of The Gentiles,
>> The Spirit of The Son."

My Content Study Aid

The Election of a Man

"The election of a man can have a profound effect.

The election of a man can change the course of nations,
        can change the course of lives,
            can change the course of man onto the path of Righteousness.

The election of a man sways the forests of knowledge and of wisdom:
            the forests overgrown with briars and supplejack—
        which hold hands with those who would resist the brash and bold:
        as such attempt to reach out to the sunlight where warmth is found
                      with Truth enabled to exist.

The election of a man can change the health of a nation,
        can change the educational sweep of universities,
                of the scholarship of learning,
                of the beliefs of students,
                of the curricula as assigned
                        to teachers.

The election of a man can change the lifestyle of the dissolute and the purview of
                            the desolate;
        can change the outlook of the job hunters—
                which empower a nation on the road to greatness;
        can recall the economics of industry and commerce to retake the
                      centre stage for impact:
        on all the lives who partake and sample that which is about to be.

The election of a man can revitalize the courts of justice where meanness of the spirit
                            gathers an agreement,
        prevails in all which is said and sealed in hindering the advance
                            of man,
            in serving up lukewarm decisions upon plates worn-out
                            and cracked.

The election of a man can spell the end of corruption,
        can stamp on the well which waters cronyism,
        can enforce with wisdom what has been lost within stupidity.

The election of a man can start the turning of the cogs,
        the rolling of the wheels,
        the ringing of the registers of cash.

The election of a man can turn on the lights in factories,
        can have them glowing in the night,
        can re-enliven each hive so filled with activity.

The election of a man can electrify a nation,
          can awaken those found sleeping at their desks,
          can encourage the disheartened to revisit the commitments:
                  when enthusiasm rules the beginning of each day.

The election of a man can bring hope and satisfaction,
          can dispel despair and dismay,
          can reach out to absorb the challenges ignored:
                  when yesterday dragged dreariness within its wake.

The election of a man can put a spring into a step,
          a dance into a song,
          a prayer into a soul,
          life into the spirit,
    awake all from their days of slumber.

The election of a man can call in the hum of machinery,
          the stamping of the presses,
          the filling of the orders,
          the recycling of the waste.

The election of a man can be justified by the busyness as generated,
          the turnaround in attitudes,
          the smiles upon the faces,
          the dissolving of the violence,
          the rejoicing in the home
            where employment reigns with hope,
            where life can now progress,
            where effort is rewarded,
            where wages can be geared,
            where purchases can be secured and holidays
                  now planned.

The election of a man can remove the threat of loss,
          can remove the thoughts of self-destruction,
          can remove the concept of being "stuck in the mud" and so unable
                  to advance.

The election of a man can bring communities to life,
          can splash the paint around,
          can arouse the sleeping giants,
          can awaken to the "spick and span" as effort is revealed.

The election of a man welcomes the neat and tidy;
              so pride retrieves its place of honour:
              in the achievements of a nation now reverting to its prime.

The election of a man can be a matter for the history books,
> can be a matter for example,
> can be a matter to be cherished,
> can be a matter to be remembered,
> can be a matter to be honoured,
> can be a matter for the records,
> can be a matter of success in building chains which will no longer
>> yield when under stress.

The election of a man restores the right to life;
> restores the understanding of accomplishments within the strength
>> of God;
> restores examples built on Righteousness where the trivial
>> is forgotten;
> restores with honour all which women hold as grievances
>> in experience denied,
>> in rewards withheld,
>> in equality usurped;
> restores all which has been stolen by the ineptitude of the
>> recent past."

My Content Study Aid

The Secrecy of God

"The secrecy of God is for the benefit of man.

The secrecy of God prevents man from saying what he thinks God wants to hear,
        to attempt to curry favour from where it is not justified,
        to attempt to mask the feelings which lie just below the surface.

The secrecy of God is not limited by man,
        is not limited by Satan,
        is not limited by any thing or any being within the creation sphere
                of God.

The secrecy of God is immune to attack,
        will not reveal the secret of life to man when faced with
                inert ingredients,
        will not permit the prodding and the probing,
            the cutting and the slicing,
            the injecting and the incubating:
        to allow man to claim success wherein a lie is present.

The secrecy of God is righteous and honourable,
        is deft and up to date,
        is synchronized and harmonized,
        is secure and unable to be breached.

The secrecy of God has no visitors to observe the starting of the cell of life embedded
                in eternity—
        upon its journey through space and time—
        for the creation cells of life as initiated by God
                within His Will and Foresight.

The secrecy of God saves man from his own destruction as he plays with clones,
        as he plays instructing cells to do his bidding,
        as he plays with mice and rats and rabbits and
                the pigs—
        a game which ends in death for life at the
                wrong end of the microscope.

The secrecy of God has encryption self-adjusting in complexity of component keys:
            within at least seven dimensions—
            where each must be present,
            correctly ordered,
            to be simultaneously applied.

The secrecy of God is well anchored in the mathematics of eternity:
> of strings and ribbons waving in the fields;
> of slugs and worms at home within the
>> moats and holes;
> of the home of exponentials which count with
>> accuracy far beyond where man can go—
>>> in thought,
>>> in reasoning,
>>> in deed;
>> in experiments on home upon the island of man
>>> or in the space of man:
> where such are at war with the conditions hostile to success.

The secrecy of God is as an archipelago,
> which stands in the absence of the sea,
> which man is unable to visit:
> is unable to attend non-existent classes;
> is unable to instruct or to receive the work of spies when such are
>> not empowered to attend—
>>> in a prevailing atmosphere of great difficulty;
> is unable to communicate in the language of high intellect;
> is unable to surmount the difficulties imposed by God—
>> in protecting the life of man in all its fullness:
>>> as it is awaited by the wise who understand the
>>>> coming Glory and the exaltation—
>> of man when in his destiny as offered for his prime.

The secrecy of God is thorough and secure,
> is necessary and correct,
> is safeguarded with the keys,
> is deep within the attributes of God.

The secrecy of God does neither bend nor yield,
> does neither tempt nor stain,
> does neither stir nor cultivate.

The secrecy of God is vital to the long-term welfare of all life,
> dwells within the spoken word of God—
>> out of earshot of the ears of man.

The secrecy of God is necessary because of the nature of man,
> because of his addiction to his purse,
> because of his jostling for position where status rules supreme,
> because of his willingness to participate,
>> to compete,
>> to jockey for the heights:
> where the morality of God is of little or even of no account at all.

The secrecy of God is not a playground for the mystics,
    is not found in the land of suppositions,
    will not yield to the palmists and the stargazers —
        the astrologers who have no Faith in what they do,
            no Faith in what they say,
            no Faith in what they write,
            no Faith within their life
                except when they choose
                    to sit upon a chair.

The secrecy of God protects the wellspring of life,
    protects the water of life,
    protects the tree of life,
    protects the journey of life in the face of adversities and trials.

The secrecy of God protects the growth patterns,
    protects the swarms,
    protects the insects,
    protects the purpose and the functioning available for each.

The secrecy of God is a volcano venting Truth;
    is a volcanic cone preventing the ultimate Truth from being misused:
        upon a bed of explanations and insincere commitments;
    is a volcanic slope where the gradient is dangerous and a fall can
                be disastrous.

The secrecy of God is a volcano biding its time,
    in warning of The Fear of God:
    for all to depart and not intrude;
    for all to walk another pathway to join The Stars of God."

My Content Study Aid

_____
_____
_____
_____
_____
_____
_____
_____
_____
_____

In The Sights of God

"In the sights of God is a dangerous place to be,
        is a blessed place to be.

In the sights of God is a testing place in which to wander,
        is a scary place to be when surrounded by problems of the day,
        is a fear-filled place to linger when a relationship is not established,
        is a disastrous place to be when a lonely soul with guilt is found
                without defence.

In the sights of God is like a spotlight on a rabbit,
        is like a searchlight on a plane,
        is like a possum in the twin moons of a car.

In the sights of God is to do with reprimands due the soul,
        with follow-ups in confirmation of the progress:
            of encouragement to the spirit to come to a blaze again.

In the sights of God speaks of the many concerns God has for man,
        of doubtful origins which bear no fruit,
        of pain and suffering which could have been prevented,
        of disasters and of risks which could so easily lead to death,
        of procrastinations still outstanding when the door to life is
                closing on mortality,
        when the grave begins to beckon and selections
            are made with much reluctance.

In the sights of God is a positioning attained without much wisdom,
        is a weary set of circumstances which wilt each day afresh,
        is a tiredness where seated in a chair is not one of contentment,
        is a recurring exasperation which never learns retreat.

In the sights of God is an awareness without commitment,
        is a looseness where firmness is a godsend with spillage
                well avoided,
        is a teasing bringing tears and where laughter starts a flood.

In the sights of God is witness to a shortage of prayers,
        is witness to what is best left unspoken,
        is witness to the suppositions and the jokes at the expense of God.

In the sights of God is the forsaking of the careless attitudes,
        of the unaccountability for the actions of Freewill,
        of the tramping round the mountain with
                eyes downcast:
        and never an upward glance ascribed to hope.

In the sights of God is participation in the games of chance,
        is the endless looking at opportunities but without the courage
                to commit,
      is the emphasis on money without knowledge of acquisition
                or retainment.

In the sights of God are the sick and lame without access to the medicines of man,
          without The Faith sufficient to engage with God,
          without the counsel and assistance to uplift a life.

In the sights of God are the liars and the false prophets,
      are those running and walking as stragglers on a downward
                sloping road,
    are those who stand in denial of The Power and The Authority:
           which rests upon The Brow of God.

In the sights of God are all those in need of Faith,
    all those still filled with doubt,
    all those still scared to commit,
    all those still dwelling in the tugs of Satan,
    all those who are yet to grasp the true reality of life,
    all those still short of Grace within their lives.

In the sights of God are the seekers and the hope-filled,
      those who believe there has to be a better way,
        who desire to know the purpose of a life,
        who desire to settle for the very best,
        who desire to seize The Promises of God in application to
                their lives:
          in which they reach fulfilment.

In the sights of God is the mayhem and the turmoil created by man within
                Freewill misapplied.

In the sights of God are the clairvoyants and astrologers,
      the mystics and the would-be "readers" of the dregs and bumps
                and palms of man,
    the soothsayers and the weavers of fantasy—
           all for the purse of man.

In the sights of God are the righteous and the committed,
    the faithful and the gathered,
    the sheep and the lambs:
        the builders of My temples with their Guest at home.

In the sights of God is man in all his various environments,
    in all his stages of understanding and acceptance,
    in all his levels of joy and celebration,
    in all his downcast stares in misery and defilement.

Arise!
> Shine!
>> For the day of man is here.
>>
>> For The Son of man has risen.
>>
>> For The Father sends His greetings.
>>
>> For My Spirit attends man in fulfilment of My Word to Him.

Arise!
> Shine!
>> Before the closure of The Age of Grace.

Arise!
> Shine!
>> While it is today—
>>> for tomorrow will not be seen by some."

My Content Study Aid

The Figurines of Man

"The figurines of man are not ideal depending on intent,
        are not ideal depending on their function,
        are not ideal if there as a devotional object.

The figurines of man can be ascribed to gods,
        can be ascribed to demons,
        can be ascribed to angels,
        can be ascribed to animals,
        can be ascribed in memory of pets,
        can be ascribed to events of little or much significance.

The figurines of man should be understood in placement before the eyes of man,
        should be there as an object of detailed beauty of an artisan,
        should be there as an instigator of a memory,
        should be there as a gift from someone known within a home,
        should be there as an image from the past with no strings attached.

The figurines of man should not be attached to a cross,
        should not dwell on that which will not be revisited,
        should not be subject to a fabricated image given
                meaning undeserved,
        should not be the subject of devotion to that which has never lived,
        should not treat as sacred that which is never due for blessings,
        should not be the basis of idolatry placed on a mistaken form.

The figurines of man should be kept off The Cross of God,
        should see The Cross of God standing both empty and vanquished,
        should see The Cross of God as an emblem of My victory,
            as a means establishing the way to life,
            as a means unique to My life on Earth,
            as a means which stands before all the
                eyes of man down through
                      The Age of Grace.

The figurines of man should see the means by which man is reconciled with God.

The figurines of man should have owners who understand the requirements for adoption,
            the requirements for a temple,
            the requirements for commitment,
            the requirements for the second birth,
            the requirements for Discipleship and
                as a sheep within the flock
                of The Good Shepherd.

The figurines of man are everywhere abounding in decoration of the life of man.

The figurines of man should be used with circumspection,
>	should be placed both as to function and the intent of the craftsman,
>	should be known as to their purpose and whether they carry sin into
>>	the home,
>>	into the sanctuary of a family of God
>>>	wherein My temples are,
>>>	wherein My Spirit dwells,
>>>	wherein holiness and purity
>>>>	are present in My Bride.

The figurines of man may be innocent and trivial,
>	may be suspect and of concern,
>	may be grotesque as birthed from within the place of nightmares.

The figurines of man are all carriers of messages,
>	are all images created by man to serve a concept,
>>	a purpose,
>>	a function,
>>	an awareness—
>>>	for all stages in the life of man.

The figurines of man must not pre-empt The Cross,
>	must not pre-empt My altars,
>	must neither pre-empt nor contaminate the sacrifice:
>>	which welcomes man in changing from the law unto Grace.

The figurines of man can keep man from eternal life,
>	can impose a barrier of impurity,
>	can speak of that which will fail to be upheld when being within
>>	the scope of idolatry.

The figurines of man must not become the idols of man,
>	must not become the receivers of offerings,
>	must not be the repose of candles lit at certain times,
>	must not be conjoined with the presence of incense,
>	must not receive either a curtsey or a bended knee.

The figurines of man should not be used as pipes bringing smoke into the lungs of man.

The figurines of man should be studied with attention and have their
>>	functioning established—
>>	for that for which they came into existence,
>>	for that for which their presence is sought,
>>	for that for which is in conflict with the long
>>>	term welfare and the life of man.

The figurines of man must have innocence of purpose to dwell within My sanctuaries,
                              to refute and not portray the
                                          idolatry of man,
                            to neither grow nor develop
                                    alternate paths to
                                      his man-made gods.

The figurines of man should be measured by artistic sense together with the portrayal of
                                                                                 the subject.

The figurines of man should not be showcased when disfigured by design,
                should be showcased in showing the skills and love evident
                                                      in production:
        the fruit of both joy and satisfaction at the outcome."

My Content Study Aid

_____
_____
_____
_____
_____
_____
_____
_____
_____
_____
_____
_____
_____
_____
_____
_____
_____
_____
_____
_____
_____
_____
_____
_____

The Hearing of My Call

"The hearing of My Call is for all so desiring in their hearts.

The hearing of My Call is for all who so desire to know where they belong within
>> The Will of God,
>> to know the outline of The Walk with God,
>> to know The Companionship of God,
>> to know a firm Relationship with God.

The hearing of My Call holds the mutual trust established as sacred within The Fear
>> of God,
> holds the forgiveness with Grace close to The Offerings
>> of Communion,
> holds Righteousness with Truth at the forefront of the soul,
> holds attention and willingness to go to stay to serve at the behest
>> of God.

The hearing of My Call requires prior loosing and binding,
> requires some preparation,
> requires the active use of My Spirit's gifts,
> requires the stance of royalty within the fields of God.

The hearing of My Call is not a once-off affair with God,
> is not open to be queried for acceptability,
> is not subject to dissent,
> is not open to procrastination,
> is not open to the imposing of conditions,
> is not a situation where the arguments of man should participate
>> in a one-sided debate.

The hearing of My Call is not made upon the deafened ears,
> upon the ears turned aside,
> upon the ears filled with idle chatter,
> upon the ears turned off with inward introspection:
>> where the music is too loud;
>> where the music is self-servicing within the
>>> stops of brevity;
>> where the music is stacked with enablement to
>>> cycle round and round.

The hearing of My Call breaks into the silence of the night,
> breaks into the silence of the day,
> breaks into the presence of My people as loosing is attached to
>> each Freewill.

The hearing of My Call can be a call by name which wakes the body in the night,
        can be a doorbell ringing in the light of day when no-one is
                found standing on a mat.

The hearing of My Call necessitates the answering so a two way conversation can exist.

The hearing of My Call is not always a necessary prior adjunct when conversing
                with God,
        can be reversed by The Call of My people whom I know,
                by The Call to Me via My Spirit is instantaneous
                      and reliable,
        can be questioning and validating,
        is secure and immune to hacking.

The hearing of My Call can answer a request for a word of knowledge,
        can answer an extended word of knowledge,
        can answer within The Will of God,
        can clarify counsel and advise according to the issues raised,
                according to the silence heard.

The hearing of My Call is not subject to interruptions when establishing a connection,
        is not subject to an impairment within the ears of man,
        is not subject to acceptance when a cacophony of sound berates
                the ears of My people,
        is not subject to close attention when distractions rule in the
                surrounds while holiness absconds.

The hearing of My Call can assist when in My ministry of proxy,
        when before a request for healing,
        when faced with the activity of a demon,
        when there is a sincere desire to be the mouthpiece
                of God,
        as when My servants testify of the "Good News" to
                The Multitudes:
                so Faith supplies the words to the mouth,
                without a stutter or a stumble—
                for My servants endowed with the mouth
                      of God will not find such
                          left empty or forlorn.

The hearing of My Call has instances where dictation is involved,
        is subject to a speed involving a record being established,
        is purposing the content for a book,
        is proposing a course of action which is best written down.

The hearing of My Call needs tests which will perceive alternative voices in the head.

The hearing of My Call should not bring confusion,
                should not bring doubt,
                should use neither profanity nor threats,
                should include neither urgency nor coercion,
                should not discuss matters of an abhorrent nature to God.

The hearing of My Call becomes more certain with experience,
                becomes more definite with constancy,
                becomes more reliable with immediacy,
                becomes more trustworthy within both regularity and time.

The hearing of My Call is consolidated within My tongues,
                is consolidated within My wisdom,
                is consolidated within the familiarity of response,
                is circumscribed by The Will of God."

My Content Study Aid

In The Service of God

"In the service of God lies the fulfilment of man.

In the service of God do the spirit and the soul unite in perfect harmony:
                                              within the glove of man.

In the service of God are miracles recorded,
        are lives changed for the better,
        are the outposts of God changed to the centrality of positioning.

In the service of God are visitors welcomed,
        are tongues proclaimed,
        are hands raised,
        are songs heard,
        are promises remembered,
        is Grace appropriated.

In the service of God do visions and dreams abound,
        do the gifts of My Spirit reach the heights of achievement,
        do the tongues of God become the tongues of man,
        do the pools and flows of water reach out in significance,
        do the signs wonders and miracles assert God is at home in support
                                of all within His service.

In the service of God is where man is supposed to be,
        is where man should be found,
        is where man should be endowed with Faith.

In the service of God is where The Multitudes are waiting,
        is where the knowledge base is thin,
        is where the willingness awaits The Call of God.

In the service of God is the face at home with portraits of amazement,
                with portraits of deep contentment,
                with portraits of much concern,
                with portraits of resolution at the outcomes,
                with portraits of gratitude at large amongst the
                        tended as Grace is found at home.

In the service of God raises the profiles of My people,
        raises their profiles before God,
        raises the relationships abroad,
        raises the memories of home,
        raises the appreciation for all which has been seen and done.

In the service of God are all The Saints of God,
    are all the members of The Bride,
    are all the committed and the trustworthy,
    are all the exuberant in earnest,
    are all the armed and dangerous with My Spirit's gifts as polished
                by much use.

In the service of God are found the thoughtful with the informed,
    are found the humble and the contrite,
    are found the earnest and committed.

In the service of God are the godly and the secure,
    are the trained and The Disciples,
    are the taught and The Believers.

In the service of God are raised the trustworthy and the faithful,
    are raised the able and the knowledgeable,
    are raised the loving the kind the thoughtful.

In the service of God do signs invigorate,
    do wonders magnify,
    do miracles invest.

In the service of God does love invade,
    does time bring Grace,
    does freedom come.

In the service of God will life improve,
    will Faith restore,
    will Saints reign.

In the service of God shall promises be kept,
    shall salvation be known,
    shall lost and sought be found.

In the service of God do days dawn more brightly,
    does Faith with Grace abound,
    is gratitude expressed.

In the service of God shall situations change for the better,
    shall eternity overcome the past,
    shall expectations surmount in triumph.

In the service of God does God come to the party,
    does God support the needy,
    does God forgive the sinner.

In the service of God is victory assur'd,
    do tongues come to the fore,
    are gifts from My Spirit.

In the service of God do the complicated become the trivial,
> do difficulties encounter resolution,
> do impossibilities bring The Power of God.

In the service of God are eyes wide in amazement,
> are ears attuned for hearing,
> are hands readied for blessing.

In the service of God is man adopted for Eternity,
> welcomed to Eternity,
> at home in The Eternity of God."

My Content Study Aid

The Ageing Of Man

"The ageing of man occurs within mortality,
        is like a butterfly grub waiting to be cocooned,
            waiting to become a chrysalis,
            waiting for the days of change,
            waiting for a rebirth where it can spread its wings,
            waiting for when it will appear in splendour and in Glory,
            waiting for when a life can be lived in all its fullness
                              of existence.

The ageing of man is limited to his mortality,
        is limited to his mortal temple,
        is limited to his time of preparation for his spreading of his wings.

The ageing of man awaits ripeness of development.

The ageing of man awaits the triggers of metamorphosis.

The ageing of man awaits the sleep of Kings.

The ageing of man awaits The Psalms of God.

The ageing of man awaits the third birth of man,
        awaits the new body to be bestowed,
        awaits the attributes of man when seen dressed and ready:
                          for eternity with God.

The ageing of man has a time of readjustment,
        has a time of segregation,
        has a time where the grave has lost its relevancy,
            where the grave has served its purpose,
            where the grave has served in demarcation of the mortal
                              from the eternal.

The ageing of man is a venture into the future with an offer accepted,
            with Grace fully in effect,
            with a commitment made binding and
                          in place,
            with an inheritance awaited in the
                    company of The Gown of Life.

The ageing of man is scheduled,
        is projected,
        is controlled.

The ageing of man is either honoured or respected,
        is either sacred or secular;
        is either religious or profane.

The ageing of man brings fulfilment to his timeframe of existence in mortality,
        brings an end to suffering with expectations built on hope or Faith,
        brings relief from the reality of a body approaching its "use by" date,
        brings a decision to the fore which impacts on the future—
                whether the location of intent or the location of default.

The ageing of man is a property of man within mortality:
                where time is present and controls,
        is absent from man when dwelling within eternity:
                where time becomes a servant with its options.

The ageing of man completes its present purpose and its functioning:
                on qualifying man for entry to the grave.

The ageing of man supervises the growth of families,
        the presenting of the babies,
        the establishing of maturity.

The ageing of man absorbs the agility of man,
        restricts man's senses in effectiveness,
        reduces man's ability to work,
        absconds with the fullness once found within his purse.

The ageing of man may introduce a time of pain,
                a time of frustration at a loss of hearing,
                      of seeing,
                      of mobility,
                      of functioning.

The ageing of man may reduce to poverty,
                to homelessness,
                to illness,
                to loneliness,
                to infirmity,
                to helplessness,
                to the need for care.

The ageing of man sees grandchildren come and go,
        sees grandchildren come and stay,
        sees grandchildren at their best and at the worst,
        sees grandchildren for what they are—
                the very youth of self.

The ageing of man should bring security of tenure,
        should bring the time to roam,
        should bring the essence of nobility,
        should bring the field of Righteousness,
        should bring The Offerings of God.

The ageing of man builds a bank of memories,
        knows what others are awaiting to experience,
        senses the rights and wrongs,
        splits the time upon demand,
        watches as the hair matches colour with the age,
                matches thatch with the age,
                matches warmth with the age.

The ageing of man is not the intent of God—
        in the absence of satanic nets,
            of demonic influence,
            of the diseases born of pestilence:
                  which man has inflicted on himself.

The ageing of man now has reconciliation through The Cross of Christ—
        may again share in eternal life,
        may again return to The Presence of his God,
        may again be blessed by God."

My Content Study Aid

The Window of Opportunity - The Floodgates of God

"The window of opportunity is closing fast,
        is closing more every day,
        is closing on Faith,
        is closing on Grace,
        is closing closing closing,
                soon to be shut firmly and in place.

The window of opportunity will not be re-opened once closed,
        will not be made available once the hourglass
                becomes empty,
        will not be permitted to grant in Grace with Faith,
        will not be possible other than to plead in Mercy,
        will not be feasible to restart or alter the clock of God
                for man:
        when the time with Faith comes to an end.

The window of opportunity has been open for millennia,
        has had very great publicity,
        has welcomed the seekers and committed,
        knows well the faithful who dwell in Grace.

The window of opportunity shares many things with man,
        shares many aspects of creation,
        shares many wonders and delights,
        shares like images galore,
        shares His sacrifice upon The Cross of God unto the life
                of man,
        shares The Inheritance of The Son with the children of
                The Father,
                with the sons of God,
                with eternity in mind.

The window of opportunity is about to open the flood gates of God as an age is closed,
        as a rule begins,
        as changes come to the fore,
        as memories are built,
                are heaped,
                are difficult to count,
                are each to survive indefinitely.

The window of opportunity initiates the flow of living water from the floodgates of God.

The window of opportunity does not stifle the flow,
> allows the living water to flow unimpeded,
> watches the living water as it reaches out with new life,
> guards the living water so it does not vanish down a
>> sink hole,
> tests the living water for both taste and vitality.

The window of opportunity seizes its namesake and expands the horizons of man:
> expands the flood so thirst is quenched,
> expands the flood so knowledge grows,
> expands the flood so wisdom comes,
> expands the flood so gifts appear,
> expands the flood so testimonies present,
> expands the flood so honour travels from
>> The Son unto The Father,
> expands the flood so My Spirit thrives in
>> The Presence of New Temples.

The window of opportunity is about to start a flood greater than in the days of Noah,
> will have greater consequences for man,
> will have much greater reach,
> will fill the voids of God—
> will fill the isolated enclaves of man—
>> with revival as The Fire of My Spirit sweeps across the
>>> surface of The Earth:
>> into every nook and cranny,
>> into ever crevasse and crevice,
>> into every cave and hole,
>> into every slum and castle.

The floodgates of God oversee the startup of a new beginning,
> follow the tribulation,
> accompany The Bride,
> prepare for The Coming King.

The floodgates of God do not bring force of arms.

The floodgates of God do bring Peace with Righteousness,
> do bring citizens with wisdom,
> do bring knowledge to the schools of children,
>> to the schools of man.

The floodgates of God are the seven semblances of My Holy Spirit:
> seen in action with their charters,
> seen in action in the reaping,
> seen in action in the instructing,
> seen in action within the reality of man,
> seen in action at the behest of The Living Loving God.

The floodgates of God will not be closed before the cynical and the proud,
                before the criminals and the insane,
                before the prisoners and the convicted,
                before the flotsam and the jetsam of life.

The floodgates of God welcome all to join the souls of God,
        welcome all to step up to eternity,
        welcome all to become adopted into The Family of God,
        welcome all to change their dwelling places to temples,
        welcome all to become the friends of God,
        welcome all outside the fold to be welcomed home where
                                          they belong.

The floodgates of God have much to offer man,
        come without a price ticket,
        have had all expenses paid.

The floodgates of God uplift gently and securely,
        uplift from the dirt into The Heavens,
        uplift from discomforts and distractions into the honouring
                                                  from God.

    The Spirit says,
        'Come!'

    The Son says,
        'Come!'

    The Father says,
        'Come!'

    God in unison says,
        'Come,
                unto the home of your belonging.'"

My Content Study Aid

_____
_____
_____
_____
_____
_____
_____

The Keepsakes of Life

"The keepsakes of life bring memories flooding back.

The keepsakes of life are silent yet do speak,
          are silent yet do catch The Son Light,
          are silent yet have recall of the soul.

The keepsakes of life are cherished for the thoughts evoked,
          are cherished for the memories both of a time and place,
          are cherished for the happy times when love was introduced,
          are cherished for a spot at sunset when the fish begin to bite,
          are cherished when Grace so sets the scene where sin no longer
                                        drives the day.

The keepsakes of life have vantage points from where complaints are never heard,
          have vantage points near beds well lit by Son shine,
          have vantage points where meals are welcomed at the table,
          have vantage points where access is not needed and just a glance
                                        will do,
          have vantage points of darkness set to flee from a handbag as it
                                        opens for a hand,
          have vantage points on fingers where sparkling can compete as if a
                                        rainbow from a storm.

The keepsakes of life are not traded in,
          are not traded up,
          are not traded down.

The keepsakes of life are not the bases for comparison,
          are not the bases for insuring,
          are not the bases for putting under lock and key.

The keepsakes of life often dwell around a neck,
          often hitch a ride upon a wrist,
          often try to hide upon an ankle,
          often find a spot right out of sight with privacy.

The keepsakes of life rarely go for resale in a pawn shop.
The keepsakes of life rarely stand in need of restoration.
The keepsakes of life rarely are thrown out in the rubbish.

The keepsakes of life can be mementos from afar,
          can be idolatry in action,
          can be the essence of nobility.

The keepsakes of life are gathered in activities destined to be remembered,
        are gathered at very little cost,
        are gathered where quality is not an issue,
        are gathered where crowding is not counted as a negative.

The keepsakes of life can be passed to another generation,
        can be held in reverence for achievement,
        can be held in honouring of standings before man,
        can be rewards for bravery,
        can be rewards for physical exertions,
        can be received from a friend to light the day.

The keepsakes of life are mass produced with appeal to visitors,
              with appeal to be added to collections,
              with appeal to collectors unable to pass by a
                              public offering.

The keepsakes of life may outstay their welcome,
        may witness a change in circumstance,
        may be a reminder of a love now lost.

The keepsakes of life cannot defend themselves,
        cannot replace themselves where a chip or breakage exhibits
                              its effect,
        cannot be easily renewed when replacement is a stumbling block,
                when a clock no longer works,
                when moths and rust wage war upon the
                              precious and the valued.

The keepsakes of life will not pass through the refiner's fire,
        are not grave goods intended for an extended life,
        are not initiated by God.

The keepsakes of life can be polished dusted and preserved,
        can be sought purchased and retained,
        can be given esteemed and held close to the heart.

The keepsakes of life can be vibrant and alluring as if a perfume in a bottle,
        can be coloured in iridescence as if a seashell from distant islands,
        can be small and very precious as if a gemstone on a finger.

The keepsakes of life can be very easily lost,
        can be very easily mislaid,
        can be very easily stolen.

The keepsakes of life can be taken out of circulation and hidden out of sight.
The keepsakes of life can vary in acceptance when the origins no longer stand in favour.
The keepsakes of life can be items endowed with a connection of a relationship
                                              with God."

I, The Lord Jesus (4)

"I,
    The Lord Jesus,
        say this day to My people destined for My garden,
            '*Have Faith* in all which you have read within My Word,
                in all which has been witnessed in the past,
                in all which speaks of an inheritance awaiting,
                in an existence of great value in a life—
                        extended far beyond the imaginings of man,
                in a return—
                        to again be dwelling within The Family of God.'

I,
    The Lord Jesus,
        say this day to My people who await My coming for My Bride,
            '*Prepare* for a change in lifestyle.
            Prepare with the gift of tongues where practise and fluency are required.
            Prepare for The Coming Kingdom and the changes to be wrought.'

I,
    The Lord Jesus,
        say this day to My people who seek to understand and to address My plans
                                                      for man,
            '*Learn* and assimilate the ways and expectations of God as He relates to
                                                      His children.
            Keep My two commandments in your daily reckonings.
            Live and rejoice in your relationship with The Living Loving God.'

I,
    The Lord Jesus,
        say this day to all people whom I love just as they are,
            '*Accept* My offer of Grace while it is today.
            Accept the reality of The Loving God who dwells among you.
            Accept the issue of sin and overcome it with a commitment which impacts
                                                          on eternity.
            Accept My promises which are applicable to all—
                        for whom I died upon The Cross.'

I,
    The Lord Jesus,
        say this day to all people whom I love but are hindered by their unbelief,
            '*Come* investigate My works in the lands of Africa.
            Seek and you shall discover all which I have laid before you.
            Find for your reward is great and easy to obtain as you leave your shackles
                                                                         far behind.'

I,
>   The Lord Jesus,
>> say to all who see and hear,
>>> '*Listen* and attend where eternal life begins.
>>> *Commit* and turn from the sinful ways of man.
>>> *Rejoice* in Righteousness as Peace comes to the fore.
>>> *Acquire* and learn The Rewarding Ways of God.'

I,
>   The Lord Jesus,
>> say to all who would speak and do,
>>> '*Forsake* the idolatry of generations past and present,
>>> *Free* the soul from curses handed down through generations of captivity.
>>> *Believe* in a new beginning where Truth and Righteousness are free to rule
>>>> within a life.'

I,
>   The Lord Jesus,
>> say to all who read My words herewith proclaimed,
>>> '*Arise shine*,
>>>> for the day of your redemption has come.
>>> *Arise stand*,
>>>> for the day of your servitude is at an end.
>>> *Arise see*,
>>>> what I have brought about within the lives of man—
>>>>> that he may be free in deed.'

I,
>   The Lord Jesus,
>> seek and gather My sheep who presently are lost,
>> seek and cuddle My lambs in their hours of need,
>> seek and save My flock unto The Family of God—
>>> as they cry out for their salvation.

I,
>   The Lord Jesus,
>> bless and keep My sheep,
>> honour and bequeath unto My sheep,
>> love and bring Grace freely to My would-be sheep,
>> love and care for all who linger outside the sheep-fold of My sacrifice—
>>> where the pasture is well below the best and nourishment is scarce.

I,
>   The Lord Jesus,
>> bless and tend The Father's flock entrusted to My care—
>>> for The Glory of The Father in an accretion to His Family.

I,
> The Lord Jesus,
>> present and gift My Spirit to counsel and to guide
>>> all those who know not what to do,
>>> all those who not where I am found,
>>> all those who desire to come and do not know the way.

Behold!
I,
> The Lord Jesus,
>> am †the way The Truth and the life—
>> no-one comes to The Father except through Me—
>>> for such,
>>>> My words of yesteryear roll down from the age of My mortality unto this end-time foretold for man.

Behold!
I,
> The Lord Jesus,
>> would rescue all the lost souls of man with their Freewill intact.

Behold!
I,
> The Lord Jesus,
>> know the way unto The Father and the testimony required.

Behold!
I,
> The Lord Jesus,
>> have sent My Spirit with the gifts the signs the wonders and the miracles to be
>>> active in His blessing of the life of man.

Behold!
I,
> The Lord Jesus,
>> say,
>>> 'I AM' and stand before the face of man as The Living Loving God who stamps
>>>> My foot upon all forms of idolatry—
>>>>> seen to be enslaving man."

Scribal Notes: 'the way the truth and the life'† Refer 'The Bible', (NKJV) John 14:6.
Similar titled item in Bk 1 'GOD Speaks of Return and Bannered', item 2 in Bk 7 'GOD Speaks to His Edifice', items 3 and 4 in Bk 8, 'GOD Speaks of Loving his Creation'.

Some others, which only partly use the 1st person pronoun, may have similar or somewhat different titles depending on the content. If desired and when encountered, such can be recorded in the 'Journaling and Notes.'

New Beginnings

"The new beginnings of man are wrapped up in his relationship with his God of sacrifice.

The new beginnings build in instalments upon the head of man,
        to test his sincerity,
        to test his ability to cope,
        to test his readiness in preparation,
        to test his commitment in past promises with significance
                      of meaning.

The new beginnings come in sequence for intent on following in the footsteps of
                            The Lord.

The new beginnings commence with the birthing of the spirit.
The new beginnings continue with the immersion of The Body for the second birth.
The new beginnings continue with the gifts of My Spirit inclusive of The Gift
                            of Tongues.
The new beginnings continue with the key of Faith which unlocks the gifts in
                            their fullness.
The new beginnings continue with the preparedness of My Bride.

The new beginnings building a foundation within mortality make a jump—
        to fulfilment on passing through the grave,
        to eternity within the destiny of choice,
        to The Garden of The Lord where all has been prepared,
        to life within My Garden as adopted into The Family of God.

The new beginnings hold great promises of the things to be,
        hold great promises which fall as an inheritance,
        hold great promises which will fulfil the expectations,
        hold great promises where the conditions are already met,
        hold great promises where The Son Light holds full sway,
        holds great promises where Grace concedes to Mercy.

The new beginnings cannot be manipulated,
        cannot be misinterpreted,
        cannot be commandeered,
        cannot be claimed as a right—
                but rather as a gift originating from Grace.

The new beginnings open a gateway needing to be approached with love and care,
>needing to be approached with Grace fully in effect,
>needing to be approached with Wisdom
>>directing knowledge,
>needing to be approached with the thought
>>processes in place,
>needing to be approached with The Tongues of
>>Heaven expressing in full fluency.

The new beginnings are incurred upon a commitment made within mortality,
>are dependent on the choice of man made while in mortality,
>are approved by My Spirit upon Freewill of a novice being seen
>>in action—
>>unaccompanied by sin.

The new beginnings in confirmation represent the cry of victory over death with sin,
>the shout of proclamation to The Heavens
>>with commitment,
>the angels with the white stone entry and
>>delivering the new garb
>>of The Gown of Life.

The new beginnings reach across the gamut from the gates of Hell to the gates
>of Heaven,
>see the Good Shepherd moving all His sheep in but one direction;
>see those subject to a destiny of default moving the other way under
>>the guard of demons as the trap so closes.

The new beginnings speak of life resolved within perfection,
>within the skill set of the angels,
>within The Spoken Word of God.

The new beginnings augment the abilities of My people,
>of all who join the throngs of God,
>of all who seek to inherit The Promises of God,
>of all who seek and find the way prepared for
>>the journeying of man,
>of all who would accept the destiny of choice:
>>which leaves the default for
>>ever dead and buried—
>>from where it can no longer have an
>>impact on the body soul and spirit.

The new beginnings bring The Promises of God within the grasp of the outstretched
>> hands of man,
> bring The Inheritance of The Son within the reality of The Saints
>> of God,
> bring The Eternal Destiny of Choice within the reach of man,
> bring The Reconciliation of man and God to now be outside the
>> boundaries of sin,
> bring The Law down on its knees as Grace is redeemed
>> by forgiveness,
> bring The Quest for Righteousness once constrained by the captivity
>> of The Law:
>> and so freed from the bottle known as Faith—
>> where the stopper is removed and sanctioned
>> on request while within the time field of man.

The new beginnings witness The Psalms of God with the fruit now nearly ripe—
> and laid open for acceptance,
> laid open with the entrance to a household of eternity,
> laid open where God opens wide his arms in welcome and proclaims:
>> "†I am the way.'"

Scribal Note: †Refer 'The Bible', John 14:6 (NKJV): 6 Jesus said to him, "I am the way, the truth, and the life. No one comes to the Father except through Me.

My Content Study Aid

Greetings From Your King

"Salutations from The King of kings speaks of words from afar,
                speaks of the written word,
                speaks of formality in action,
                speaks of the kingly distancing within His rule
                              and reign.

Salutations from The King of kings sets up boundaries which cannot easily be crossed,
                sets up a sternness in presentation which brings
                              frigidity to the air,
                sets up the 'fear' of the King of kings with a
                              completely different meaning,
                sets up an approach where handshakes are quite stiff,
                        where bows are quite precise,
                        where protocols are strict and
                              hide behind obedience,
                        where eye contact is not the first
                              choice of the day.

Salutations from The King of kings is to be thrown out with the 'soup' of yesterday,
                is to be detached from the throne of God,
                is to be banished from His kingdom,
                is to go to where the used frowns pile up in a corner
                              to await the rubbish tin,
                is to be treated as 'past the use by date' and not to
                              rear up in presenting its imaging or voice again.

    For the coloured stallions,
            the red the black the pale,
            have run their dash across the landscapes of man.

    For the rider of the white horse leads His retinue in victory,
            has won the hearts and souls of man.

Hearken to The Call of The Lord ringing out within His courts of praise and worship:
            with The Song of The Lamb,
                The Anthem of The King;
            with the fanfares of immediacy heard trumpeting:
                        'Greetings now and forever more.'

For He is risen.
    He is risen in deed.
    And His Bride is welcomed home.

'Greetings from your King' acknowledges His love and presence,
        acknowledges His caring and provisioning,
        acknowledges His success and victory.

'Greetings from your King' acknowledges His presence amongst His Saints,
        His presence before His people,
        His presence with His Bride.

'Greetings from your King' speaks of His inheritance from The Father,
        speaks of the coronation of The Son by The Holy Spirit in
        The Presence of The Father—
        as The Three-in-One,
        The Holy Trinity of God,
        speaks of The Kingdom's crown established firmly in its
                place upon the rightful heir.

'Greetings from your King' greets the refreshed and responsive,
        greets the enthused and eager,
        greets the active and ambitious.

'Greetings from your King' reveals fidelity due The King,
        reveals a throne now fully occupied,
        reveals fealty as a tribute from within The Fear of God.

'Greetings from your King' should serenade the souls of The Saints,
        should comfort the spirits of The Bride at home within their
                places as prepared,
        should affirm the safe harbour of the bodies of the
                committed within their gowns of eternal life.

'Greetings from your King' says all is well within The Kingdom,
        all is well upon a throne,
        all is well in terms of governance.

'Greetings from your King' speaks of sanctity of being,
        speaks of accomplishment of a goal,
        speaks of a transition from a time of preparation to the
                completion in eternity.

'Greetings from your King' is a call upon the status of the co-heirs of The Kingdom,
        of responsibilities inherited and
                now shared,
        of judgement and of Truth as
                determinators of justice—
        for the heart the soul the body in a time foregone.

'Greetings from your King' reminds of reverence retained,
        of supervision still required,
        of governance as propounded for the gatherings of man.

'Greetings from your King' declares order is determined,
    declares order is preserved,
    declares evil is overcome.

'Greetings from your King' is the reserve of kings,
    is the reserve of responsibilities,
    is the reserve for those instated by The Lord—
        for all as drawn from among His Bride.

'Greetings from your King' reverberates among The Heavens,
    resonates upon The Earth."

My Content Study Aid

Welcome to My Garden

"The welcome to My garden is as a welcome home.

The welcome to My garden has a protocol of acceptance,
        has a protocol of governance,
        has a protocol enabling the fulfilment of expectations.

The welcome to My garden has a protocol declared for the guidance of My Bride.

The welcome to My garden is much more than as seen within mortality,
        introduces a whole new expanse of God opening up to the
                new senses of man.

The welcome to My garden bestows the walkways and the pathways,
        the rugged and the smooth,
        the glorious and the sublime,
        the high and the low:
            to the evaluation of each child of God.

The welcome to My garden is one of permanence and longevity,
        is one of wisdom and of understanding,
        is one of life exposed by God to examination by His Bride.

The welcome to My garden has variance and variability,
        has records and the reasoning,
        has the myths and mayhem from within the tales of man:
            within the reality of God.

The welcome to My garden encourages investigations,
        encourages the eyes of wonder,
        encourages the tongues of thought.

The welcome to My garden encourages the mastery of thought transmission
                and reception.

The welcome to My garden has 'catch-up' schools for those who were taught that the
        tongues of God did not exist,
        were of no avail,
        were to be ignored,
        were not relevant,
        were a demonic babbling of the day.

The welcome to My garden is not extended to those who instructed that tongues:
        were a lapsed short term gift,
        had stopped in the times of the first apostles,
        were not intended for The End-time of progression—
        despite the evidence to the contrary in the lives of My
            people who knew Me and conversed.

The welcome to My garden is the richest of rich experiences,
        displays beauty in all the categories imaginable by man,
        sustains beauty in all the musical works available in Heaven,
        showcases the artistic endeavours of all the attendees of
                My garden.

The welcome to My garden can bring emotion to the fore,
        can bring tears to the eyes,
        can amaze the face when the first glimpse is observed and
                understanding dawns.

The welcome to My garden appreciates the innocent and the well-behaved,
        appreciates the sturdy and well-founded,
        appreciates the wise and well-informed.

The welcome to My garden appreciates the enlightened and well-prepared:
        that they may feel at home,
        that they may make comparisons,
        that they may seize the opportunities with which they
                are surrounded.

The welcome to My garden is there for many cultures,
        is enabled to cultivate and blend,
        is capable of thought in all the tongues of Heaven,
            in all the tongues of man,
        where response is instantaneous and accurate in the serving
                of intent.

The welcome to My garden is not to a set piece in an environment which does
                not change,
        in an environment where seasons
                are unknown,
        in an environment where snow and ice
                are absent,
        where water is a scarce commodity,
        where change is slow and inconspicuous.

The welcome to My garden is to a place which lives,
        is to a place where life is real and on-going,
        is to a place with interest and endeavour,
        is to a place modified by those who live and dwell therein.

The welcome to My garden is to a place where accidents are short-changed by the fuse
                of God,
        where feet are not subject to a stumble,
        where havens are not subject to intrusion
            bringing noise and levels of activity:
        seen to be boisterous and approved by the
        noise-makers and the activists at large.

The welcome to My garden has The Sincerity of God,
                has The Promises of Surprises,
                has the joy and relaxation endemic to The Psalms of God,
                has the love and reflections of happiness abounding in the
                              enchanting layers of discovery:
                  within My garden prepared and readied for My Bride."

My Content Study Aid

My End-time Environment for Man

Of Temples	216
Of End-time Prophecy	218
Coming Day of The Lord	222
Of End-time Events	225
Cutover of God	229
Dissemination of The Multitudes	232
Wisdom Sought and Found	234
My Heralds with The Parts	237
What are The End-time Psalms of God? *or The End-time Homilies of God?*	241
Habakkuk 2:1-3	242
Renaming of The Book Series	243
My Nine Volumes' Indexing	244
Cross-indexed 'Category' Study Aid	246

Of Temples

"The second temple had its time expire upon My rising from the grave.

The second temple's fate was sealed upon the renting of the curtain in The Holy
>> of Holies,
> for it was then that was witnessed the transference of The
>> Presence of God:
> from the temple built by man to The Temples built by God.

For the day of Pentecost would follow in its path.

For the day of Pentecost would usher in the era where the heart of man would
> become the dwelling place of My presence.

For the day of Pentecost would announce the new locations of The Temples of God
> wherein My Spirit would be seen to dwell,
> would My Counsel be forth coming,
> would My Gifts be presented for acceptance,
> would the pathway to My Presence be ensured by Faith with
>> Grace in leading My people back:
>>> to the source of eternal wisdom,
>>> of eternal light,
>>> of eternal life.

The second temple's fate was aligned with the promise made to Abraham with
> his descendants,
> was taken down and scattered within The Will of God,
> has already been rebuilt in many different locations
>> from where My Spirit dwells,
>> from where the living water flows,
>> from where My Gifts are evidenced,
>> from where salvation's message is proclaimed,
>> from where Faith flows forth as a mighty river
>>> with rivulets galore:
>> as Grace abounds to cleanse and inundate both sides of all
>>> the banks.

The second temple's fate was shattered into splinters,
> had fulfilled its purpose,
> was about to be surpassed,
> was not able to equip The Coming Saints of God,
> was not able to complete The Presence of God among His people,
> was not part of the fulfilment of The Inheritance of The Cross,
> was not able to make the switch from the edifice of law to The
>> Field of Grace.

So The Ark of The Covenant had a new covenant to embrace,
        a new covenant to uphold,
        a new covenant to honour and protect—
            within the life of My people with their destiny of choice:
                  with the tools of God available—
        so all may be able to find their way home to dwell
                  within The Family of God."

My Content Study Aid

Of End-time Prophecies

"The end-time prophecies of God have been strained through the voices of My prophets:
>> as they guided and directed with My Word,
>> at their times upon The Earth.

The end-time prophecies of God are now the recipients of attention;
> the ordering into understanding,
> the presenting with opinions running wild,
> the see-sawing back and forth
>> as confusion is spread,
>> as misinterpretation flourishes by the hour,
>> as variants seek publicity,
>> as The Word of God is churned,
>> as the complexity generated by man
> causes its placement in the 'too hard' basket—
> where neither wisdom nor meaning is present:
>> so My people don't prepare.

The end-time prophecies of God were placed in the concepts of the day in which they
>> saw The Light,
> were placed in the fields of hope and Faith and visions:
>> that My people may not perish,
>> that My people may be sustained,
>> that My people would ponder on what
>>> their future holds.

The end-time prophecies of God have been served up to the populace of God—
> contaminated by the selective emphasis applied—
>> by those with agendas undeclared,
>> by those without the ear of God,
>> by those who walked as lone wolves
>>> in a forest:
>> whose howl called strangers to their side
>>> in the monasteries of man.

The end-time prophecies of God serve a distinct and valued purpose,
> will function as intended,
> will be seen to harness The Will of God to The Freewill
>> of man,
> will lead man along a path where the hand of God
>> is evident;
>> where the hand of God is raised unto a season;
>> where the hand of God says,
>>> 'Stop and Behold';

where the onward rush of man is leading him to
a destiny:
which will not be to his liking;
where the objective of the few is set
on misdirection:
of the would-be flock of God.

The end-time prophecies of God are for the benefit of My people,
are sacrosanct and sacred,
are awe-inspiring and formidable:
in all that they propose,
in all that they convey,
in all that they superimpose upon the life of man.

The end-time prophecies of God as applied by man are not necessarily The End-time
prophecies of God as applied by God.

For man is missing information critical to his studying,
critical to his theses,
critical to his assumptions and conclusions,
critical to that for which he lays the responsibility at
the feet of God,
critical in the attribution of words to cling to that for
which they were not intended.

The end-time prophecies of God,
as called by man,
include prophecies to do with situations in the days of the prophets:
in situations not recorded for which the prophecies remain
in perpetuity,
in situations which have come and gone,
in situations apparent within just two or three generations
beyond the life of a prophet,
in situations where the textual transmission of My Word is
split at the will of man—
into partial sentences,
into broken paragraphs,
into broken scenes,
into broken themes—
where 'attractive' substantive substance is taken at the behest of man,
to be misapplied to that which fits a plausible end-time situation:
for which it was not intended;
for which it has been extricated;
for which it has been polished and reset:
in presentation for a very different age and function
from that in which it was submitted to My prophets:
as a cautionary for events long passed and overlooked in history—

so to become invisible as the 'unrecorded' outside the time line of
My Word.

The end-time prophecies of God do not transplant The Truth from relevance to
the unrelated,
do not transfer an event across the time pages of man,
do not alter a correct relationship as presented in the
past with intended applicability to the present.

The end-time prophecies of God from a distant past are not numerous in their numbers,
are not intended to invite guesswork,
are not the harbingers of confusion,
are not to be composed of partial
mixtures from different times
and places,
are not selected by the 'matchings' of
man where similarities are treated
as affirmation of relationship:
which breeds a conclusion born of error."

Scribal Note:
Compare the difference which a new covenant makes— with The Temples of The Lord abounding everywhere:
Jeremiah 3:16
"Then it shall come to pass, when you are multiplied and increased in the land in those days," says the Lord, "that they will say no more, 'The ark of the covenant of the Lord.' It shall not come to mind, nor shall they remember it, nor shall they visit *it,* nor shall it be made anymore.

with: Revelation 11:19
Then the temple of God was opened in heaven, and the ark of His covenant was seen in His temple. And there were lightnings, noises, thunderings, an earthquake, and great hail.

and especially refer to Revelation 11:19 *with the* Divine Commentary, His Bk 2; 'GOD Speaks to Man on the Internet'.
Divine Commentary:

"So The Temples of God are opened on completion,
are opened after transition,
are opened for inspection where there,
in the place of highest honour,
resides the heart of man—
the ark which carried safely home The Covenant with God.

So was the excitement of Heaven,
the celebrations,
the jubilation at each success,
so conveyed to John to be so described to man."

and also to 'The Ark of The Covenant', His Bk 7 'GOD Speaks to His Edifice'.

New King James Version (NKJV) Scripture taken from the New King James Version®. Copyright © 1982 by Thomas Nelson. Used by permission. All rights reserved.

My Content Study Aid

The Coming Day of The Lord

"The coming day of The Lord is a sequence borne of the need for restoration.

The coming day of The Lord asserts The Wrath of God upon the plight of man:
      upon his treating of his home;
      upon his doping and his drives;
      upon his selfishness and greed;
      upon his idolatry and carnality.

The coming day of The Lord will cleanse The Earth of its smudges and its blurs,
      its hypocrisy and its cesspits,
      its iniquity and its hard-heartedness,
      its selfishness and its enmity both to
          brotherhoods and God.

The coming day of The Lord will root out the infestations of false belief,
    will root out the lazy and the blasphemers,
    will root out the parasites and the worms,
    will root out the vain and the proud—
        those who have no fruit,
        who know no fruit,
        who develop no fruit,
        who carry no fruit—
        which lasts beyond the grave of man.

The coming day of The Lord will readjust the boundaries of man:
    will examine the grudge bearers without a valid cause,
    will examine the carriers of hearts of evil intent,
    will examine the bearers of hearts consumed by vengeance,
    will examine the hate mongers of hearts encumbered with a
          score to settle,
    will examine the princes and the generals of hearts in
          preparation for a war.

 Beware of those who fail their examination:
  for they will have no cause for hope,
    no reason to assume success,
    no possibility of enticing to entrapment,
    no justification for the taking of the profile of the murderer.

The coming day of The Lord will follow the testimony of My Word;
      the prophecies of the prophets whom I know;
      the course declared by valid
         introspections interpreting:
      the ways and means of the footfalls of God
          upon The Earth.

The coming day of The Lord lays waste and reconfigures.

The coming day of The Lord clears landscapes from contamination of like with like.

The coming day of The Lord elevates My people to due prominence under Grace.

The coming day of The Lord hears and acts on the calls of My Saints.

The coming day of The Lord checks the rise of evil with the spread of violence.

The coming day of The Lord consolidates The Earth in readiness for its future.

The coming day of The Lord prevents infestations from spreading to areas of interest.

    For as The Heavens speak so The Heavens do.

    For as The Lord intends so The Lord affirms.

    For as Satan plots so his plans are foiled.

The coming day of The Lord finally approaches its fulfilment,
>> finally is to be implemented on the status of The Earth,
>> finally is declaring a warning to His people within The New
>>>> Covenant of The Cross.

The coming day of The Lord sees a flash within the skies,
>> indicates the time of imminence,
>> allows for the wise and the righteous to evacuate:
>>>> to shelter within The Earth,
>>>> under The Earth,
>>>> in the shadows of The Earth—
>> so protection is assured from the streaming of the skies:
>> so safety is released after three cycles of the hour hands:
>>>> those of the wound clocks of man.

The coming day of The Lord witnesses the streaming of My vengeance,
>> the streaming of My wrath,
>>>> the streaming of My corrections as impacting on
>>>>>> the surface areas of The Earth:
>> where the conflicts of man know of no forgiveness,
>>>> know of neither Grace nor
>>>>>> of Mercy,
>>>> know of neither resolution nor
>>>>>> of peace:
>> while the misplaced Faith of the resolute will neither yield
>>>>>> nor negotiate—
>> without placing a lie upon the paper:
>> there to be adorned with the signatures of man.

The coming day of The Lord will not be re-released on man,
>> will not recur as His carrier of vengeance,
>> will not re-inflict The Wrath of God.

The coming day of The Lord is an indicator of the proximity of My return,
of My second advent,
of My coming for My Bride,
of My instatement with
My Kingdom as a
colony of Heaven,
of the governance of My
Kings and Queens—
each replete with
their inheritance.

The coming day of The Lord upholds The Promises of God,
the oversight of The Father,
The Presence of The Holy Spirit—
with the participation of The Hosts of Heaven:
in upholding righteous life upon The Earth."

My Content Study Aid

Of End-time Events

"The end-time events of God are not resequenced by man.

The end-time events of God are imposed upon man in his mortality:
>> in all his Fear of God,
>> in all his Wisdom gained,
>> in all his Knowledge acquired,
>> in all his Understanding realized,
>> in all his Adoption of The Truth,
>> in all his Walk in Righteousness,
>> in all his Commitment to The Bride
>>>> of Christ,
>> in all his Selection or rejection of
>>>> a destiny with God.

The end-time events of God bring a new beginning in extending the horizons of man.

The end-time events of God are worthy of deep consideration.

The end-time events of God speak of The Immortality of God about to enter the mortality
>> of man.

The end-time events of God introduce man to the results of the application of Freewill,
> introduce accountability for the past,
>> introduce transitioning to a differing lifestyle.

The end-time events of God bring Certainty replacing Faith,
> bring Reality replacing Hope,
> bring Mercy replacing Grace,
> bring Pleading replacing Conviction,
> bring Royalty on schedule replacing the governance of man,
> bring The Edifice of Heaven replacing the edifice of man,
> bring The Thrones of God replacing the thrones of man.

The end-time events of God are in clarity of occurrence:
>> as to impact on The Multitudes;
>> as to impact on My Bride;
>> as to impact on The Time of Preparation.

The end-time events have arrived,
> grow in their ferocity as they berate The Earth.

The end-time events are acquiring the practice of laying waste and of wrecking,
> are acquiring the tempests of the fire and of flooding,
> are acquiring the inundations of the surging of the seas,
> are acquiring the invasions of the cyclones on the move,
> are awaiting the candles with their plumes and flows.

The end-time events sweep and clean the crowded sin fields from The Earth,
        toss and turn the overflowing sin bins of the cities,
        suck and blow the sinning hidey-holes of man.

The end-time events sprout and serve the violence of man:
              the senseless with the savage;
              the murderous with the looting;
              the mobs with the brainwashed—
                    all as filled with the rampaging souls of man.

The end-time events introduce and dismiss the insurrections against the state:
              the rebellions against authority,
              the coups with the betrayals,
              the blood letting with the killing:
       where Mercy is unknown,
       where Grace has long fled the fields of battle and of death;
       where the soul of man is welded to Satanic motivations in
                    the evil seeking of attention:
              when no value is placed upon a life.

The end-time events shudder and retreat,
        pause and refresh,
        shake and advance.

The end-time events climb and escalate the viciousness of man,
              the viciousness of climate,
              the viciousness of activities:
                      previously unseen by man.

The end-time events introduce barbarians running wild,
        soldiers without command,
        mercenaries looking for an outlet—
            where they can maim and injure,
            where they can confront and butcher,
            where they can set the children one against another.

The end-time events bring forth pleas to be ignored,
        bring forth calls to be silenced,
        bring forth screams shortened by a blow,
        bring forth shouts of impatience,
        bring forth orders without substance,
        bring forth the guns—
                the weaponry of man—
                    to be pointed at the innocent as fingers tighten on
                                  the triggers,
        bring forth the sound of firing which speaks of the break-up of
                                  the families:
              as members fall lifeless on The Earth.

The end-time events create those who willingly would flee,
        who willingly would leave,
        who willingly would hide,
        who willingly would join the refugees:
            if such had the means,
            if such could reach a place of safety where options
                still prevail,
            if such had the ability to transport their possessions:
                in the absence of the fire enveloping their homes,
                in the absence of the fire issuing from the barrels,
                in the absence of the fire targeting their hopes and
                    dreams and life its very self.

The end-time events witness the death scenes of man,
        witness man's inhumanity to man,
        witness the hand of God moving as it both cleanses and purifies:
            the landscapes and the seascapes of The Earth—
            from the sinners with their residues of sin.

The end-time events build into a crescendo of destruction,
        where the deaths of man can be no longer counted,
        where the bodies lie where they have fallen,
        where the birds do feed and peck,
            do rip and tear,
            do fight and squabble:
        where life has forsaken the mortal gloves of man,
        where life has likely bypassed the selection of
            a destiny,
        where life with the ownership of an entry in The Book
            of Life may only be known by God.

The end-time events have the preparation of The Bride:
        the separating of the goats from My sheep,
            of the kids from the lambs,
            of the tares from the wheat;
        the practising of My Spirit's gifts;
        the fluency in tongues,
        the decorating of the gowns of life,
        the storage of the jewels on the far side of the grave,
        the attending to the soon-to-be shortages of life,
            the necessities of life—
                of water and of food,
        within a sanctuary of God—
        where defence is likely to be necessary—
        when dwelling within the zones of the troubling of man.

Wise is he who has at hand the means of his defence in a coming time of violence,
who has the necessities of life stored securely—
as supply chains are broken,
as shortages rule both the day and the night,
as weight loss becomes a problem which focuses the mind:
on the recurring need for seizures of replenishments.

Scribal Note: *Refer also* 'The Days of Thunder', His Bk 2; 'GOD Speaks to Man on The Internet', *and* 'The Days of Thunder (2)', His Bk 8 'GOD Speaks of Loving His Creation'.

My Content Study Aid

_____
_____
_____
_____
_____
_____
_____
_____
_____
_____
_____
_____
_____
_____
_____
_____
_____
_____
_____
_____
_____
_____
_____
_____

The Cutover of God

"When The Earth goes into turmoil for its season of correction
　My people are to stand above it,
　　　　are to stand upon the sidelines while the cleaning is in action,
　　　　　　　　while the calls are being made,
　　　　　　　　while the corrections are in progress.

　My people are to live their lives in Faith in that they will dwell:
　　beyond the flood waters brought by iniquity to cascade upon the structures which
　　　　　　　　conceal all that is abhorrent to The Living God;
　　beyond the fire brought to purify the sinners in denial of the thoughts within the
　　　　　　　　souls wherein the lies are generated;
　　beyond the wind storms brought by unforgiveness,
　　　　　　within the blackened hearts,
　　　　　　　　where activities which challenge The Will of God
　　　　　　　　　　still linger and expound;
　　beyond the surges of the sea brought to remove the contaminants in need
　　　　　　　　　　of cleansing—
　　　　　　from the foreshores of the land where the greed of
　　　　　　　　man prevents his sharing—
　　　　　　　　as selfishness is seen to rule;
　　beyond the reach of the shaking of The Earth where the idolatry of man in all its
　　　　　　　　ramifications and appearances:
　　　　　　are no longer to be tolerated to arise before
　　　　　　　　The Face of God;
　　beyond the reach of marauding bands set on plunder and on sacking as they seek
　　　　　　　　and loot in violence—
　　　　　　with the blood trails as evidenced—
　　　　　　to so testify within their localities of familiarity.

　For such will be the cleansing of The Earth.

　For such will be the stage as set for a new beginning.

　For such will be the resetting of what has been and is to be no more.

　For such will settle the new pathways to guide and so direct the future of man into
　　　　　　　　　　his full potential—
　　　　　　　　in The Presence of The Kings and Queens.

　For such will bring the encountering of a new Banner,
　　　　　　a new Flag,
　　　　　　a new Standard—
　　　　　　　　to testify,
　　　　　　　　to state,
　　　　　　　　to claim,

    that which has long been expected yet had failed to appear.
For such is about to appear before the face of My people;
  while The Multitudes at large search and are sustained with full validity of
        past hopes and the supporting of activity—
 in acknowledgement of The Faith and Grace long held in trust—
 in such acts by those who knew the keys of The Kingdom developed to be held
      and turned when dwelling side-by-side
     in the three-fold fields of Righteousness,
        of Truth,
        of Faith,
       within the mortality of lives:
  so being committed to a greater conviction of the heart,
    which will surely lead each home.

For by The Ways of God will man attain his full potential.

For by The Ways of God shall man receive his kinfolk of adoption.

For by The Ways of God will man achieve his destiny as approved by God,
        as made possible by God,
        as prepared by God.

For by The Love of God was man brought into existence.

For through The Love of God can man attain his full potential.

For in The Love of God shall man achieve the reality of eternity.

For as man grows so a knowledge of God is expected.

For as man matures so his time for preparation diminishes.

For as man leaves mortality so the third birth lies in readiness.

For the preparedness of God oversees the preparedness of man.

 The angels of God are extremely tearful when their charge is unprepared,
       is ill-prepared,
       is non-prepared—
   and so forsakes The Loving Care of God.

For the summit of achievement,
 the mountaintop of perseverance,
The Firebrand of The Spirit—
speaks of the success of The Freewill of man being in alignment with The Will of God.

So man achieves his Destiny of Choice,
 deletes his Destiny of Default:
    to live forever within The Extended Family of God.

So the optional purposing of God in approaching The Freewill of man marries with the
    intent of man to seek the outstretched hand of God.

And there within the twilight of man on Earth,
                        as he has come to know it,
now carries him into a life with a new beginning in The Company of God."

My Content Study Aid

The Dissemination of The Multitudes

"The dissemination of The Multitudes is all across The Earth,
   is not focussed on The New Zion,
   is not concentrated on The New Jerusalem,
   is not concerned with the land of inheritance where history is not established,
         where kinfolk have no established claim of nationhood,
           where all is as the same wherein The Multitudes are concerned.

The dissemination of The Multitudes is open and explicit,
        is to be development with security,
        is to be livelihood with success,
        is to be culture with respect,
        is to be growth within the similarity of their tongues.

The dissemination of The Multitudes cannot breach the walls of jealousy;
        are turning down the offer of the centuries,
        are failing a second time for a willingness to commit,
           when Grace and Faith are available to all,
   will soon have to handle the plea for Mercy and of Judgement—
              at The Great White Throne,
        where The Multitudes are all promised to attend—
          as laid before them with a knowledge band,
             before it is too late.

The dissemination of The Multitudes will not be disenfranchised,
        will not be banished,
        will not be imprisoned without cause—
where a trial with justice will prevail within the fields of Truth and Righteousness,
        will be admitted as kingdom citizens applicable to
           the lands wherein they dwell,
        will have access to the advantages which citizenship
              rightfully possesses:
  unless in denial of The King when citizenship is withdrawn with expulsion,
           to the wastelands of The Earth—
        so to wander where they will.

The dissemination of The Multitudes is not a movement choice,
        is not an action with a welfare benefit,
        is not a subsidy to sweeten the concept of disposition,
        is not recompense for moving to a job,
        is a continuation of working with their skillsets
            of employment.

The dissemination of The Multitudes is not the inauguration of mass transition across
            previous boundaries,

      is not the subjugation of the families struggling for survival,
      is not the subject of procrastination where delay removes the intensity of feelings.
The dissemination of The Multitudes is the orderly organisation of life for the betterment
                                  of all involved,
      is the affirmation of a supreme change in leadership,
      is the understanding of the responsibility as it affects an individual's Freewill actions:
              where accountability may be required if morality is breached—
                        with an injustice as the end result.

The dissemination of The Multitudes sees a higher standard for each in dealing with
                                  their fellow man,
      for the installing of The Golden Rule as the guideline for behaviour,
      for the promoting of a healthier way of life where drugs leading to addiction are no
                                  longer tolerated,
              shall not be available from any market servicing A Kingdom,
              shall lead to A Kingdom citizen suffering loss of the citizenship
              which may be seen as very unattractive:
                      as a life starts to seize up,
                            as life support is seen to vary downwards,
                                until the senses are recovered—
                      as addiction no longer rules a life.

The dissemination of The Multitudes is not a drawn-out affair,
              has solutions for the incapacitated,
              has health options assured to overcome the issues of the day
                                and of the night,
              has pain no longer as a by-product of ill health,
                        or something not meshing as it should—
            as pain is permanently banished from the body by a throne in action.

The dissemination of The Multitudes is an enormous step up for all who understand,
    can only be surpassed by the making of a commitment that opens the gates of God,
        which leads to the supremacy of existence,
                to the wonderland of creation,
                to the be all of life within the stars
                            with the close companionship of God,
            in welcoming eternity as man and God clasp hands together—
                            in the handshake of creation."

My Content Study Aid

_____
_____
_____

Wisdom Sought and Found

"Wisdom sought and found needs to have its location known,
                needs to have its extent established,
                needs to be available both by day and by night.

Wisdom sought and found is offered as the supplement to Truth,
                is offered to wean man away from foolishness,
                is offered so man may be mature in all his thinking
                                      and his actions.

Wisdom sought and found extends the vocabulary of man,
        aids his thinking and responses,
        amplifies the effect of both his tongue and his mouth,
        catches the attention of an audience with the crowning of his words,
        spreads the concepts grounded in wisdom to both the far and wide.

Wisdom sought and found is a joy to behold,
                brings succinctness of expression,
                exposes weakness in defence,
                greets the morning of the day with both Truth and specificity,
                closes out the day with a signature of prayer from
                                      a thankful heart.

Wisdom sought and found can be overwritten by a gusher of exuberance,
        by a volcano of the mouth in full eruption,
        by a certainty of expression for a concept hiding in confusion,
        by an exposition of flamboyance which catches the imagination,
        by a reticence to share with others that which wisdom has declared.

Wisdom sought and found has no echo of correction,
                has no thought patterns in denial,
                has no subjectivity placing doubt upon The Truth.

Wisdom sought and found is recognized when encountered on the highway governing
                        both the spoken and the written word,
            encourages a lingering of assessment of the depth encountered,
                    requires a decision of involvement for silence,
                              for amplifying,
                              for correction—
        as each situation is considered as to the dominance of wisdom.

Wisdom sought and found is a pearl of great price,
                is the value put on speech,
                        on writing,
                            which carries through the centuries,
                where later adjustments denigrate rather than enhance,

        where the adjectival superlatives are often quite unnecessary
            to bring emphasis to a point already well made,
        where the 'more' is found quite often not to meet the
        expectations as silence brings the blessings of a mouth at rest.

Wisdom sought and found has its primacy of origin within the gifts of God,
    has its reception dependent on a prayer request of understanding,
    has its downloading to The Temple of The Spirit within the functioning of
        the gift of tongues,
    has its positioning in the voice patterning dwelling within The Will of God,
    has its reliability in superimposing The Words of God onto the words of man:
        with the specific surrendering of The Freewill speech of man—
    to the over-riding guidance and direction of The Divinity as present
        with The Spirit.

Wisdom sought and found knows the fall of Grace,
    follows on the fall of Faith,
    is best when anchored in a commitment to The Tongues of Heaven,
    becomes a wonder of a witness when applied by personal Freewill consent:
        within The Will of God.

Wisdom sought and found is not of the ability of man unless within the wisdom
        of the flesh.

Wisdom sought and found varies according to the origin,
    according to the nature,
    according to the conceptual stance.

Wisdom sought and found is at its most fulfilling,
    its most rewarding,
    when allowed to reign within a life,
        within a temple,
    when allowed to create the choice of words being uttered,
    when allowed to supervise that which the heart of man desires to
        express with the deepest understanding,
            sincerity,
            and belief,
        to the world at large.

Wisdom sought and found should be sought from God.

Wisdom sought and found is perfect when authorised for Impartation by God.

Wisdom sought and found magnifies and espouses The Freewill of man best
        when subjugated to The Will of God.

Wisdom sought and found is in its epitome of usage when in the field of speech
        as overseen by The Divine.

Wisdom sought and found should be a Godly given adjunct to all that man would say.

Wisdom sought and found is the advantage received from The Heavens for enabling man's full expression on The Earth."

Scribal Note: Refer to The Bible, NKJV, Luke 7:35
"But wisdom is justified by all her children."

My Content Study Aid

My Heralds with The Parts of The End-time Psalms of God

"My Heralds,
    arise and take control!
    Arise and set the agendas!
    Arise and ensure success!

My Heralds,
    arise and fund!
    Arise and rate returns!
    Arise and seek the market place of man!

    Arise and feed the hungry and the starving—
        those who seek and want and need the fare,
        as such are laid before the hearts and minds of man:
            where My altar is yet to be disclosed.

My Heralds,
    set My fare before the eyes of man!
    Set My fare on the table of The Lord!
    Set My fare where green pastures grow with nourishment aplenty!

My Heralds,
    set My fare within My Churches,
        the gathering points of The Lord,
            where the sacred are at home,
            where My Bride is fed and watered,
            where My Bride is taught to practise tongues as part of the gifts of
                                    My Spirit,
            where My Bride should prepare and be ready,
            where My Bride should be armed with the weapons of self-defence.

My Heralds,
    scatter where the birds do feed!
    Scatter where The Multitudes are present!
    Scatter where the secular do not encounter The Divine!
    Scatter far and wide as dispersion is carried on the voice of man,
            as dispersion is carried on the winds of change,
            as dispersion is carried by the caravans of trade.

    Scatter where My books are seen with availability!

Scatter My books abroad so they may be handled,
>> so the browsing may be completed by access to
>>>> the pocket,
> so The End-time Psalms of God may be completed
>>> to fulfilment:
>> where a new beginning is both practical and assured—
>> in being furnished with both the means and the
>>>> knowledge of the way.

My Heralds,
> gather testimonies from the readers with an incentive to comply—
>> for the labourer is worthy of his hire.

Gather testimonies which are short and sweet,
> which are brief and to the point,
> which validate both the source and the journey's end.

Gather testimonies which can be used for all modes of My books:
>> the soft covers,
>> the casebound,
>> the electronic,
>> and the audio,
> that all may be fed and encouraged to develop within the niches
>> where each dwells:
>> so each may bring honour to My Name—
>> so I may bring honour to The Father.

My Heralds,
> understand the process of distribution and acceptance,
>> of enabling sales throughout The English speaking world:
>> in order that The End-time may be filled with triumph—
>>> as Satan's dominion diminishes,
>>> as Christ becomes esteemed,
>>> as Righteousness brings peace,
>>> as Truth prevents the lies,
>>> as Accountability impacts on Freewill,
>>> as Evil is overcome and fused into The Light of Life:
>>>> which shall not dim.

My Heralds,
> do not leave what is seen to be amiss!
> Strengthen and support!
> Rectify and correct!
> Challenge and suggest!
> Persevere and sway the reticence of man!
> Enthuse and inspire the would-be fence sitters:
>> who know not on which side to fall!

My Heralds,
>   follow-up and suggest!
>   Record and verify the numbers on the records:
>   >   that all may be correct and true,
>   >   that all may be accurate and final,
>   >   that all may be trusted as a sure foundation
>   >   >   which will not topple in a storm,
>   >   >   which will not stand in need of correction,
>   >   >   which will not throw doubt upon the level of acceptance of
>   >   >   >   My books in The End-time Psalms of God.

My Heralds,
>   check on the acceptance of the shopping chains of man—
>   >   where the leadership acknowledges The Ways of God!
>
>   Request tables in the premises where The Multitudes can browse!
>
>   Check also on the secular where display space is at a premium,
>   >   and the attractiveness of the wares are not perceived from behind a veil:
>   >   >   which is yet to be lifted from the eyes.
>
>   For in these end-times I am lifting veils from eyes!
>   >   I am speaking to the deaf!
>   >   I am uplifting man to a higher plane!

My Heralds,
>   do not underestimate The Power and The Authority of God bestowed upon
>   >   His End-time books:
>   >   with their origin divine;
>   do not underestimate The Counselling of My Spirit as He watches and leads the
>   >   passers-by:
>   >   >   to stop and to enquire of The End-time Psalms of God,
>   >   >   to stop and so acquire The End-time Psalms of God.

My Heralds,
>   approve and confirm the potential
>   >   within the preparation for the widespread distribution of God,
>   >   within the widespread marketing of God,
>   >   within the servicing of the layers of the marketplace all open to acceptance—
>   >   with ready access to My books,
>   >   with an allowance in setting the time frames of acceptance:
>   >   >   so the initial impressions can become the sales of record.

My Heralds,
> do not leave a stone unturned!
> Do not leave premises empty of My books!
> Do not turn your backs while the prospect of achievement still opens wide
> > the doors of Heaven and so,
> > the doors of Earth!"

Scribal Note: 'The Lord gave the word;
> Great was the company of those who proclaimed it:'
> > The Bible, Psalm 68:11 (NKJV)

Sample Adjuncts: *Website; Flag, Banner, Standard, (all in 2 sizes); Cap (multi-fitting); sleeved T shirt (various sizes); Emblem sticker (2 sizes); Fanfares (3 commissioned and recorded).* Also 'The Anthem of The King of Kings' with lyrics, melody, and guitar chords in Keys of G and Eb in the form of Sheet music in Bk 6 'GOD Speaks to His Bridal Presence'.

My Content Study Aid

What Are The End-time Psalms of God?
or The End-time Homilies of God?

"The End-time Psalms of God seize this moment for attention,
        hold the interest of these hands,
          welcome this presence of the intellect of
                      My would-be Bride.

The End-time Psalms of God stretch both time and space,
        stretch the past into the present,
        stretch the present into the future:
        stretch the mind of man;
        stretch the extensibility of knowledge into wisdom.

The End-time Psalms of God bear The Reality of God,
        bear the reality of His return,
        bear the reality of Heaven and of Hell,
        bear the reality of adoption into The Family of God,
        bear the reality of the need for preparation of My Bride,
        bear the reality of My gift of tongues wherein fluency
                      is sought.

The nine parts of The End-time Psalms of God speak of a new beginning,
        is the voice of God appearing in dictation,
        is the reality of God made known within
            The End-time now awaiting My return."

Scribal Note:
These volumes in this series form The Parts of The End-time Psalms of God.
These may probably be better known by man in his naming as 'The End-time Homilies of God' - in being 'Religious discourses which are intended primarily for spiritual education rather than doctrinal instruction.

1. GOD Speaks of Return and Bannered

2. GOD Speaks to Man on The Internet

3. GOD Speaks as His Spirit Empowers

4. GOD Speaks to Man in The End-time

5. GOD Speaks in Letters of Eternity

6. GOD Speaks to His Bridal Presence

7. GOD Speaks to His Edifice

8. GOD Speaks of Loving His Creation

9. GOD Speaks Now of a Seal Revealed

Habakkuk 2:1-3

I will stand my watch
And set myself on the rampart,
And watch to see what He will say to me,
And what I will answer when I am corrected.

Then the LORD answered me and said:
"Write the vision and make it plain on tablets,
That he may run who reads it.

For the vision is yet for an appointed time;
But at the end it will speak, and it will not lie.
Though it tarries, wait for it;
Because it will surely come,
It will not tarry."

The Bible - NKJV
'Used by Permission'

Bible Commentary on the above verses:

Five Keys to Hearing God's Voice,
PROPHETIC DREAMS AND VISIONS.

Hearing the voice of God is the birth-right of the born-again
(John 10:27, 28
  "My sheep hear My voice, and I know them, and they follow Me. "And I give them eternal life, and they shall never perish; neither shall anyone snatch them out of My hand.

Acts 2:17, 18 Quotes Joel 2:30

Revelation 3:20
  "Behold, I stand at the door and knock. If anyone hears My voice and opens the door, I will come in to him and dine with him, and he with Me.).

Like Habakkuk, we can take a posture before God that enables us to hear His voice.

1) <u>Meet</u> with The Lord regularly in a special place of prayer: "I will stand my watch."

2) <u>Look</u> for God to speak to you in dreams and visions: I will "watch to see."

3) <u>Listen</u> for the word of The Lord: "He will say to me."

4) <u>Keep</u> a journal of things that God says: "Write the vision."

5) <u>Wait</u> for God to bring it to pass: "It will surely come."

(Hosea 12:10/Matthew 2:12) J.W.R.
New Spirit Filled Life Bible - NKJV
'Used by Permission'

The Renaming Of My Book Series

Scribal Note: At 4.47am Tuesday 22nd March 2016, *I heard The Lord saying,* "**The End-time Psalms of God**". *It was so imperative that I wrote it down with the time.*

Then, at 12.50pm, Good Friday 25th March 2016, *while I was looking at the above sheet of paper on my lounge table, I heard The Lord saying,* "**This is the naming of the grouping of My books.**"

These books were currently then collectively regarded as "**The Works of God**". This being inherited when the website builders applied it to the front page image of a replacement website (a new wineskin!) then under construction.

Then, for the next several days, I was thinking about the far-reaching implications of this, and of what, exactly, was meant by "**The End-time Psalms of God**" *and of what they were comprised?*

Then at 6.15 – 7.37, 8.56 – 9.39am Saturday 26th March 2016, the item with the above name was dictated by The Lord for inclusion in this eighth book. On completion, He indicated that each book is to be considered 'a part' *of* 'The End-time Psalms of God' *and that on each book's cover and/or early in the book is to appear somewhere the text:*
A Part of The End-time Psalms of God

A day later (Easter Saturday) in a time of interesting and relevant discussion (RR) The Lord was also in agreement to this text being placed out of sequence at the beginning of Book 8 or indeed in every book at a selected point of significance, as excerpts or in completeness, with the guidance based on the experience and expertise of the Publishers in handling The End-time Psalms of God.

The Lord also says either 'The Works of God' or 'The End-time Psalms of God' are both acceptable and can be taken as being interchangeable. *These volumes in this series form* The Parts of The End-time Psalms of God.

These may probably be better known by man in his naming as 'The End-time Homilies of God' - in being 'Religious discourses which are intended primarily for spiritual education rather than doctrinal instruction.

My Content Study Aid

_____
_____
_____
_____
_____
_____

My Nine Volumes' Indexing

"The indexes to My End-time Psalms should all be complete and accurate,
>> *My End-time Homilies* should be ordered and so structured,
>>>> should all supply the categories of the content to
>>>>> the selection availability of
>>>>>> both man and My people.

The indexes to My nine books should be consistent in their approach,
>> should be familiar with the handlers and the readers,
>>> the inspectors and the browsers,
>>> the assimilators and the impatient,
>>> the committed and the seeking.

The indexes should be guiding and directing,
>> summarising and collective,
>> imparting and grouping,
>> simplifying and determining.

The indexes require the guidance of My Spirit as to where selection starts and stops,
>>> as to where selection approves and indicates,
>>> as to where selection reigns in Truth and in
>>>> integrity of content.

The Indexes are the highways to the repository of knowledge laid in wisdom—
>>> for the discovery of man,
>>> for the encouragement of My people,
>>> for the preparation of My Bride.

The indexes are the explanatories of locating,
>> of mining,
>> of evaluating:
>> of acceptance or denial as progression is imparted—
>>> to the drawing of conclusions from the content fare.

The indexes are approved of God,
> are contained within His books,
> are explicit in their details,
> are essential in avoiding faces of exasperation,
>>> of puzzlement,
>>> of frustration.

The indexes are personalized by inscribing the pages of the 'Journaling and Notes':
>>> with references and highlights to that
>>>> which is attractive to the eye,
>>>>> to the spirit,
>>>>> or to the soul—

>   at the transfer of end-time information as
>   the seal is broken in readiness—
>   for a walk into Truth and Righteousness.

The indexes provide the readied access for The Stars of God,
> provide the readied references where memory is not explicit,
> provide the readied reckoner for availability and interest,
> provide the readied finder for reviewing what has already gone before,
> provide the readied means of searching to isolate a choice in need of
>   a revisiting,
> provide the readied ability of finding like on like—
>   where there is a commonality of purpose
>   present in the dictations of The Lord."

"The indexes of My nine volumes—
> the parts of The End-time Psalms of God, or as The Works of God,
>   *or as the parts of The End-time Homilies of God:*
> are as the pathways for the feasting of each spirit and each soul:
> as laid as fare upon The Altar where the hungry are sated—
> as an offering for The End-time communion of man into The
>   End-time Will of God."

My Content Study Aid

_____
_____
_____
_____
_____
_____
_____
_____
_____
_____
_____
_____
_____
_____
_____
_____
_____

Cross-indexed 'Category' Study Aid

The Nine End-time Psalms of God *or The End-time Homilies* of God
'Contents - Category' Summary

	Bk1	Bk2	Bk3	Bk4	Bk5	Bk6	Bk7	Bk8	Bk9	Totals
Communication	20									20
DivCom Daniel		13								13
DivCom Ezekiel			48							48
DivCom Revelation		23								23
Edicts of The Lord	1						23			24
Edifice of God	5			1		2	7	1		16
Encouragement					15	21				36
Eternity Beckoning	10			2	11	7	19			49
Fear of God	1					4	1			6
Freewill of Man	5			6	5	5	7			28
Good News	11	7	4							22
My Banner	23	1	1			1	1			27
My Counsel	30			26	19	17	41			133
My Creation					7	6		9	1	23
My Garden	2							22		24
My Grace	4	15	5	5	2	4	3	3	2	43
My Harvest	5			9	6	15	9			44
My Kingdom on Earth	5			8	3	6	12			34
My Love	9	15	3	5	5	9	10	5	7	68
My Return	9	7	1	6	4	3	7	8	3	48
Preparation	13	47	28	9	6	5	41	21	10	180
Thanksgiving of Man									7	7
The Cross	1	7	2		1	1	3		1	16
The End-time	13	24	1	16		6	15	22	2	99
The Trinity	5			4	8	7	9		1	34
Tongues					1	1	1		8	11
Vision & Dream	5									5
Website of The Lord		17		1						18
Wisdom	1	3		2			1	1		8

Appendix

Alphabetical Listing of The End-time Psalms of God *or as The End-time Homilies of God*	248
The 9 Books of either The End-time Psalms of God *or as The End-time Homilies of God*	261
4 Companion Books End-time Flowers of God	262
4 Synopses of The Flowers of God	*262*
About the Scribe	*263*
Journaling and Notes (1)	*264*
Journaling and Notes (2)	*265*

Alphabetical Listing of The End-time Psalms of God
or as *The End-time Homilies of God*

(2, 3, 4 ...) Denotes following items with a similar or same name as earlier ones

A

Aberrations of Man	Bk5
Abilities of Man	Bk1
Ability of Support	Bk4
About My Little Book	Bk9
Absence of Entity	Bk7
Absence of God	Bk3
Acceptance of Authority	Bk7
Accepting of My Bride	Bk6
Achievement of The Goal	Bk5
Achieving of My Garden	Bk8
Actions of The Spirit	Bk9
Activities of God	Bk2
Activities of My Servants	Bk6
Acts of God	Bk2
Adhering to The Commitment	Bk7
Adultery of Man	Bk7
Advent of The Lord	Bk1
Afflictions of Man	Bk4
Agape Love of God for Man	Bk6
Age of Grace	Bk1
Ageing of Man	Bk8
Agency of Life	Bk7
Aggravation of The Soul	Bk3
All in The Kingdom - Edict 8	Bk7
Allergies of Man	Bk3
Alphabetical Listing of The End-time Psalms of God	Bk8
or The End-time Homilies of God	
Altar of The Lamb	Bk2
America, The Beautiful	Bk2
Anthem of King of Kings	Bk6
Anthem of The King	Bk1
Apocrypha of Man	Bk8
Appeal of Jesus (2)	Bk9
Appeal of The Lord	Bk2
Arcana of Life	Bk6
Archetypal Year	Bk6
Ark of The Covenant	Bk7
Armourer of God	Bk6
Arms of Adoration	Bk2
Arms of The Lord	Bk1
Arrowheads of God	Bk8
Arrows of The Bowman	Bk3
Aspects of Revival (Queries)	Bk4
Assault in Violence	Bk4
Attacks Upon Man's Heart	Bk1
Attendants of The Bride	Bk1
Attention to The Details	Bk7
Authoring of God	Bk2
Awakening of My People	Bk5

B

Banner Affirmed as His Will	Bk1
Banner as A Signpost	Bk1
Banner at Home	Bk1
Banner Brings Response	Bk1
Banner Comes Forth	Bk1
Banner Defined	Bk1
Banner in its Presence	Bk1
Banner in The Role	Bk1
Banner Named, Introduced	Bk1
Banner of Assails	Bk1
Banner of Design	Bk1
Banner of Destiny	Bk1
Banner of Effects	Bk1
Banner of The Battle	Bk1
Banner of The Cross	Bk9
Banner of The Kingdom	Bk7
Banner of The Protocols	Bk1
Banner on The Way	Bk1
Banner Prepared	Bk1
Banner Setting Forth	Bk1
Banner Speaks of Unity	Bk1
Barbarity of Man	Bk2
Barn of Righteousness	Bk6
Battlements of The Mind	Bk1
Beating of A Drum	Bk8
Beauty of My End-time Books	Bk6
Beauty of My Garden	Bk8
Beauty of The Earth	Bk1
Beauty of The Morning	Bk4
Behaviour of Man - Edict 22	Bk7
Behold The Bride of Christ	Bk5
Belief of Man in His Loving God	Bk2
Believe Be Guided Be Warned	Bk7
Beneficence of God	Bk7
Benevolence of Grace	Bk3
Bespoke Enemies of God	Bk4

Bespoke from The Tailor	Bk5
Beyond The Grave of Man	Bk5
Birth of Man	Bk1
Birthday of A Saint	Bk1
Birthday of The Son	Bk2
Birthing of a Chrysalis	Bk5
Blasphemy	Bk6
Bleating of My Sheep	Bk8
Blessed are They	Bk6
Blessed are They (2)	Bk6
Blessing of A Pet	Bk7
Blessing of My Lands	Bk4
Blessing of The Sunlight	Bk6
Blessings of God	Bk6
Blessings of The Earth	Bk7
Blessings of The Faithful	Bk3
Blood of The Lord	Bk7
Blooming into Life – Edict 16	Bk7
Blooming of The Youth	Bk7
Blue on The Banner	Bk1
Boats of God	Bk7
Body of Man 1 – Designed	Bk1
Body of Man 2 – A House	Bk1
Body of Man 3 – A Temple	Bk1
Body of Man 4 – Protected	Bk1
Body Parts of Man	Bk7
Bones of The Earth	Bk1
Book of Life	Bk1
Book of Life (2)— Records	Bk9
Boredom of Man	Bk3
Boundaries of The Earth	Bk5
Boundlessness of Sin	Bk7
Bounty of The Earth	Bk4
Bow of a Ship	Bk8
Bowing of The Seas	Bk4
Brainwave of Endeavour	Bk5
Bride of Christ	Bk6
Bride-in-Waiting	Bk6
Broken Spoke	Bk6
Bubbling Brook	Bk6
Butterflies of Heaven	Bk1
Buzzing of The Bees	Bk4

C

Cadence of The Lord	Bk6
Call of Gathering	Bk4
Call of My Spirit	Bk7
Call of The Lord	Bk9
Camaraderie of The Soul	Bk5
Candles of The Lord	Bk1
Canker of Man	Bk2
Capacity of Man	Bk5
Carriers of God's Wisdom	Bk1
Casting of The Net	Bk4
Catalysts of Destiny	Bk4

Categories Indexed (9 Volumes):
- Communication   20 Bk1
- Div Com Bk of Daniel   13 Bk2
- Div Com Bk of Ezekiel   48 Bk3
- Div Com Bk of Rev.   23 Bk2
- Edicts of The Lord   1 Bk1, 23 Bk7
- Edifice of God   5 Bk1, 1 Bk4, 2 Bk6, 7 Bk7, 1 Bk8
- Encouragement   15 Bk5, 21 Bk6
- Eternity Beckoning 10 Bk1, 2 Bk4, 9 Bk5, 7 Bk6, 19 Bk7
- Fear of God   1 Bk1, 4 Bk6, 1 Bk7
- Freewill of Man   6 Bk1, 6 Bk4, 4 Bk5, 5 Bk6, 7 Bk7
- Good News   11 Bk1, 7 Bk2, 4 Bk3
- My Banner   23 Bk1, 1 Bk2, 1 Bk3, 1 Bk6, 1 Bk7
- My Counsel   30 Bk1, 26 Bk4, 19 Bk5, 17 Bk6, 41 Bk7
- My Creation   7 Bk5, 6 Bk6, 9 Bk8, 1 Bk9
- My Garden   2 Bk1, 22 Bk8
- My Grace   4 Bk1, 15 Bk2, 5 Bk3, 5 Bk4, 2 Bk5, 4 Bk6, 3 Bk7, 3 Bk8, 2 Bk9
- My Harvest   5 Bk1, 9 Bk4, 6 Bk5, 15 Bk6, 9 Bk7
- My Kingdom on Earth   5 Bk1, 8 Bk4, 3 Bk5, 6 Bk6, 12 Bk7
- My Love   9 Bk1, 15 Bk2, 3 Bk3, 5 Bk4, 5 Bk5, 9 Bk6, 10 Bk7, 5 Bk8, 7 Bk9
- My Return   9 Bk1, 7 Bk2, 1 Bk3, 6 Bk4, 4 Bk5, 3 Bk6, 7 Bk7, 8 Bk8, 3 Bk9
- Preparation 13 Bk1, 47 Bk2, 28 Bk3, 9 Bk4, 6 Bk5, 5 Bk6, 41 Bk7, 21 Bk8, 10 Bk9
- Thanksgiving   7 Bk9
- The Cross   1 Bk1, 7 Bk2, 2 Bk3, 1 Bk5, 1 Bk6, 3 Bk7, 1 Bk9
- The End-time   13 Bk1, 24 Bk2,

	1 Bk3, 16 Bk4, 6 Bk6,	Coming of The Kingdom (2)	Bk2
	15 Bk7, 22 Bk8, 2 Bk9	Coming of The Lord	Bk2
The Trinity	5 Bk1, 4 Bk4, 8 Bk5,	Coming of The Lord (2)	Bk4
	7 Bk6, 9 Bk7, 1 Bk9	Coming of The Son	Bk1
Tongues	1 Bk5, 1 Bk6, 1 Bk7, 8 Bk9	Coming of The Spirit	Bk1
Vision & Dream	5 Bk1	Coming of The Trumpet Call	Bk1
Website of The Lord	17 Bk2, 1 Bk4	Coming of the Tulips	Bk8
Wisdom	1 Bk1, 3 Bk2, 2 Bk4,	Coming of The Turmoil	Bk1
	1 Bk7, 1 Bk8	Coming Saints of God	Bk7
Census of God	Bk1	Coming Storm	Bk3
Ceremonies - Edict 15	Bk7	Commitments of Man	Bk1
Chains of Choice	Bk1	Complacency of Man	Bk7
Challenge of Mortality	Bk4	Complaint	Bk4
Champions of God	Bk7	Compulsion of The Soul	Bk5
Change of God	Bk6	Conditional Promises of God	Bk7
Changing Thrones	Bk7	Confines of The Spirit	Bk1
Chaperone of Life	Bk6	Conflicts of Man	Bk4
Character of Man	Bk1	Consecration of A Child	Bk7
Character of Man (2)	Bk6	Consensus	Bk4
Charging of My Envoys	Bk7	Consequences of Sin	Bk2
Chariot of The Lord	Bk9	Consternation of Man	Bk2
Cheerleader of My Garden	Bk8	Consumption	Bk4
Chemistry of Man	Bk2	Courts of Heaven	Bk7
Children of God - Edict 18	Bk7	Courts of Justice - Edict 19	Bk7
Children of God (2)	Bk7	Covenant of The Cross	Bk2
Choice of Man	Bk7	Cow and The Bull	Bk7
Choices of Man	Bk5	Cradle of The Lord	Bk6
Christmas Day	Bk1	Creation Plan of God	Bk2
Churches in The Mountains	Bk1	Cross-dressing of Man	Bk7
Circle of Fire	Bk6	Cross-index Category Study Aid	Bk8
Circumcision of The Heart	Bk4	Crossing of The Dialects	Bk4
Clavicles of Grace	Bk5	Crossing of The Threshold	Bk5
Climax of Eternity	Bk7	Crossroads of Eternity	Bk7
Clouds of Conquest	Bk2	Crown Jewel of Creation	Bk1
Clouds of Conquest (2)	Bk4	Crown of Life	Bk7
Clouds of Conquest (3)	Bk6	Cruelty of Man	Bk7
Clustering of My People	Bk2	Crying of A Child	Bk7
Coatings of The Soul	Bk6	Crying of The Whales	Bk8
Collars of The Shepherd	Bk6	Cup of The Fruit of The Vine	Bk1
Collisions	Bk4	Curtain of The Veil	Bk4
Comfort of Man	Bk7	Cutover of God	Bk8
Comfort of The Lord (1)	Bk1		
Comfort of The Lord (2)	Bk1	**D**	
Comfort of The Lord (3)	Bk8	Database of God	Bk7
Coming Day of The Lord	Bk8	Day of Restoration	Bk2
Coming King of India	Bk7	Day of The Lion	Bk2
Coming of The King	Bk2	Day on which I, The Lord, Arose	Bk2
Coming of The Kingdom	Bk1	Days of Change	Bk2
		Days of Christmas	Bk3

Days of Embitterment & Accord	Bk8
Days of Hindering	Bk7
Days of Leanness	Bk3
Days of Loneliness	Bk2
Days of Pentecost	Bk4
Days of The Aspirations of Man	Bk2
Days of Thunder	Bk2
Days of Thunder (2)	Bk8
Death of Man	Bk1
Death of Man (2)	Bk7
Death of Mortal Man	Bk2
Deceit	Bk4
Decoration of The Heavens	Bk5
Defeats of Man	Bk7
Defilement of The Spirit	Bk1
Departure of Faith with Grace	Bk4
Dependencies of Man	Bk5
Despair of Man	Bk7
Destiny of Lucifer	Bk9
Diet of My Sheep	Bk4
Dignity and Worth of Man	Bk6
Disappointments of God	Bk5
Discourses of Man	Bk6
Dispelling of The Shadows	Bk1
Dissemination of The Multitudes	Bk8
Distractions of Man	Bk1
Div Com Bk of Daniel – Intent	Bk2
Div Com Bk of Daniel Ch 01	Bk2
Div Com Bk of Daniel Ch 02	Bk2
Div Com Bk of Daniel Ch 03	Bk2
Div Com Bk of Daniel Ch 04	Bk2
Div Com Bk of Daniel Ch 05	Bk2
Div Com Bk of Daniel Ch 06	Bk2
Div Com Bk of Daniel Ch 07	Bk2
Div Com Bk of Daniel Ch 08	Bk2
Div Com Bk of Daniel Ch 09	Bk2
Div Com Bk of Daniel Ch 10	Bk2
Div Com Bk of Daniel Ch 11	Bk2
Div Com Bk of Daniel Ch 12	Bk2
Div Com Bk of Ezekiel – Intent	Bk3
Div Com Bk of Ezekiel Ch 01	Bk3
Div Com Bk of Ezekiel Ch 02	Bk3
Div Com Bk of Ezekiel Ch 03	Bk3
Div Com Bk of Ezekiel Ch 04	Bk3
Div Com Bk of Ezekiel Ch 06	Bk3
Div Com Bk of Ezekiel Ch 07	Bk3
Div Com Bk of Ezekiel Ch 08	Bk3
Div Com Bk of Ezekiel Ch 09	Bk3
Div Com Bk of Ezekiel Ch 10	Bk3
Div Com Bk of Ezekiel Ch 11	Bk3
Div Com Bk of Ezekiel Ch 14	Bk3
Div Com Bk of Ezekiel Ch 15	Bk3
Div Com Bk of Ezekiel Ch 19	Bk3
Div Com Bk of Ezekiel Ch 20	Bk3
Div Com Bk of Ezekiel Ch 21	Bk3
Div Com Bk of Ezekiel Ch 22	Bk3
Div Com Bk of Ezekiel Ch 24	Bk3
Div Com Bk of Ezekiel Ch 25	Bk3
Div Com Bk of Ezekiel Ch 27	Bk3
Div Com Bk of Ezekiel Ch 28	Bk3
Div Com Bk of Ezekiel Ch 29	Bk3
Div Com Bk of Ezekiel Ch 30	Bk3
Div Com Bk of Ezekiel Ch 31	Bk3
Div Com Bk of Ezekiel Ch 32	Bk3
Div Com Bk of Ezekiel Ch 33	Bk3
Div Com Bk of Ezekiel Ch 34	Bk3
Div Com Bk of Ezekiel Ch 36	Bk3
Div Com Bk of Ezekiel Ch 37	Bk3
Div Com Bk of Ezekiel Ch 38	Bk3
Div Com Bk of Ezekiel Ch 39	Bk3
Div Com Bk of Ezekiel Ch 40	Bk3
Div Com Bk of Ezekiel Ch 41	Bk3
Div Com Bk of Ezekiel Ch 42	Bk3
Div Com Bk of Ezekiel Ch 43	Bk3
Div Com Bk of Ezekiel Ch 44	Bk3
Div Com Bk of Ezekiel Ch 45	Bk3
Div Com Bk of Ezekiel Ch 46	Bk3
Div Com Bk of Ezekiel Ch 47	Bk3
Div Com Bk of Ezekiel Ch 48	Bk3
Div Com Bk of Revel'n – Intent	Bk2
Div Com Bk of Revelat'n Ch 01	Bk2
Div Com Bk of Revelat'n Ch 02	Bk2
Div Com Bk of Revelat'n Ch 03	Bk2
Div Com Bk of Revelat'n Ch 04	Bk2
Div Com Bk of Revelat'n Ch 05	Bk2
Div Com Bk of Revelat'n Ch 06	Bk2
Div Com Bk of Revelat'n Ch 07	Bk2
Div Com Bk of Revelat'n Ch 08	Bk2
Div Com Bk of Revelat'n Ch 09	Bk2
Div Com Bk of Revelat'n Ch 10	Bk2
Div Com Bk of Revelat'n Ch 11	Bk2
Div Com Bk of Revelat'n Ch 12	Bk2
Div Com Bk of Revelat'n Ch 13	Bk2
Div Com Bk of Revelat'n Ch 14	Bk2
Div Com Bk of Revelat'n Ch 15	Bk2
Div Com Bk of Revelat'n Ch 16	Bk2
Div Com Bk of Revelat'n Ch 17	Bk2
Div Com Bk of Revelat'n Ch 18	Bk2

Div Com Bk of Revelat'n Ch 19	Bk2
Div Com Bk of Revelat'n Ch 20	Bk2
Div Com Bk of Revelat'n Ch 21	Bk2
Div Com Bk of Revelat'n Ch 22	Bk2
Div Intent Bk of Ezekiel Ch 05	Bk3
Div Intent Bk of Ezekiel Ch 12	Bk3
Div Intent Bk of Ezekiel Ch 16	Bk3
Div Intent Bk of Ezekiel Ch 17	Bk3
Div Intent Bk of Ezekiel Ch 18	Bk3
Div Intent Bk of Ezekiel Ch 23	Bk3
Div Intent Bk of Ezekiel Ch 26	Bk3
Div Intent Bk of Ezekiel Ch 35	Bk3
Div Intent, Servants *(Scrib'l Nte)*	Bk3
Divine Commentary	Bk1
Divine Scriptural Revelations	Bk1
Doorway of Mercy	Bk5
Doves of God	Bk3
Dressing of My Garden	Bk8
Drumbeat of The Tree	Bk2
Dungeons of The Heart	Bk1

E

Ear of God	Bk6
Earth of God	Bk1
Earthquakes of Man	Bk2
Ecclesia of My Kingdom	Bk6
Ecology of Man	Bk4
Edicts of The Lord	Bk7
Edifice of God	Bk1
Edifice of God (2)	Bk7
Edifice of God (Present) (3)	Bk7
Edifices of God (4)	Bk7
Educating of The Young	Bk7
Education - Edict 13	Bk7
Effects of The Fall on Man	Bk1
Eggs of Life	Bk2
Elect of God	Bk7
Election of a Man	Bk8
Embarking on A Journey	Bk5
Embitterment of Man	Bk7
Emblem of The Spirit	Bk1
Emissaries of God	Bk6
Enclaves of The Lord	Bk2
Encounter at The Cross	Bk2
End-time Psalms of God	Bk8
or End-time Homilies of God	
End-time Speaks	Bk4
End-time Summary of God	Bk9
End-time Vision From God	Bk4

Also Refer Of …	Bk8
Endowing of My People	Bk2
English (Saxon) Gold (1)	Bk2
English (Saxon) Gold (2)	Bk2
English (Saxon) Gold (3)	Bk2
English (Saxon) Gold (4)	Bk6
English (Saxon) Gold (5)	Bk6
English (Saxon) Gold (6)	Bk6
Enquiring of My Spirit	Bk3
Entrance into Hell	Bk2
Entrance to Heaven	Bk1
Entreaties of The Heart	Bk6
Entry to My Garden	Bk8
'Escape' of Man	Bk5
Escaping Through The Flames	Bk7
Eternity of God	Bk5
Events of Man	Bk4
Evolutionary Question Mark	Bk5
Example of the Philistines	Bk8
Excessive Wealth of Man	Bk4
Exorcizing of Demons	Bk1
Experience of Man	Bk2
Experience of Tribulation	Bk4
Extraction of Man	Bk1

F

Fabric of Life - Edict 14	Bk7
Facelift of The Earth	Bk7
Facilities of God	Bk6
Facilities Unknown	Bk3
Failure of a System	Bk4
Fairies of The Earth	Bk2
Faith Filled Faithful Servants	Bk5
Faith of Man	Bk5
Faith of The People	Bk9
Fall of a House of Hell	Bk1
Fall of Authority	Bk7
Fall of Empires	Bk3
Fall of Grace	Bk4
Fall of Grace (End-time 2)	Bk6
Fanfares (3), Anthem	Bk6
Fashion House of My Church	Bk7
Fate of The Damned	Bk9
Favour of The Lord	Bk1
Favour of The Lord (2)	Bk2
Fear of God	Bk1
Feast of The Incarnation	Bk1
Features on A Landscape	Bk7
Feeding of The Faithful	Bk4

Feeding of The Sheep	Bk1	Fruits of Man's Efforts	Bk2
Fertility of Man	Bk7	Frustrations of God	Bk1
Fickleness of Man	Bk1	Fulfilment of The Cross	Bk2
Fiefdom of The Lord	Bk1	Functioning of Tongues	Bk9
Fields of Wonder	Bk8	Functioning of Unity	Bk6
Figments of Man	Bk7	Funding of God	Bk7
Figurines of Man	Bk8	Fungus of Restraint	Bk4
Final Birth of Man	Bk2	Funnels of The Mind	Bk2
Fire and The Tribulation	Bk1	Future of Man	Bk7

G

Fire of God	Bk6	Galleons of Service	Bk1
Fire of Heaven	Bk6	Game Hunters of The Earth	Bk5
Fire of Life	Bk7	Games of Young Men	Bk2
Fire of The Harvest	Bk2	Garden of God	Bk4
Fire of The Lord	Bk6	Garden of God (2)	Bk8
Fire of The Lord (2)	Bk9	Garden of Peace & Tranquility	Bk6
Firestorm of My Spirit	Bk5	Garden of The Cross	Bk8
Firmly Written For Man	Bk2	Garden of The Lord	Bk1
Fishing in The Seas	Bk3	Gardening of Man	Bk8
Flag of The Kingdom of God	Bk2	Gate To Life	Bk9
Flag, Standard, and Emblem	Bk7	Gathering of The Bride	Bk1
Flash Call to The Body	Bk2	Generosity of Man	Bk5
Floodgates of God	Bk8	Genetics of Man	Bk2
Flowering of Man	Bk7	Gentleness of God	Bk7
Fodder of The Sheepfold	Bk2	Gethsemane of The Christ	Bk6
Followers of Evolution	Bk7	Ghosts of Man	Bk7
Food Source of My Garden	Bk8	Giants of The Earth	Bk2
Foolishness of Man	Bk4	Gift of Tongues	Bk3
Footfalls of Man	Bk2	Girding of The Loins	Bk7
Footpaths of The Lord	Bk1	Glory of Achievement	Bk5
Footprints of The Youth of Man	Bk2	Glory of Enthronement	Bk3
Forbearance of God	Bk6	Glory of God	Bk1
Forest of Fire	Bk6	Glory of My Garden	Bk8
Foretaste of Heaven	Bk1	Glory of The Kingdom	Bk1
Foundation of My Kingdom	Bk3	Glory on Man	Bk5
Fountain of Youth	Bk3	Goals of A Young Woman	Bk2
Four Living Creatures	Bk9	God of Love	Bk2
Fragrance of My Spirit (2)	Bk4	God of Man	Bk5
Fragrance of The Spirit	Bk2	God of Purpose & Function	Bk7
Free In Deed	Bk8	Golden Bow of God	Bk6
Freewill of Man	Bk7	Goliaths of Man	Bk1
Freewill of Man (2)— spirit, flesh, soul, temple	Bk9	Gospel of The Lord	Bk1
Frequency of Listening	Bk7	Governance in My Lands	Bk4
Frequency of Response of Man	Bk2	Government of a People	Bk6
Friendships of Man	Bk5	Grace of God	Bk6
Friendships of The Earth	Bk2	Grain of Wood	Bk5
Fruit of My Church	Bk6	Grateful Heart	Bk6
Fruit of One's Endeavours	Bk7	Gratitude of Man	Bk3
Fruit of The Bride	Bk6		

Grave of Man	Bk7
Greetings from Your King	Bk8
Grouping of My People	Bk6
Growth in My Lands	Bk4
Growth of Man	Bk6
Guidance of God	Bk1

H

Habakkuk 2:1-3	Bk8
Hackers of The Body	Bk1
Hand of Man	Bk6
Handshake of Creation	Bk1
Harried and The Haunted	Bk7
Healing of A Child	Bk7
Healing of Man	Bk1
Health of My Flock	Bk6
Hearing of My Call	Bk8
Heralds of God (1)	Bk6
Heralds of God (2)	Bk6
Heresy	Bk7
Hesitancy of My Flock	Bk6
Hiding Place of Sin	Bk7
Highways to The Destinies	Bk7
History of The Book(s)	Bk1
Holding of My Gold	Bk7
Holdings of The Lord	Bk6
Holiness of God	Bk3
Holiness of God (2)	Bk4
Holy Days of God	Bk7
Holy Spirit Chasers	Bk7
Home of Godly Wisdom	Bk5
Homing of My Bride	Bk2
Honour Your Family - Edict 5	Bk7
Humming of The Wires	Bk4
Hurdles of Man	Bk1

I

I Love My People	Bk1
I, The Lord	Bk1
I, The Lord (2)	Bk7
I, The Lord, Call, Listen, Share	Bk9
I, The Lord Jesus (3)	Bk8
I, The Lord Jesus (4)	Bk8
I, The Lord, Shall Co-Reign	Bk6
I, The Lord, Speak, Hear, Warn	Bk9
I, The Lord, Speak to My Bridal	Bk6
Idolatry of Man	Bk3
Immersion of The Faithful	Bk2
Imminence of My Coming	Bk6
Importance of The Soul	Bk7
Imposing of Correction	Bk7
In Love	Bk1
In the Service of God	Bk8
In the Sights of God	Bk8
Incubation of Man	Bk2
Incubators of Man	Bk5
Incumbency of Christ	Bk7
India is A Land	Bk3
Indwelling of My Spirit	Bk4
Inheritance of Christ	Bk7
Inheritance of Man	Bk1
Invasion by The Multitudes	Bk4
Inside of The Eyelids	Bk5
Intent of The Lord	Bk1
Investiture of Man	Bk4
Invitation to The Dance	Bk6

J

Journey of Exaltation	Bk2
Journey of Man	Bk1
Journey Through Life	Bk7
Journeying of Life	Bk7
Journeying of Man	Bk5
Joy of The Lord	Bk5
Judgement of God	Bk4
Judgement of Man	Bk2
Justice in Judgement	Bk1
Justness of God	Bk2

K

Keepsakes of life	Bk8
Keys of The Kingdom	Bk1
Kingdom of God	Bk7
Kings of The Kingdom	Bk7
Kissing of God	Bk6

L

Lacerations of God	Bk6
Lack of Faith	Bk4
Lamb of God Presents	Bk7
Lamb's Book of Life	Bk2
Land of Goshen	Bk5
Land of Plenty	Bk1
Landing on A Comet	Bk7
Languages of Heaven	Bk9
Last Call To Man	Bk2
Liars & Wastrels in My Lands	Bk4
Lick of The Lion	Bk1
Life After Death	Bk7
Life on Life	Bk7
Life with The Lord	Bk6

Life within America	Bk6	Miracle of Christmas	Bk1
Life within My Garden	Bk8	Mischief-Makers of The Earth	Bk7
Life within The Kingdom	Bk7	Misery of Man	Bk3
Lifeline to God	Bk3	Misery of Man (2)	Bk5
Lining of Peru (Nazca Lines)	Bk8	Missing from My Garden	Bk8
Lion and The Lamb	Bk7	Mission of My People	Bk1
Lion of Judah	Bk1	Moment of Inspection	Bk2
Lion of Judah – Tree of Life	Bk7	Morality of God	Bk1
Lion of Judah in Readiness	Bk1	Mortality of Man	Bk4
Lion of Judah Reigns	Bk1	Mountaintop of Life	Bk7
Lion Offers All, His Ways	Bk1	Movement of The Soul	Bk8
Lion Purring (*also see 'Purring'*)	Bk1	Movements of Man	Bk2
Lioness and Lion (*also 'Roar'*)	Bk1	*Musical and Verse Addenda*	Bk6
Livery of God	Bk3	Mustering of The Bride	Bk1
Location of Man	Bk5	My Book of Love	Bk9
Locus of The Lord (Website)	Bk2	My Book of The Storm	Bk3
Lord Will Come	Bk9	My Book Seven Status	Bk7
Love Note to My Children	Bk5	My Children of The World	Bk5
Love of Money	Bk2	My Church on Fire	Bk7
Love of Our God	Bk9	My Divinity in My Lands	Bk4
Loving God of Man	Bk2	My End-time Calls for Man	Bk4
Loving of A Child	Bk7	My Heralds with The Parts	Bk8
Lumps of Clay	Bk5	My Kingdom Rules	Bk7
Lyrics/Songs, Anthem, Fanfares	Bk6	My Letter Especially to You! Yes, to YOU!	Bk5

M

		My Letters From The Son	Bk5
Maestro of The Intellect	Bk8	My Little Book	Bk9
Magnificence of God	Bk5	My Messengers of Fire	Bk7
Man into his Own - Edict 10	Bk7	My Missives For My Bride	Bk6
Man of Righteousness	Bk2	My Missives Going Forth	Bk6
Man shan't Tinker - Edict 11	Bk7	My Nine Volumes' Indexing	Bk8
Management of God	Bk8	My People	Bk4
Mantle of A King	Bk2	My People of The Internet	Bk2
Marching of The Saints	Bk2	My Prophets of This Age	Bk2
Mark of The Beast	Bk1	My Relationship With Man	Bk5
Marriage of Two People	Bk7	My Saints in Action	Bk7
Martyring of Man	Bk7	My Saints in Celebration	Bk7
Marvels of The Ancients	Bk7	My Servants Empowered	Bk7
Maturing of The Earth	Bk2	My Sheep and The Goats	Bk7
Means of Man	Bk5	My Sheep within the Saleyards	Bk8
Measure of A Man	Bk1	My Youth Enflamed	Bk7
Mediation by the spirit of Man	Bk7	Mystery of Life	Bk1
Meeting of The Minds	Bk8		

N

Memory of Freewill	Bk2		
Mercy Call - Edict 9	Bk7	Name Above All Names	Bk7
Message of Compassion	Bk1	Naming of Creation	Bk2
Message of Healing	Bk1	Need of My People	Bk4
Messages of Life	Bk1	Needs of Life	Bk1
Ministry of My Servants	Bk4	Nettings of God	Bk7

Networking of God	Bk2
Never Before	Bk7
New Beginnings	Bk8
New Day	Bk1
New Life	Bk2
New Prince is Born	Bk5
New Signs in Use	Bk1
New Signs of The Kingdom	Bk1
New Wineskin	Bk7
No Blaspheming God - Edict 3	Bk7
No Broken Abjurations - Edict 7	Bk7
No Idols on The Earth - Edict 2	Bk7
No Laying Waste - Edict 4	Bk7
No Other Gods - Edict 1	Bk7
Non-vindictiveness of God	Bk5

O

Occultists and Sympathizers	Bk7
Of End-time Events	Bk8
Of End-time Prophecies	Bk8
Of Temples	Bk8
Offer of My Grace	Bk2
Offerings to The Lord	Bk7
Oil of The Spirit	Bk2
Onslaught of Disasters	Bk2
Onward Journey of Man	Bk2
Outreach of My people	Bk5

P

Partnering of Man	Bk7
Passing of a Cloud	Bk8
Passion of The Lord	Bk4
Pasture of God	Bk6
Pathway of The Son	Bk1
Pathway of The Stars of God	Bk8
Pathways of The Rain	Bk1
Paucity of Hope and Faith	Bk4
Pearls of God	Bk6
Peril of The Unprepared *Hell*	Bk7
Perspicacity of Man	Bk5
Pestering of Man	Bk4
Pets of The Earth	Bk1
Picking up The Remnants	Bk5
Plank of A Nation	Bk1
Plans for My Scrolls	Bk7
Playground of The Stars	Bk7
Plight of A Child	Bk2
Plunder of The Soul	Bk1
Policy of The Lord	Bk2
Polishing of The Soul	Bk1

Portals of The Kingdom	Bk1
Potential of Man	Bk7
Power of God	Bk4
Power of My People	Bk4
Power of Speech	Bk7
Power of The Holy Spirit	Bk1
Power of The Spirit of Man	Bk1
Prayer of Thanksgiving	Bk7
Prayer of The Lord	Bk9
Prayer of The Saved	Bk9
Prayer of The Servant	Bk9
Prayers of Just & Unjust	Bk9
Prayers of The Faithful	Bk9
Prayers of The Indwelt	Bk9
Prayers of The Justified	Bk9
Prayers Within Eternity	Bk7
Precept upon Precept	Bk1
Preparedness of Man	Bk1
Presence of Man	Bk5
Presence of The Angels	Bk2
Presenting of Fire	Bk6
Presenting of The Saints	Bk7
Pride of Judah's Lion - Edict 6	Bk7
Preternatural Infancy of Man	Bk6
Priesthood of Believers	Bk7
Prime Directive to Man	Bk6
Procrastination of Man	Bk2
Profanity of Man	Bk1
Progressing of My Bride	Bk6
Promises of God	Bk1
Prongs of Satan	Bk4
Property of God - Edict 17	Bk7
Protocols of Heaven	Bk6
Provisioning of God	Bk2
Psalms of God	Bk8
Purity of My Bride	Bk4
Purring of The Lion	Bk1
Pursuits of God	Bk3
Pursuits of Man	Bk3

Q

Quest for Happiness	Bk6
Quest for Holiness	Bk6
Quest for Know'dge One's God	Bk7
Questioning of The Saints	Bk2
Quivering of Man	Bk7

R

Race of The Righteous	Bk1
Railway of Life	Bk7

Raining of Jerusalem	Bk2	Satanic Influence	Bk7
Rancour of the Reeling	Bk5	Saving Children of Today	Bk4
Readiness of God	Bk7	Scales of God	Bk6
Readiness to Jump	Bk5	Scenery of God Abroad	Bk5
Readying of The Bride	Bk6	Scepticism of Man	Bk6
Reality of God	Bk7	Scissors of The Lord	Bk7
Reasoning of Man	Bk7	Scope of God	Bk2
Recalibration	Bk4	Scream of Agony	Bk8
Receptiveness of Man	Bk4	Screens of God	Bk2
Record of The Spirit	Bk9	Screens of Man	Bk2
Recovery from a Sinkhole	Bk4	Scripts of Man	Bk2
Red Cross	Bk1	Scrolls of The Lord	Bk2
Refuges of The Saints	Bk7	Sea of Faces	Bk8
Reins of God	Bk6	Sea of Fire	Bk6
Reins of Power	Bk8	Sealing of The Temple	Bk5
Relationships Within My Garden	Bk8	Season of The Heralds	Bk2
Relay Centres of My Temples	Bk4	Seating on A Throne	Bk2
Renaming of The Book Series	Bk8	Secrecy of God	Bk8
Replevin of The Lord	Bk1	Secrecy of Gov'ments of Man	Bk2
Requiem of Man	Bk8	Secreting of Goals	Bk4
Rescuing of Man	Bk6	Seed of Faith	Bk6
Resilience of Man	Bk5	Seeding of Wealth	Bk7
Responsibility of Freewill	Bk1	Seeping of The Blood	Bk5
Responsibility of God	Bk6	Sequence of Salvation	Bk2
Restlessness of Man	Bk5	Sequences in My Garden	Bk8
Restraints - Edict 21	Bk7	Sequencing of Time	Bk1
Return of The Shepherd	Bk1	Sermon of The Lord	Bk2
Revelation 6:1-8 plus Others	Bk9	Servants in India	Bk3
Rewards of Faith	Bk8	Servants of The Lord	Bk1
Rhythm of The Saints	Bk6	Servants, D Int (Scribal Note)	Bk3
Rich and Wasteful - Edict 12	Bk7	Service to God	Bk6
Ridicule from The Ignorant	Bk7	Serving in Heaven	Bk9
Righteous in Preparation	Bk1	Set My People Free	Bk7
Righteousness	Bk3	Settlement of Man	Bk4
Ring of Salvation	Bk7	Settlers within My Garden	Bk8
Rise of Ashkelon	Bk1	Settling of The Son	Bk3
Rising of The Son	Bk1	Shadow Life of Man	Bk7
River of Fire	Bk6	Shadows of Man	Bk6
Roar of The Lion	Bk1	Shaming of Politics	Bk4
Roar of The Lion of Judah	Bk1	Shell of Man	Bk6
Roar of Zion	Bk1	Shortfall of Man	Bk2
Robustness of A Trial	Bk4	Shouting of Man	Bk4
		Signalling The Teatime	Bk5
S		Silence of God	Bk1
Sacrifice of Self	Bk5	Sin Beneath The Veil	Bk1
Saints in Song	Bk6	Sin Resident Within	Bk6
Sanctification	Bk4	Sky Signs of God	Bk5
Sanctity of Life	Bk1	Slaughter of The Innocent	Bk1
Satan's Nest Eggs	Bk7	Smaller Becomes Better	Bk5

Snowfields in My Garden	Bk8	Swamp of Man	Bk6
Social Media at Work	Bk4	Swan of Regality	Bk8
Son Shines	Bk5	Swimming Pool of Life	Bk6
Song of The Lord	Bk9	Sword of Vengeance	Bk9
Song of The Saved	Bk9	**T**	
Song of The Servant	Bk9	Table of The Lord	Bk9
Songs/Lyrics, Anthem, Fanfares	Bk6	Tableting of Man	Bk8
Songsters of God	Bk8	Tares among The Wheat	Bk7
Soul of God	Bk9	Tasks of Responsib'ty - Edict 20	Bk7
Soul of Man	Bk2	Teaching of A Child	Bk7
Soul of Man (2)	Bk6	Teapots	Bk6
Soul of Man (3)	Bk7	Teardrops of My Children	Bk4
Sound of Laughter	Bk7	Tears of Man	Bk2
Sourcing of Evil	Bk8	Tears of Man (2)	Bk6
Sourcing of The Living Waters	Bk4	Tears of The Lord	Bk1
Sparkle of A Diamond	Bk8	Temperature of The Day	Bk8
Spectacles of Heaven	Bk1	Temperature of The Soul	Bk1
Spirit Structures	Bk9	Template for The Future	Bk5
Spreading of Socialism	Bk4	Temple of The Body	Bk1
Squanderings of Man	Bk2	Temples of The Testimonies	Bk7
Squirrels of The Earth	Bk4	Tenants of The Mind	Bk1
Stalling of Man	Bk7	Terror of The Seas	Bk8
Standard of The Kingdom of God	Bk2	Testimony Day of The Lord	Bk1
Star and its Positioning	Bk1	Testimony of My Book of Scrolls	Bk2
Stepping Stone of Mortality	Bk5	Testimony of My Book of Storm	Bk3
Stepping Stones of The Lord	Bk1	Thankful are the Poor in Spirit	Bk4
Stones of The Earth	Bk5	This Day	Bk2
Storm of Fire	Bk3	Those with Freewill Choice	Bk7
Storm of God	Bk3	Threshold of Existence	Bk7
Storm of Man	Bk3	Threshold of God	Bk4
Storm of Satan	Bk3	Threshold of The Lord (2)	Bk6
Storm of The Earth	Bk3	Throne of God	Bk6
Storm of The Wealth of Man	Bk5	Thrones of God	Bk2
Storming of The Citadels	Bk7	Timetable of A Cat	Bk7
Storming of The Seas	Bk3	Timetable of God for Man	Bk7
Story of Our God	Bk9	Tin-lizzies of The Skies	Bk8
Stream of Life	Bk7	To The Victor Goes The Prize	Bk6
Strength of The Lord	Bk1	Tongue of Fire	Bk1
Superintendency of God	Bk8	Tongue of Lucifer	Bk9
Superstitions of Man	Bk7	Tongue of Praise	Bk9
Supplicant of God	Bk4	Tongue of Prayer	Bk9
Supremacy of God	Bk4	Tongue of Worship	Bk9
Supremacy of Love	Bk4	Tongue(s) of The S(s)pirit	Bk9
Surges of The Sea	Bk7	Tongues of Angels	Bk9
Surprises of Man	Bk5	Tongues of Demons	Bk9
Surroundings of Man	Bk4	Tongues of Demons (2)	Bk9
Survival of My People	Bk4	Tongues of God	Bk7
Survival of The Flock	Bk1	Tongues of Heaven	Bk3
Sustaining of a Vision	Bk8		

Tongues of Man	Bk9		Ventures into Lying	Bk4
Trail of Miracles	Bk7		Venturing of Man	Bk2
Transfer of Existence	Bk7		Vestibule of God	Bk6
Transfer of Time	Bk2		Viceroy of India	Bk5
Transgressors of The Soul	Bk1		Vicissitudes of Man	Bk6
Trials of God	Bk7		Victors of The Soul	Bk1
Tribulation of Life	Bk7		Victory of My Kingdom	Bk7
Trickle of The Foe	Bk1		Vision	Bk1
Trinkets of The Heart	Bk1		Vision of My Banner	Bk7
Triumphs of Man	Bk7		Vision Scriptures	Bk1
Triumvirate of God	Bk9		Visionaries of God	Bk6
Troops of The Lord	Bk1		Visions for The Future	Bk8
Troubling by Man	Bk2		Visions of My People	Bk4
Tuning Forks of God	Bk6		Visitation of India	Bk3
Turning Points in Life	Bk1		Visitation of The Earth	Bk1
Twisted Faiths of Man	Bk7		Visiting India	Bk7
Twisting of the Tongue of Man	Bk5		Visiting My Garden (2)	Bk8
Twisting of The Votes	Bk4		Visiting of Megiddon	Bk5
			Visitor from Afar	Bk7

U

			Visitor from Afar (2)	Bk7
Ultimatums of God	Bk6		Visitors to The Garden	Bk1
Ups and Downs of Life	Bk7		Vitality of A Nation	Bk4
Urgency of Man	Bk7		Vitamins of Life	Bk7
Utterance of A Promise	Bk1		Voice in The Wilderness	Bk4
			Voice of God	Bk2

V

Vacancies of My Spirit	Bk4		Voice of Man	Bk5
Vacancies within My Garden	Bk8		Volatility of Man	Bk6
Vacuum of Space	Bk5		Volleyball of Man	Bk4
Vagaries of Man	Bk2			

W

Vagaries of Man (2)	Bk7		Wailing of The Innocent	Bk3
Vagrancy of The Youth	Bk5		Walk into Eternity With God	Bk7
Vagrancy without Inhibitions	Bk4		Walk into The Countryside	Bk7
Valediction of Man	Bk6		Walk of Man	Bk2
Valour of My Saints	Bk6		Walk Upon A Hill	Bk7
Value of a Goal	Bk7		Warlord of The Nations	Bk6
Value of Speech	Bk7		Warmth of God	Bk6
Vanguard of My Spirit	Bk5		Warring of My People	Bk2
Vanity of Man	Bk6		Washing of The Clothes	Bk5
Vanity of Man (2)	Bk5		Washings of Mortality	Bk7
Vanquishing of The Foe	Bk2		Wastelands of God	Bk5
Vapours of The Earth	Bk1		Watching at The Crossroads	Bk5
Variance of Man	Bk5		Watchtowers of The Saints	Bk3
Variant Scriptures of My Word	Bk6		Waterfalls of Life	Bk7
Variations in The Sea Level	Bk8		Waters of Baptism	Bk6
Variety in Heaven	Bk7		Waters of Life	Bk1
Variety in the Flock of God	Bk6		Waterways of God	Bk5
Variety of Choice	Bk1		Wave of Unity	Bk2
Variety of Man	Bk3		Waves of God	Bk2
Veins and Arteries	Bk5			

Way Home	Bk1		White Stone of Life	Bk7
Way Stations of The Lord	Bk5		Whitebait of The Seas	Bk4
Wayfarer of God	Bk3		Wiles of Woman	Bk3
Ways of God	Bk1		Willingness of God	Bk6
Ways of God (2)	Bk2		Willingness of God (2)	Bk2
Ways of God (3)	Bk6		Will of God in Victory	Bk4
Ways of God (4)	Bk7		Willow and The Oak	Bk6
Ways of The Spirit	Bk9		Wind of My Spirit (2)	Bk5
Wayward Wind	Bk5		Wind of My Spirit (3)	Bk6
Wealth of Man	Bk1		Wind of The Spirit	Bk2
Weather of God	Bk3		Window of Opportunity	Bk8
Weathering of Man	Bk6		Window of Wonder	Bk1
Website of The Lord	Bk4		Window of Wonder - Parable	Bk1
Website of The Lord (Attempts)	Bk2		Windows of Earth	Bk7
Website of The Lord (Content)	Bk2		Winds of Change	Bk2
Website of The Lord (Enables)	Bk2		Wings of Heaven	Bk1
Website of The Lord (Eternity)	Bk2		Wisdom	Bk4
Website of The Lord (Foghorn)	Bk2		Wisdom of God	Bk2
Website of The Lord (Intent)	Bk2		Wisdom of God (2)	Bk2
Website of The Lord (Morsels)	Bk2		Wisdom of The Ages	Bk7
Website of The Lord (Net)	Bk2		Wisdom on Time	Bk4
Website of The Lord (Offers)	Bk2		Wisdom Sought and Found	Bk8
Website of The Lord (Presence)	Bk2		Wise of Man	Bk2
Website of The Lord (Purpose)	Bk2		Wishing of Man	Bk8
Website of The Lord (Reason)	Bk2		Withering of The Vine	Bk8
Website of The Lord (Results)	Bk2		Wonder of The Eye	Bk7
Website of The Lord (Serves)	Bk2		Wonderment of Eternity	Bk5
Website of The Lord (Tells)	Bk2		Wonders of The Earth	Bk6
Website of The Lord (Update)	Bk2		Wonders of The Heavens	Bk7
Website of The Lord (Abilities)	Bk2		Wool of My Sheep	Bk5
Wedding Feast of The Lamb	Bk6		Worldliness of Man	Bk7
Welcome of The Centuries	Bk5		Worthiness of My Bride	Bk6
Welcome to My Garden	Bk8		Wrath of God	Bk1
Welfare of Man	Bk3		Wrath of God (2)	Bk4
Well of Life	Bk7		Writings of God	Bk5
Wellspring of Life	Bk7			

Y

Youth of My Church	Bk7
Youth Outside My Church	Bk7

What are The End-time Psalms	Bk8
Wheels of Commerce	Bk4
Wherewithal of Man	Bk1
Wherewithal of Man	Bk4
Whirlwind of Man	Bk6
Whistler in The Wind	Bk8
White Cross	Bk1

Scribal Note:

This Alphabetical index includes 1135+ items from all Nine Volumes.

As at 20th June 2019

The 9 Books of either The End-time Psalms of God or as The End-time Homilies of God

	Pages	Total Words
1. GOD Speaks of Return and Bannered	418	90,840
2. GOD Speaks to Man on The Internet	498	126,842
3. GOD Speaks as His Spirit Empowers	272	68,205
4. GOD Speaks to Man in The End-time	248	62,358
5. GOD Speaks in Letters of Eternity	236	56,766
6. GOD Speaks to His Bridal Presence	326	77,905
7. GOD Speaks to His Edifice	512	127,491
8. GOD Speaks of Loving His Creation	280	71,115
9. GOD Speaks Now of a Seal Revealed	124	25,030

Scribal Note:
These 9 volumes in this series form The Parts of The End-time Psalms of God.
These may probably be better known by man in his naming as 'The End-time Homilies of God' - in being 'Religious discourses which are intended primarily for spiritual education rather than doctrinal instruction.

My Content Study Aid

The 4 Companion End-time Flowers of God

	Pages	Total Words
10. GOD End-time Updates Ancient Alien History	310	84,011
11. GOD End-time Updates His Call to The Multitudes	166	46,152
12. GOD End-time Updates The Bride of My Son	180	47,267
13. GOD End-time Updates The Guardianship of Friends	280	82,610

4 Synopses of The Flowers of God

Book Ten 'God End-time Updates Ancient Alien History' delves into the distant past of Flying Saucers with Alien strangers cross- and interbreeding to generate Neanderthals, and where the discovered new element of Moscovium disintegrates over time into an antigravity fuel, which enables flying saucers to fly the way they do, and where ancient knowledge tells of the extermination of the dinosaurs because of being predators. The current situation, with crop circles and Flying Saucers with real live Aliens, brings history up to date.

Book Eleven 'God End-time Updates His Call to The Multitudes' here The Lord Jesus speaks throughout The Earth— to all who would prepare for an ongoing life with Him. He is reaching out to have The Multitudes come to an understanding and awaits a response in answer to the question of the thoughtful: Why is the Freewill of man of such importance to God? Why is the Freewill of man such a determinant of the ultimate destiny of man? Why is the Freewill of man either respected or honoured by God? Why is the Freewill of man 'Honoured' by his movements within the new covenant?

Book Twelve 'God End-time Updates The Bride of My Son' as dictated by The Father. The Father loves and enfolds as He chooses to bring before The people of The Lord all those who are close to His Heart especially as the wisdom of the centuries has been nurtured in the heavens, is often obvious when spoken, raises eyebrows at the thoughts revealed, silences while matters are considered as to the best way forward. The wisdom of the centuries is a gift from God, is an enlightening of speech, is the victory of expression. The wisdom of the centuries is an expansion of vocabulary.

Book Thirteen 'God End-time Updates The Guardianship of Friends' with eighty six divinely selected scrolls dictated by Jesus: where The Curtain Call of God stimulates: in growth, in Faith, in righteousness, in expression, in quests, in being friendly and inviting. It affirms the value: of being under The Faith Field of Mortality, the confirmation of The Righteous Field of Morality, the requested availability of The Cleansing Field of Grace, the necessity of Seeking The Field of Preparation, The gifts of My Spirit as on The Day of Pentecost, the benefit of attaining fluency in The Heavenly Gift of Tongues, access to the given opportunity to select: the destiny of choice as the goal of life, to be so set in Faith for Freewill Activities— with righteousness prevailing as the destiny is assured. It closes out the time of Grace, opens up the time of Mercy at The Bema Seat.

About The Scribe

Updated 11 April 2020

Anthony is 79, having been married to his wife, Adrienne, for 56 years. They have five married children: Carolyn, Alan, Marie, Emma and Sarah and fourteen grandchildren: Matthew, and Ella; Phillipa, and Jonathan; Jeremy, Ngaire, and Trevor; Jake, Finn, Crystal, and Caleb; Bjorn, Greta, and Minka.

Anthony was raised on a dairy farm in Springston, Canterbury, NZ in the 1940s. He graduated from Canterbury University, Christchurch, NZ with a B.Sc. in chemistry and mathematics in 1962. He was initially employed as an industrial chemist in flour milling, with linear programming applications.

These used the first IBM 360 at the university for determining least cost stock food formulations and production parameters for determining quantities of raw materials, packaging and sacks for the purchasing division. Later he was involved in similar applications on the refining side of the oil industry in Britain, Australia and New Zealand. This was followed by sales and managerial experience in the chemical industry.

The family moved to a Bay of Plenty, NZ, town in 1976 when Anthony took up funeral directing, as a principal, expanding an initial sibling partnership until the close of the century. Anthony acquired practical experience in accounting, business management, and computer usage (early Apples— including The Lisa) from within their business.

Upon retiring from active funeral directing in 2000 and selling his interests, he then commenced the promotion and the writing of funeral management software for the NZ funeral environment. Rewarded with national success in NZ, with his son also expanding recently (2019) into Australia, he has now retired completely, as from 2007, from the active management of that interest. He lives near some of his family in Hamilton NZ.

Anthony was brought up in the Methodism of his father until his mid-teens, his mother's side was Open Brethren. He is Christian in belief within an Apostolic Pentecostal Charismatic framework of choice (since the 1990s) having been earlier in the Mormon church for several years. Thereafter he was in the Baptist denomination followed by finding a home within the NZ Apostolic church movement for some years, and where in recent times all have made him welcome while Jesus has dictated His 13 books.

He and his wife, who has visited a number of Asian countries, have been to India in 2011, 12, 13, 16 and 18 on The Lord's tasks and have witnessed and participated in many miracles which befall His People and The Multitudes.

His forbears William Henry Eddy and Margaret Jane Eddy, née Oats, emigrated to New Zealand from Gulval, Cornwall, England in 1878 on a sailing ship, with a very slow passage time of 79 days, and with their three month old infant child, Margaret Anne, dying 21 October 1878 from Congestion of the brain on board the Marlborough while en route to NZ. The Marlborough sailed London 19 September 1878, via Plymouth 26 September 1878, and arrived Lyttelton 14 December 1878 with 336 assisted immigrants. His grandfather, Alfred Charles Eddy, then but three years old, together with an older brother aged four, obviously survived the trials of the sea voyage to become a part of a family with a further eleven New Zealand born siblings all living to maturity.

Journaling and Notes (1)

Journaling and Notes (2)

www.ingramcontent.com/pod-product-compliance
Lightning Source LLC
Chambersburg PA
CBHW060047230426
43661CB00004B/696